330.9
D49

132736

DATE DUE			

DEVELOPMENT AND THE
RURAL-URBAN DIVIDE

DEVELOPMENT
AND THE
RURAL-URBAN DIVIDE

Edited by
John Harriss and Mick Moore

FRANK CASS

First published in Great Britain by
FRANK CASS AND COMPANY LIMITED
Gainsborough House, 11 Gainsborough Road,
London E11 1RS

and in the United States of America by
FRANK CASS AND COMPANY LIMITED
c/o Biblio Distribution Centre
81 Adams Drive, P.O. Box 327, Totowa, N.J. 07511

British Library Cataloguing in Publication Data

Development and the rural-urban divide.
1. Economic development   2. Equality
3. Geography, Economic
I. Harriss, John   II. Moore, Mick
330.9   HD82

ISBN 0-7146-3241-4

This group of studies first appeared in a Special Issue on 'Development
and the Rural-Urban Divide' of *Journal of Development Studies*, Vol. 20,
No. 3, published by Frank Cass & Co. Ltd.

Printed and bound in Great Britain by
T. J. Press (Padstow) Ltd, Padstow, Cornwall

CONTENTS

Editors' Introduction

There is a rural-urban dimension to most analyses of economic growth and societal change, especially in poorer countries with large agricultural sectors. The subject of rural-urban relations is potentially vast. This collection makes no attempt to deal with the theme as a whole, but is rather focused on a debate which has emerged in development studies over the last two decades. This debate is centred around the work of four scholars, notably Michael Lipton [*1977*], but including also M. J. Mamalakis [*1969 and 1971*], Ashok Mitra [*1977*] and Robert Bates [*1981*] (for details see the first paper in this collection). There are two themes central and common to their work. First, in attempting to explain national level patterns of economic resource allocation within a political economy framework, they use the concept of economic sectors, mainly the rural/agricultural versus urban/industrial categorisation, to supplement and partly substitute for the more conventional class categorisation. Second, they suggest in varying degrees that the way in which sectoral conflicts influence the allocation of economic resources through state action has been the prime cause of slow rates of economic growth (and, in Lipton's work, of growth biased against the poor) in developing countries since the Second World War. Most evidently in Lipton's work, inter-sectoral relations are elevated to a position where they compete with the grand theoretical frameworks of modernisation, dependency and modes of production.

Such claims have inevitably been contested. Most debate has centred around the claims by Mamalakis (on Latin America), Lipton (on developing countries generally) and Bates (on tropical Africa) that the Third World development policy has been characterised by some form of urban bias. (Mitra makes a more limited counter-claim about the emergence of rural bias in post-Independence India.) Many of the critiques, including all those in this collection, are focused mainly on the validity of the analytic models put forward to account for urban bias. However, there is generally not even a consensus in development studies that there is a set of phenomena characteristic of developing countries which can best be explained by adopting sectoral categories and models. There are at least two major reasons for dissenting from this dissent: for believing that there *is* something to explain, and that notions of urban bias are a useful point at which to begin seeking explanation. The first is now well-documented: the prevalence in developing countries of economic policies which bias prices in various markets against agriculture.

The contrast with industrial countries, which generally protect and subsidise agriculture, is almost complete [e.g. *Bale and Lutz, 1981*]. And incidentally, as Lipton states in his paper here, some of the developing countries which he had earlier listed as being exceptions to the general rule of urban bias are not in fact exceptions at all.[1] The second reason, which Lipton also reiterates in his paper here, is that differences between average rural and average urban incomes are far greater in contemporary developing countries than in the now-industrialised countries at a comparable level of development.

Sceptics might suggest that the last observation can be explained without resort to inter-sectoral analysis. Perhaps it is because contemporary developing countries have access to and use technology and capital equipment from the industrialised nations which is very productive compared to poor country agricultural technology, thus generating high urban and industrial incomes and high urban-rural income differentials. The explanation of high urban to rural income ratios lies in technology and international economic relations, not in inter-sectoral relations and their effect on government policy within developing countries.[2] There remains a strong case for examining theories of inter-sectoral relations seriously and on their own terms.

The examinations of these theories presented here are generally critical in tone. The five case studies by Ellis, Harriss and Harriss, Moore, Nolan and White, and Redclift take Lipton's model of urban bias as a point of departure. All in some way tend to agree that it has some plausibility especially at first sight, but that it is also inadequate and incomplete in various respects. The focus is on the validity of the model in explaining how governments influence the allocation of material resources. Most criticisms relate to two issues introduced by Moore in the first paper.

The first is the descriptive and analytic adequacy of the notion of distinct and homogeneous rural and urban economic sectors. Frank Ellis [see also Bates, 1981] deals with two countries, Tanzania and Fiji, which are more representative of most developing countries than the model country (India) around which Lipton's and Mitra's analysis is framed. Agriculture and thus agricultural politics are not focused solely or mainly around the production of foodgrains. There are large tropical export crop sectors. Food and export crop growers produce for different destinations, have their products marketed and surpluses appropriated (if at all) through different channels, and are potential prey to different exploiters and appropriating mechanisms. Mick Moore argues for Sri Lanka that there are major intra-rural regional differences in the extent of dependence on agriculture, on type of crop produced, in agrarian structure and in degree of effective access to political influence. For a series of contingent reasons a core-periphery continuum is a more useful framework than the rural-urban divide for beginning to examine both the economics and the politics of policy, especially agricultural policy. Barbara and John Harriss examine rural-urban economic relations over time at the level of a single Indian market town and its hinterland, and illustrate the problems involved in applying macro-level arguments about sectoral relations to micro-level data. They argue that, while it may be possible to demonstrate the existence of financial resource flows from the hinterland to the town which lend credibility to the idea of 'the exploitation of the countryside by the town', this phenomenon is *not* sufficiently explained by the sectoral model.

The questions raised by John and Barbara Harriss about the explanatory value of Lipton's urban bias model in particular point to a second major set of criticisms, concerning the usefulness of the sectoral framework for the analysis of politics. Most contributors question this, including Nolan and White, who find the rural-urban dichotomy useful for their economic analysis. Several contributors make a criticism that Lipton uses the term 'urban bias' both as an explanatory variable, to refer to a pattern of political alliances shaping policy, and as a dependent variable – as a description of the resultant pattern of resource allocation. While Lipton has conceded the point in principle, he does not make the distinction in his response to his critics published here. Ellis argues that Lipton's postulated alliance of the rural rich with the urban sector to form a single 'urban class' makes the latter improbably comprehensive, and defines away the phenomenon of intra-rural differentiation. As Moore puts it: 'It is ... unlikely that any political science study would lead to the identification of categories of political actors as broad, discrete and stable as Lipton's rural and urban classes-cum-interest groups.' Nolan and White show that in China what appears as 'urban bias' in policy has not necessarily flowed from urban political forces and that this, and 'industrial bias', have other roots and are susceptible to other explanations. Their analysis shows that, to the extent that the relative political influence of urban and rural interests and orientations have affected development strategy, the relation between policy objectives and actual results has been paradoxical. An underlying criticism is that the sectoral framework as used by Lipton is reductionist, because it depends on the view that classes defined by their relations to means of production are simultaneously interest groups in the political sphere. It is rather ironic that Lipton, who is so critical of Marxist thinking, himself reproduces a fundamental flaw of much Marxist political analysis. We may add that Lipton's version of the sectoral political framework is often believed to be so broad and open to such fluid interpretation that it is difficult to derive falsifiable propositions from it. It is perhaps for this reason that it has stimulated a good deal of heated debate but rather little empirical research.

It would be surprising if a set of attempts to evaluate a general theory through case studies of individual areas, countries and regions did not detect many problems and suggest modifications. That does not in itself invalidate the original attempt to find a model to explain what do, after all, appear to be widespread empirical phenomena in some way suggestive of 'urban bias' (see above). The concluding paper by Lipton incorporates a powerful defence of such a search. Whether the universe for such an enterprise should be all poor countries is perhaps the main question to be faced by those who have some sympathy with Lipton's approach. Michael Redclift's paper is relevant to answering that question. He argues, in conformity with the 'dependency' tradition in Latin American development studies, that within Latin America the relationships between urban and rural sectors cannot be adequately understood without placing them in a context of international economic relations and dependency. Urban areas form part of the chain of dependency. He also shows that the small size of the rural sector in Latin America and the rapid recent growth of capitalist agriculture raise doubts about the usefulness of 'urban bias' ideas which seem to relate mainly to the poorer continents of Africa and Asia. One implication which could be drawn from his paper is that refinements of inter-sectoral theories and models might best focus on groups of relatively homogeneous countries rather than on the Third World as a whole [*e.g. Bates, 1981*]. A second and less direct implication is that the nature of inter-sectoral conflicts might depend on overall income levels. As Bates [*1983: 123*] suggests, increased average income levels tend to dampen producer-consumer conflicts over food prices and thus the extent of at least some aspects of urban bias in national economic policy. The models of sectoral bias discussed here were all framed to deal with situations of poverty. There is perhaps scope for a more dynamic theory which tries to explain the superficially paradoxical association between urban biased pricing policies in poor agricultural countries and rural biased policies in industrial countries. Such a theory should and could refrain from attempting to force too much material on social relationships into an inter-sectoral mould. There remain many issues genuinely in the province of inter-sectoral analysis which have not yet been adequately or completely explored.

NOTES

1. From the small list of countries that Lipton cited as not being urban-biased [1977:74], one could on his criteria omit China [Nolan and White, this volume], Tanzania [Ellis, this volume], Malawi, which has been biased towards large farms [Jonathan Kydd, private communication], and until the early 1970s, Taiwan [Lee, 1971] and South Korea [Kim and Joo, 1982].
2. This point was suggested by Diana Hunt in a University of Sussex seminar.

REFERENCES

Bale, M. D. and Lutz, E., 1981, 'Price Distortions in Agriculture and Their Effects: An International Comparison', American Journal of Agricultural Economics, Vol.63, No.1.
Bates, R. H., 1981, Markets and States in Tropical Africa. The Political Basis of Agricultural Policies, Berkeley: University of California Press.
Bates, R. H., 1983, Essays on the Political Economy of Rural Africa, Cambridge: Cambridge University Press.
Kim, D. H. and Joo, Y. J., 1982, The Food Situation and Policies in the Republic of Korea, Paris: OECD.
Lee, T. H., 1971, Intersectoral Capital Flows in the Economic Development of Taiwan 1895–1960, London and Ithaca: Cornell University Press.
Lipton, M., 1977, Why Poor People Stay Poor. Urban Bias in World Development, London: Temple Smith.
Mitra, A., 1977, Terms of Trade and Class Relations, London: Frank Cass.
Mamalakis, M. J., 1969, 'The Theory of Sectoral Clashes', Latin American Research Review, Vol.4, No.3.
Mamalakis, M. J., 1971, 'The Theory of Sectoral Clashes and Coalitions Revisited', Latin American Research Review, Vol.6, No.3.

Political Economy and the Rural-Urban Divide, 1767–1981

*by Mick Moore**

Recent theories of urban and rural bias in Third World development are premised upon the notion of a relatively clear rural-urban divide in terms of ecology, occupation and social and political organisation. As is the case with development economics generally, these theorists have drawn upon the societal assumptions and methodological postulates of classical political economy and of its Marxian offshoot. The concept of a clear rural-urban divide is deeply embedded in classical political economy, in Marxian political economy, and in sociological theory. The relevance of this concept to the contemporary Third World is implicitly questioned.

INTRODUCTION

In her review of Michael Lipton's book on 'Urban Bias' [*Lipton 1977a*] Judith Hart [*1977*] complained at the allocation of excessive space to discussion of the genesis of ideologies of urban bias in the work of classical and early Marxian political economists. Their world was too different from the contemporary Third World for their ideas to have any current relevance, while the real task was to get on and do something about urban bias today. Impatience with what might appear as purely academic indulgence is at the very least understandable in a Minister for Overseas Development. One might easily agree with Judith Hart that the classical political economists provide no guide to action in the modern world. Yet it would be a mistake to believe that the works of the classicals can safely be ignored by those attempting to understand and evaluate the kinds of ideas about urban (or rural) bias propounded by Michael Lipton and other contemporary scholars whose work is discussed below. For these contemporary theorists, especially Lipton and Ashok Mitra [*1977*], are not only building, like all economists, on a corpus of concepts and theories rooted in part in the works of the classicals. Further, their work is in some respects, both in spirit and in substance, nearer that of the classical political economists than of the dominant school of neo-classical economics which supplanted the classicals in the late nineteenth century. Among contemporary students of development Lipton and Mitra are not exceptional in owing a debt to classical political economy. It is in large part through the medium of development studies that the classical (including the Marxian) tradition has re-entered Western social science in the last three decades or so.

*Institute of Development Studies, University of Sussex. The author acknowledges a debt to John Harriss for help with this paper, especially for a set of notes on Marx, and to John, Don Funnell and Michael Redclift for very helpful comments on an earlier draft, not all of which he has been able to respond to adequately.

This conscious debt that Lipton, Mitra and others owe to the classicals[1] is one reason for examining how the classicals have influenced the contemporary study of rural-urban relations. Another is that one can find embodied in the classicals certain basic concepts and approaches which continue to prevail in contemporary analyses of rural-urban issues made from a variety of disciplinary and ideological viewpoints. (Here one must include also the classics in sociology — see below.) Above all, one finds in the classicals the very basic conception that the rural-urban dichotomy is useful and robust: that it is a categorisation central to the understanding of societies and economies widely separated by space and time. One of the purposes of this collection is to question this basic proposition.

To conduct this questioning one must look first at the terms 'rural' and 'urban'. What do they mean? One does not need to investigate the tautologies of the dictionary definitions to realise that the terms have a wide variety of implicit and overlapping references. They relate to one or more of the following sets of differences: ecology or landscape; size and density of human population; patterns of economic activity, especially where rural is equated with agriculture and urban with non-agriculture; economic function in the geographer's sense (central places and all that); and characteristic patterns of human interaction of the kind mentioned below in the discussions of sociological theory.

'Rural' and 'urban' are very flexible terms of universal application to all societies. What is for everyday purposes a very convenient economy in vocabulary may however pose considerable problems for scholarly analysis. Not only is one virtually forced to use the same terms to describe very different entities, but one is also discouraged from asking whether the basic dichotomy between rural and urban is always appropriate. Admittedly terms like 'suburban' and 'peri-urban' permit some sub-categorisation of urbanness, and in any particular circumstance one can class towns by size. But for any general conceptual discussions vocabulary does not permit any alternative to the rural-urban dichotomy without recourse to neologisms or specialists' jargon.

It is within neither our purpose nor competence to develop a new language for analysing those questions coming under the rubric of rural-urban relations. One must be content to use existing vocabulary, while at the same time attempting to combat the tyranny it can exercise over the expression of ideas. The intent of this paper is to sketch out the way in which contemporary analyses of rural-urban relations draw sustenance from the classical traditions of social science, paying special attention to the way in which these classical traditions have encouraged the relatively uncritical acceptance of the rural-urban dichotomy as a basic analytical concept.

THE FOUNDERS OF POLITICAL ECONOMY

Sir James Steuart and the Classical Foundations

Contemporary theorists of rural-urban relations have been particularly influenced by the *British* political economy tradition, from which Marxian political economy developed. While Adam Smith is normally honoured as *the* founder of classical political economy, it is appropriate to start with a contemporary, Sir James Steuart, whose major work on political economy emerged from the press nine years before Smith's [*Steuart, 1767*]. In fact most of what Smith had to say on the rural-urban question closely parallels Steuart's work. The first point that they have in common is that, like all the classical political economists, their basic unit of economic analysis is the nation state, and their main focus on economic interrelationships within the national economy. Certainly both Steuart [*1767: Book 2*] and Smith [*1776: Book 2, Chapter 5; Book 4*] have a great deal to say on foreign trade. But their perspective is that of wealthy nations for which foreign trade represents a stage of economic growth and an adjunct to the domestic economy.

Within this 'nation-state' context, Steuart does not appear to have felt any necessity to justify either his use of a basic dichotomy between 'agriculture' and 'industry' or the identification of agriculture with the countryside and industry with towns [*Steuart, 1767: 40 and passim*]. And this despite a recognition that at the time a great deal of manufacturing actually took place in the countryside on a domestic basis [*e.g. Steuart 1767: 90*]. One might also note his dual usage of the term 'industry' to refer both to manufacturing and to the spirit of entrepreneurship or capital accumulation [*Steuart, 1767: 146*]. This elision appears to foreshadow the tendency of later political economists to view manufacturing as subject to more dynamic economic motivations and forces than agriculture [*Lipton, 1977a: 92-100*].

Yet Steuart was no proponent of priority for manufacturing. The focus of his Book 1 is the proper balance between agriculture and industry. And indeed 'balance' is exactly what he advocates, although his criteria appear crude in the light of modern economics. He advocates keeping as many people on the land as are required to keep the whole population well-fed, and diverting the remainder, the 'free hands', into industrial employment. His conception is one of fundamental harmony between rural and urban interests. Not only do cities absorb 'free hands' but their populations are easily taxable, urban growth enhances the value of adjacent land, and urban and industrial growth lead to the development of roads and canals to the benefit of the rural population [*Steuart, 1767: Book 1, Chapter 10*].

As proponents of 'balance' between agriculture and industry, Steuart and Smith were attempting to correct what they saw as the excessive pro-agriculture bias of the dominant pre-existing political economy school, that of the (mainly continental) Physiocrats [*Roll, 1973: 128-37*]. It is surely in their defence of the new industrialism that one must find at least part of the explanation why Steuart, Smith and others, in violation of their recognition of the quantitative significance of rural domestic manufacturing, adhered so implicitly and unquestioningly to the notion of a fundamental divide between the rural agricultural and the urban industrial sector. Manufacturing was not new, but factory production was. While not all early factories were located in towns, urban factory production must have appeared very novel and of great potential significance. The attempt to deal with the implications of this new form of economic and social organisation must partly explain why the classicals were so willing to draw a line between this and the older, mainly agricultural sector. They consigned rural domestic manufacture to an analytical void from which

Marx was to rescue it temporarily, only to cast it explicitly into the scrap heap of history (see below).

It is of more than passing interest that a later and different school of political economy treated domestic manufacturing in a less cavalier fashion. In the mid-nineteenth century a partially indigenous school of political economy in Germany treated domestic manufacturing as a separate analytical category and made it the subject of much empirical research [*Kriedte et al., 1981: 1-4*]. By implication, the rural-urban dichotomy appeared less complete here than in the British tradition.

From the contemporary viewpoint there appears to be an unanswered question about the ease with which early British political economy adopted the notion of the rural-urban sectoral divide. For one of the elementary tools of economics has long been the division of the economy into primary (agriculture and extractive), secondary (manufacturing) and tertiary (services) sectors. Much service industry is relatively recent. It is almost an axiom of economic history that the importance of this sector tends to increase with economic growth. Yet some service activities, notably transport, storage and trade, were of great significance in the eighteenth century, and essential to the very market-orientated agriculture then found in the British Isles. Why in the work of the classicals does the service sector not find more recognition and, correspondingly, the rural-urban categorisation a less universal and uncritical acceptance? To answer this question one must recall another fundamental postulate of classical political economy: that productive activities were defined as the production of *goods*. The performance of service functions, even if in some sense admitted to be essential,[2] was correspondingly relegated to the 'non-productive' category. It was only in the latter half of the nineteenth century, in conditions of greater material abundance, that the question of economic *choice* – rather than the priority for increasing material production – began to feature prominently in the agenda of political economy. The newly-emergent neo-classical economics school was eventually able to sweep most of the board with an analytical method which specified that value lay in the amount of money that purchasers were prepared to pay.[3] Since purchasers were prepared to pay for services, then the performance of services was deemed as productive as the production of goods of equivalent market value. This opened the way to the categorisation of economies into primary, secondary and tertiary (service) sectors.[4] By this time – in Britain and the United States at least – agriculture was sufficiently capitalist and small that rural-urban issues ceased to pose any major analytical challenge in economics.

Adam Smith and Sectoral Bias

The contemporary student of rural-urban relations reading *The Wealth of Nations* is likely to be impressed above all by a few brief sections in which Smith sketches out scenarios of 'urban bias' which parallel very closely the work of present-day scholars like Michael Lipton. Smith's argument that returns to capital investment are greater in agriculture than in non-agriculture [*Smith, 1776: Book 2, Chapter 5; compare Lipton, 1977a: 184-215*] may be dismissed as quirky and distinctly unsophisticated in the light of contemporary economic method. It is founded on the claim that nature is always labouring for free in support of capital invested in agriculture, and the returns are higher because the total input effort (capital and nature) is greater than when an equivalent amount of capital is placed in non-agriculture. Much more significant is Smith's argument that in Europe[5] the selling prices of urban manufactured goods had generally been raised to artificially high levels through political forces. Starting from his repeated concern at the tendency for producers and traders in the same line of activity to collude with one another − a concern which many latter-day 'free market' proponents of Smith's work have found it convenient to ignore − he claims that urban producers find collusion much easier than do scattered rural populations. Urban producers generally succeed both in directly raising their own selling prices above free market levels and in persuading governments to allow them to be raised further by restricting imports of competing manufactured goods.

> The enhancement of price occasioned by both is everywhere finally paid by the landlords, farmers and labourers of the country who have seldom opposed the establishment of such monopolies. They have commonly neither inclination nor fitness to enter into combinations; and the clamour and sophistry of merchants and manufacturers easily persuade them that the private interest of a part, and of a subordinate part of the society, is the general interest of the whole. [*Smith, 1776: Book 1, Chapter 10, Part 2*]

This, in a nutshell, summarises a large part of Michael Lipton's argument in his *Urban Bias*!

Since Lipton detects in Smith's work, and especially in what he terms 'development and distortions of Smith's ideas' [*Lipton, 1977a: 99*], the roots of 'urban bias' in both classical and neo-classical economics there is scope for a debate on whether or not Smith was 'urban-biased'. And here the evidence seems to point all ways. Lipton detects incipient 'urban bias' in (a) Smith's stage theory of economic growth and the claim that the role of agriculture is to provide 'surpluses' for urban manufacturing development; and (b) in Smith's view that the potential for the division of labour and thus for technical progress and output growth is larger in manufacturing than in agriculture [*Lipton, 1977a: 92-7*]. One might well juxtapose to this Smith's explicit glorification of the virtues of rural life,[6] and conclude by taking at face value his claims that *in the process of economic growth* the interests of town and country were mutual and harmonious [*Smith, 1776: Book 3, Chapter 1*]. It is implicit in Smith's presentation that rural-urban economic conflict and exploitation is a feature and perhaps also a cause of general economic stagnation. It is not in evidence during periods of economic progress (see also note 5).

Smith fits into our characterisation of classical political economy less for his historical analysis of rural-urban relations at particular times and places than for his basic approach to the question. He shares with Steuart the basic presumption about the usefulness of the rural agricultural v. urban manufacturing dichotomy (see above), but adds to this in ways which bring him nearer to contemporary theorists of rural-urban relations. In various ways Smith helped to effect an implicit change in the meaning of the word 'political'

in 'political economy'. For Sir James Steuart, for example, 'political' had referred essentially to policy: he was concerned to develop principles for the wise
management of the nation's economic affairs [*e.g. Steuart, 1767: Preface*].
Smith moved the subject along a road which was to be pursued even further
by his successors, notably Ricardo and, above all, Karl Marx: a concern with
'politics' in the sense of competition over material resources [*Mitra, 1977:
Chapter 2*]. Among the themes which are evident in Smith's works and
developed by Ricardo and Marx are: the presumption that society comprises
classes of people defined in relation to the means of production – owners
of capital, owners of land, and providers of labour [*Smith, 1776: passim*];
the belief that a major concern of political economy should be to explain how
the fruits of productive activity are 'naturally distributed among the different
Ranks of the People'[7] in the form of rent for landlords, profit for capital and
wages for labourers;[8] and the implicit assumption, evident from the discussion above of his model of 'urban bias' in Europe, that economic classes
organise to put pressure on the state to improve their own position in the
exchange economy – that classes defined by their relation to the means of
production are simultaneously interest groups in the political sphere.

Ricardo

It is characteristic that Ricardo appears to have little to say in his major economic texts on the structure of the society with which he dealt. Like most of his
contemporaries, he accepted that Smith had laid the foundations and established the agenda of political economy. Ricardo concerned himself with tidying
up loose ends, correcting errors and, above all, in establishing political economy as a deductive discipline in which valid general conclusions could be drawn
from a few basic assumptions and postulates [*Deane, 1978: 74-8*]. Among his
basic assumptions, so evident to him as not to require justification, was a
'Smithian' model of society of the kind sketched out above: one in which the
main classes were capitalists, landlords and labourers, and which was in turn
categorised into an urban manufacturing sector, populated by capitalists and
labourers, and a rural agricultural sector in which landlords featured prominently alongside capitalist farmers and rural labourers [*Ricardo, 1817: passim*].
    Of all the classical political economists Ricardo's name is now most closely
associated with the analysis of rural-urban relations. For like many of his
contemporaries, but in ways which give him a claim to intellectual pre-
eminence, much of his work was concerned with the question of import
production for British agriculture – the debate on the repeal of the Corn Laws
– and the implications both for the distribution of income and for economic
growth. It is not necessary here to discuss Ricardo's theory of rent, its relation
to the Corn Law debate or his intellectual disputes with Malthus and other
advocates of import protection for agriculture [*see Deane, 1978: Chapter 5;
and Mitra, 1977: 11-20*]. It is important simply to note how far the basic
outlines of this debate – the categorisation of society into rural and urban
sectors and into classes defined in relation to the means of production; and
the presumption that politics is orientated around the pursuit of class interests
– foreshadow the recent scholarship discussed below.

Karl Marx

In relation to rural-urban questions, as to so many others, it is becoming increasingly difficult to identify a single Marxist or Marxian position or approach, and increasingly foolhardy to attempt general conclusions without being prepared to back them with detailed textual research. However, it is understandable to this author that the strong anti-rural and anti-peasant strain in Marxism should be allocated first place in the demonology of those scholars who view 'urban bias' as an important cause of human misery and inadequate rates of economic growth in the Soviet Union and the contemporary Third World. The spirit of Mitrany's [*1961*] denunciation of *Marx Against the Peasant*, closely reflected in Lipton's more subtle attack on ideologies of 'urban bias' [*1977a: 107-21*], is an understandable response to the marked anti-rural emotive and programmatic themes in Marxism. 'For Marx, the whole rural scheme of things is tantamount to idiocy as far as its impact on human thought is concerned' [*Nisbet, 1967: 67*]. Anti-ruralism was the emotive and programmatic handmaiden of Marx's (historically unwarranted) conviction that the distinctive feature of rural society – small-scale family farming – was destined to disappear in the face of capitalist competition.[9] That the formally Marxist-Leninist government of China has been less automatically urban-biased [*Nolan and White, this volume*] might in some sense balance, but not exonerate, the dominant European Marxist tradition.

Marxist theory as a whole, including in China [*Nolan and White*], has certainly inherited the classical presumption that the rural-urban divide is analytically (and politically) robust and useful. That however is not quite all which needs to be said on the subject here. For in Marx's work there are hints of a more subtle and historically-informed approach to rural-urban relations than the simple assumption that rural and urban are given analytical categories standing above all history.

There are clear ambiguities in Marx's use of the terms rural and urban, as indeed there are in his references to many other issues which he never pursued in depth. Take, for example, the following quotation from *Capital*: 'The foundation of every division of labour that is well developed, and brought about by the exchange of commodities, is the separation between town and country. It may be said, that the whole economic history of society is summed up in the movement of this antithesis' [*Marx, 1867: 352*].[10] At first sight, the second sentence appears to suggest that rural and urban, understood as socio-economic categories rather than simply as descriptions of contrasting landscapes, are historically universal categories, and that a (conflictual) relationship between them is both equally universal and a prime motor of societal change. Yet the first sentence, when placed in its context of Marx's analysis of the replacement of domestic (often rural) manufacture by urban factory production, implies something very different: that the clarity and nature of the rural-urban divide is not historically invariant. The distinction has been sharpened by the disappearance of (rural) domestic manufacture and the concentration of non-agricultural production in the towns:

> Modern Industry alone, and finally, supplies, in machinery, the lasting
> basis of capitalistic agriculture, expropriates radically the enormous

majority of the agricultural population, and completes the separation between agriculture and rural domestic industry, whose roots – spinning and weaving – it tears up. [*1867: 748-9*]

That Marx has some concept of historically contingent patterns of rural-urban relations becomes very clear as he envisages a future in which capital brings agriculture up to the same standards of productivity and cultural progressiveness as industry (this author's emphases added):

> The irrational, old-fashioned methods of agriculture are replaced by scientific ones. Capitalist production completely tears asunder the *old bond of union which held together agriculture and manufacturing in their infancy*. But at the same time it creates the material conditions for a *higher synthesis* in the future, viz. the union of agriculture and industry on the basis of the more perfected forms they have each acquired during their *temporary separation*. [*1867: 505*]

One might tentatively conclude that the two quotations immediately above should be interpreted merely as formal concessions to theoretical and normative consistency: expressions of confidence that the society which will succeed capitalism will resolve, along with all others, the rural-urban contradiction which did not exist at the primitive stage of social development and which is a by-product of the advance of capitalism. Or one might prefer to go for the honoured formula of 'unarticulated insights': to detect the outlines of a theory of rural-urban relations based on historical stages in the development of commodity and capitalist production and in the relationship between agriculture and non-agricultural production. The latter interpretation however awaits a Marxian scholar who will do for rural-urban relations what Harvey [*1973 and 1982*], for example, has done for urbanisation: drawn together Marx's 'unarticulated insights' and the way in which he 'captures the interaction effects that led to the rapid agglomeration of production within cities' to develop a Marxian analysis of the urbanisation process. At present the Marxian tradition cannot be said to have broken with the classical assumption that the rural-urban divide is fundamental.

SOCIOLOGICAL THEORY

The rural-urban dichotomy *per se* barely features in the conceptual apparatuses of Comte, Durkheim, Le Play, Saint-Simon, Tocqueville, Tonnies, Troeltsch, Weber and the other scholars who can claim to have helped found sociology as a discipline in the late eighteenth and, more especially, the early and mid-nineteenth centuries [*Nisbet, 1967*]. Yet their dominant collective concern with the adverse consequences on social relations of contemporary economic, social and political changes made an analagous dichotomy between communitarian and non-communitarian forms of social organisation into the most fundamental conceptual tool of sociology [*Nisbet, 1967: Chapter 3*]. Communitarian forms of social organisation, 'characterised by a high degree of personal intimacy, emotional depth, moral commitment, social cohesion, and continuity in time' [*Nisbet, 1967: 47*], were not seen by the founders as exclusive to rural society. They were equally the attributes of such institutions as the family and craft and municipal guilds. But the dominant perspective was that community in all its forms was disappearing in the face of the pressures for individualistic, contractual, instrumental, amoral and simplex (i.e. single-stranded) social relationships associated with the dynamic forces of modernism: industry, factory production, urban living and political democracy. It was therefore but a short step from associating community with disappearing forms of social organisation to associating it with the apparent antithesis of modernity: rurality and agriculture. And this is a step which, as Newby [1980] has argued at length, later sociology has rarely refrained from taking. Sociology, especially rural sociology (by virtue of its very existence), has committed itself to the view that differences between rural and urban forms of social organisation, whether conceived in terms of dichotomy or continuum, are fundamental. It may be true that the 'rural-urban continuum now lies generally discredited' [Newby, 1978: 5], but this view is not yet universally accepted. Sociology has long given sustenance to the belief that the concepts of rural and urban are fundamental and indispensable to macro-level social analysis.

CONTEMPORARY ANALYSES OF RURAL-URBAN RELATIONS IN THE THIRD WORLD

Even in the early stages of development studies (i.e. the 1950s) considerable concern was expressed as to whether there was not, from a Western-centred historical perspective, something abnormal or even pathological about the pattern of both urbanisation and of rural-urban relations in the Third World. Take, for example, the much derided school of 'modernisation theory', which represented the single most coherent general approach to the study of Third World development in the 1950s and 1960s. At its crudest the 'modernisation' approach was centred around the hypothesis that the development path of poor nations could broadly be expected to replicate, and could be evaluated against the (?) path which had been followed by the non-industrialised nations. Yet in the 1950s Hoselitz, a leading modernisation theorist, was already drawing attention to apparently pathological features of urban growth in the Third World: unemployment; urban destitution; a division between what were later termed the 'formal' and 'informal' urban economic sectors; and overall, indications of 'overurbanisation' [Singer, 1977: 14].[11]

From the rural side there were in the 1950s and 1960s similar empirically-based concerns about what would now be termed 'urban bias'. These concerns were broadly of two kinds. In the first place, writers like Schickele [1968: Chapter 5] saw evidence of consistent urban bias in economic policy of a kind sketched out by Adam Smith long before (see above). He suggested that the state tended consistently to divert resources from rural agricultural to urban industrial sectors by depressing agricultural produce prices, taxing agricultural exports, taxing agriculture more heavily than industry, and obliging the rural sector to meet the reproduction costs of the industrial work force. Like the classicals, Schickele also added a class dimension to the sectoral divide: the surplus extracted from agricultural producers by landlords and moneylenders was diverted to the urban sector, not reinvested in agriculture to generate rural livelihoods.

In the second place Schickele [*1968: Chapters 5 and 6*] and other scholars like René Dumont [*1966*] and Thomas Balogh [*1966: 238-44*], both of whom were concerned primarily with African developments, were drawing attention to the deleterious effects on agricultural development and rural living standards of another aspect of state activity, one which would have been totally foreign to Adam Smith. This was the way in which the state's welfare expenditures, especially education and health programmes, and its administrative efforts to promote development, were consistently biased against rural areas. The central focus of concern was the way in which human capital development failed to benefit rural areas: formal education was simultaneously fitting rural youth for urban jobs and alienating them from agriculture and rural life; salaries and living conditions of public servants were tending to concentrate most of the public service, but especially the more able public servants, in urban areas and in departments catering to urban needs and concerns. There was simultaneously a general feeling that public investment of all kinds was unduly concentrated on urban and industrial facilities. These concerns would have been alien to Adam Smith and the other classicals because they had no experience of the 'welfare state': a policy in which the state assumed overall responsibility for economic progress and the living standards of its population.

The concerns of Schickele, Dumont, Balogh and others may be termed as 'empirical' in that they emerged simply from observation: there was no attempt to link them to any overreaching theory of development. Such attempts were however underway. In the late 1960s and 1970s three development economists – Lipton [*1977a*], Mamalakis [*1969*] and Mitra [*1977*] – put forward general theories which claimed to explain slow economic progress in the Third World by prevailing rural-urban relationships. Mitra [*1977: 20*] described a class analysis approach to rural-urban relations as 'one of the grandest problems classical political economy has dealt with'. For the first time since the debates on the British Corn Laws the rural-urban relations issue was back as a major item on the agenda of political economy.

There are a range of differences between Lipton, Mamalakis and Mitra in focus and approach. For example, Mamalakis attempts to explain low growth in Latin America since the 1930s, Mitra tries to explain the falling-off of the rate of economic growth in India in the 1960s, and Lipton tries to explain both low growth and, even more importantly, the persistence of mass rural poverty in most of the Third World since the Second World War. Lipton argues that 'urban bias' – the diversion of resources to urban areas – is the cause of low growth and poverty. Mitra, operating with a very similar politico-economic model, argues virtually the exact opposite: that in India and perhaps other countries it is the ability of the rural rich to distort terms of trade in their favour which has emerged as the major constraint on economic progress. Mamalakis' argument is similar to Lipton's except that his model comprises several economic sectors, not simply rural and urban. It is, however, the urban sector which he identifies as the bloodsucker.

It is convenient to start with a sketch of Michael Lipton's work, not so much because it is the most widely known and claims the widest application but because it bears more similarity to the work of Mamalakis and Mitra than they bear to each other.

Michael Lipton: 'Why Poor People Stay Poor'

The most important class conflict in the poor countries of the world today is not between labour and capital. Nor is it between foreign and national interests. It is between the rural classes and the urban classes. The rural sector contains most of the poverty, and most of the low-cost sources of potential advance; but the urban sector contains most of the articulateness, organisation and power. So the urban classes have been able to 'win' most of the rounds of the struggle with the countryside; but in so doing they have made the development process needlessly slow and unfair. Scarce land, which might grow millets and beansprouts for hungry villagers, instead produces a trickle of costly calories from meat and milk, which few except the urban rich (who have ample protein anyway) can afford. Scarce investment, instead of going into water-pumps to grow rice, is wasted on urban motorways. Scarce human skills design and administer, not clean village wells and agricultural extension services, but world boxing championships in showpiece stadia. Resource allocations, within the city and the village as well as between them, reflect urban priorities rather than equity or efficiency. The damage has been increased by misguided ideological imports, liberal and Marxian, and by the town's success in buying off part of the rural elite, thus transferring most of the costs of the process to the rural poor. [*Lipton, 1977a: 13*]

'This opening paragraph summarises all the main arguments in Lipton's book *Why Poor People Stay Poor. Urban Bias in World Development*. For present purposes they can be reduced to the following seven propositions:

1. In direct contradiction to the 'dependency' type of analyses which were becoming so prominent in development studies at the time that Lipton was writing, the main explanations of economic and political phenomena within Third World countries are to be found in relationships internal to individual countries.[12]
2. Countries can be clearly divided into rural (agricultural) and urban sectors.
3. There are major conflicts of interest between these two sectors.
4. The sectors are each internally divided into two main class categories whose interests may diverge and conflict.
5. Groups designated by sectoral and class location appear as solidary political actors pursuing the group interest in politics.
6. The urban sector is generally more successful in politics, but only through 'buying off' the rural elite.
7. The resultant pattern of resource allocation is inefficient in terms of aggregate growth and inequitable to the cost of the rural poor.

The validity of proposition 7 will not concern us in this paper, which is focused on the analytical viability of the rural-urban sectoral divide. The first point to be made about the first six propositions is how closely they correspond to the basic analytical frameworks of classical political economy sketched out above. Lipton's awareness of the classicals has already been noted. There is also implicit in his work an awareness of contemporary Marxian perspectives and a clear attempt to engage Marxists on their own

– and thus also on the classicals' – terms by focusing on questions of class, inequality and the use of public power to advance class interests.

Michael Lipton on the Rural-Urban Divide

Unlike the classicals, Lipton felt the need explicitly to refute – albeit more by assertion than by reference to evidence – potential criticisms that the city-country line was not clear cut. We are told [Lipton, 1977a: 57-60] that in terms of settlement geography the blurring of the line is rare and exceptional, that 'the bias diagnosed in this book stems from and benefits large towns of ten to twenty thousand people and more' [Lipton, 1977a: 58], that there is no major tertiary or 'rurban' sector to blur the line significantly, and that he is not talking of metropolitan or capital city bias rather than general urban bias.[13] Lipton also diverges slightly from the classicals in that he does not fully equate 'urban' with 'industrial': almost all industrial activity is urban, but the urban sector both includes many other activities and anyway obtains political leverage from the very fact of its urbanness – its tight clustering around the seats of power [Lipton, 1977a: 60-2].

In his defence of the city-country line against the suggestion of 'capital city' bias Lipton exposes himself to criticisms which have been widely voiced in relation to many aspects of his book, and which are almost unavoidable given the scope of his argument: generalisation about most developing countries by reference to evidence from a few. In this particular case the identity of 'the few' is of some interest. Not only are most of the references to India, but Lipton chooses to focus on large countries, naming India and Nigeria:

> Socio-economically, 'capital city bias' obscures the link between towns *as a whole* and the urge to industrialise, modernise and 'westernise' – an urge as readily expressed in ports, tourist resorts or company towns (and by their beneficiaries) as in capital cities, which often reflect only a long-established need for a trading and administrative centre. The newly expanded secondary cities are often the real, new centres of power. The economic power behind urban bias rests – to speak in nineteenth-century British terms – in Manchester, not in London. Politico-administratively, especially in a big federal country such as India or Nigeria, the greater strength and immediacy and sophistication of urban pressure groups is often much *less* serious in the capital city than in other towns, especially than in centres of provincial administration. To some extent, politicians and administrators in Delhi acquire distance from and capacity to play off, the sort of urban-industrial pressures that overwhelmingly weigh upon decisions in a state capital like Patna. [Lipton, 1977a: 59]

Rather than closing the debate, Lipton's defence of his city-country line appears to open it wide. Suppose that instead of defending it by reference to India and Nigeria he had chosen one of that far more numerous category of developing countries whose history – and sometimes origins – had been determined by their emergence as exporters of primary products to Europe in the nineteenth century, if not before: Ghana, Liberia, Senegal, Argentina, Guyana, Sri Lanka, Thailand, Burma, etc. Here a single metropolis, built around a port, dominates absolutely; other urban centres are few and tiny in relation to the metropolis. Here we could certainly apply the city-country divide in a formal sense, in most cases dividing the metropolis from the rest. But would we be making the same kind of division as in India or Nigeria, where the urban sector comprises many individual and widely scattered towns? Lipton's own arguments suggest not, for in the quotation above he introduces, albeit in passing, the notion of conflicts of interests between different urban settlements. And it is a notion that must have more substance than he implies. If individual urban centres do indeed pursue a collective interest, then there are potential intra-urban sector conflicts in India which will not emerge in Senegal or Argentina. To speculate on whether the nature of urban bias differs between such metropolitan-centred countries and countries like India would be to delve too far into the hypothetical. The main point is that, leaving aside both class analysis (see below) and any questions about which smaller towns are to be included in the 'urban sector' (see *Harriss and Harriss, this volume*) in any particular case if the hypothesis of 'urban bias' is to be tested, there are important questions about the similarity and unity of interests of different urban centres.

Similar kinds of questions can be raised about the homogeneity of the rural sector (for the question of class interests, see below). Lipton (and Mitra) appear to ignore three major variables in (implicitly) asserting this homogeneity. The first is the far from complete separation between rural areas and manufacturing. As Ho has illustrated for Taiwan and South Korea, manufacturing is far from being an exclusively urban activity before, during or after industrialisation. In 1930 84 per cent and 63 per cent of manufacturing employment in South Korea and Taiwan respectively was located in rural areas. In 1975 (Korea) and 1971 (Taiwan), after a period of very rapid industrial growth, the figures were 46 per cent and 51 per cent [*Ho, 1982: 974 and 981*]. The second variable is cropping patterns. Lipton and Mitra both use models in which foodgrains are the main rural product, an assumption generally valid for India, but not for many developing countries, where non-food agricultural exports feature prominently. The interests of cash crop producers may conflict with those of food producers [*Moore, this volume*] and the mechanisms through which their surpluses are appropriated may differ [*Ellis, this volume*]. The case study by Moore explores the implications of the other major variable ignored by Lipton and Mitra: the way in which space − distance from the capital city − produces systematic differences in both the objective interests and the political power of the rural population. Following the traditions of the classical and Marxian political economists, and indeed of most British − as opposed to French − social science,[14] the effect of distance on socio-economic relationships does not feature at all in the work of Lipton and Mitra. They simply divide countries into an urban space or sector and a rural space or sector. Variations among the rural areas in access to cities are not dealt with at all; the perspective of economic and political geography is totally absent.

Implicit in the above paragraphs is a criticism of Lipton's work which has already been raised by Seers [*1977*] but in a less than fully satisfactory fashion: whether Lipton's work is not ultimately concerned mainly with India. Seers suggests that the book seems 'to reflect primarily the socio-economic structure of India', and observes that India features very prominently in the empirical evidence [*Seers, 1977: 9*]. He notes that India's size and the resilience of its traditions and institutions mean that external influences weigh less heavily there than in most countries [*Seers, 1977: 11*]. His suggestion that the rural-urban contrast is stronger in India than elsewhere [*Seers, 1977: 6*] might have been supplemented by the observation that India has a particularly 'balanced' distribution of major cities. Delhi is primarily an administrative centre, and other urban and manufacturing interests are concentrated in a range of other large cities – notably Bombay, Calcutta, Madras, Bangalore and Hyderabad – spread fairly evenly over the map of India.

These criticisms are, at least in part, validly answered by Lipton's response that the degree of urban bias is less in India than elsewhere [*Lipton, 1977a: 18; 1977b: 30-1*]. But that is not to agree that the claim about the 'Indian bias' is misplaced. For Seers did not adequately stress and develop the point that it is the basic analytical framework of Lipton's book which is 'Indian', not that India is especially urban biased. The analytical framework is 'Indian' firstly in the sense that it was originally developed to deal with Indian material [*Lipton, 1977a: 18*]. Lipton's first writings on urban bias were on India [*e.g. Lipton, 1968 and 1972*]. It is 'Indian' secondly in that various empirical features of India make the model more applicable there than most developing countries: a relatively 'balanced' distribution of large towns (see above); the absence, except in Kerala [*Lipton, 1977a: 57*] of densely populated semi-rural, semi-urban urban peripheries containing large proportions of the population;[15] the relatively small role of tropical export crops and the corresponding importance of foodgrains in agricultural production (see above); a very long established and relatively clear division between rural and urban social groups;[16] and the relatively high level of insulation from external political, cultural and institutional influence (see above). Thirdly, and perhaps most importantly, Lipton's work is 'Indian' in the sense that it arises from, and contributes to, an established Indian tradition of seeing the rural-urban divide as a central feature of social organisation: 'The striking aspect of the Indian concern with issues of distribution is its concentration on a single focus of attention: the urban-rural dimension.' 'Most other issues ... seem to be treated under this larger rubric.' [*Kothari, 1970: 351-2*]. This obsession with the rural-urban divide presumably arises at least in part from the very clarity of the divide in India; it (the obsession) is certainly not common to all Asian cultures.[17] It is also likely that this basic predisposition has been strengthened in contemporary Indian social science by the widespread diffusion of Marxian ideas, which perpetuate the British political economy tradition of assuming a clear rural-urban divide (see above). Reference has already been made above to the irony of the situation in which Lipton and Mitra should be working at the same time on the economics of rural-urban relations, operate with the same politico-economic model (which in Mitra's case is avowedly Indian), and yet conclude that in India there is 'urban bias' and 'rural bias' respectively. Their methods and models unite them more than their ideologies and policy preferences divide them,[18] and it is mainly in India that their methods and models were forged.

Class and Politics in 'Urban Bias'

In the several dozen reviews which have appeared of Lipton's work the most common single theme, apart from tributes to his intellectual ability and the basic plausibility of much of the argument, is probably critical questioning of his use of the concept of 'class' and the relation of the concept to the rural and urban sectoral categories. At the risk of over-simplifying one can identify two basic perspectives from which critiques are made.

The first, which one might call the 'political economy' critique, is made by those adhering to one of the fundamental tenets of political economy: that the primary motivation behind political action is the pursuit of material class interests, however they may be defined. The main criticism of this school centres around issues which are ultimately terminological, although they do have considerable ideological and emotive connotations: whether Lipton has indeed justified his claim that 'The most important class conflict in the poor countries of the world today is not between capital and labour .... It is between the rural classes and the urban classes' [Lipton, 1977a: 13].

The issues here are familiar to anyone who has read Lipton's book and the reviews.[19] On the one hand Lipton talks of the rural-urban clash of interests. On the other hand he does not abandon class analysis of the more conventional kind, and indeed argues that the rural 'elite' – the larger farmers who sell surplus foodgrains to the town – are in fact in alliance with urban interests. In return for accepting policies which depress market prices for food and concentrate public investment in urban activities, the rural 'elite' are rewarded through policies which subsidise scarce agricultural inputs like fertiliser and irrigation pumps to which only the elite have effective access, but which they use less efficiently than poor small farmers. The critics then respond with the query that, if part of the 'rural' population in fact benefits from urban-biased policies, why talk of sectoral clashes at all, since conventional class terminology can describe the same phenomena more accurately? Seers makes the same point in response to Lipton's claim that racial inequality in South Africa is essentially an expression of urban bias:

> It is true that a bigger proportion of blacks than of whites live in rural areas, but one could turn the argument round the other way: it is because of racial discrimination ... that blacks tend to live where they do – and in both town and country are deprived of the economic and political power to earn more. Surely urban bias leads to a model of the Republic with less explanatory power than one which rests on race, as do its politics and laws. [Seers, 1977: 6-7]

Further pursuit of this argument here does not seem fruitful, although one might note Michael Lipton's more recent suggestion (this volume) that his 'rural elite' are in fact an *urbanising* class. Let us turn instead to the second kind of critique of Lipton's political analysis, which has received far less attention and which might be termed the 'political science' critique. Take as the starting point the fact that both Lipton and Mitra share the methodological presumption, common to both Marxian and non-Marxian political economy, that since classes pursue class interests in politics, in order to demonstrate that a class is pursuing its interest it is adequate to demonstrate that it benefits from policy. The study of politics – how interests are conceptualised, aggregated and mobilised politically – is of little or no significance. At no point does Lipton give examples of *how* the class alliances which he posits have actually operated politically. One might note that there is an apparent causal connection between the method of assuming a given pattern of politics and his dual use of the term 'urban bias'. As he now agrees, he uses it both as explanatory variable (a pattern of political alliances and activities) and as explanandum (the pattern of public and private resource allocation which emerges from politics).

The political economist might respond that the method of assuming that X interest is powerful if X interest actually benefits from policy is, if not totally adequate, then a fairly good indicator of the pattern of politics. So it is, but only if one is looking in detail at particular cases and has available adequate data to see the whole picture. It is not too difficult in any polity to find examples of a policy benefiting a particular interest. Before concluding that the 'urban' or any other interest group was dominant, one would need to examine a wide range of policy outcomes.

As Corbridge has explained, the fundamental problem with the method of political analysis pursued by Lipton (and Mitra) is that it involves the equation of two very different concepts: 'class' and 'interest groups':

> Firstly, any attempt to define a class as an interest group must share the inadequacies attaching to this general equation. Very briefly ... these inadequacies are an indeterminacy and an instability: indeterminacy in that each and every interest group, to be consistent, must then define and locate a specific class, which leads to a fruitless multiplication of classes rendering the whole concept valueless; and instability in that members of a particular class are prone to rapid and recurring shifts in their membership patterns. Indeed, any individual might at the same instant be affiliated to two, possibly contradictory, class locations. This is well evinced in the particularly problematic position of the rural elite, at least in Lipton's analysis. With regard to food prices supposedly, and certainly with regard to the provision of transport and educational facilities, the rural elite is the natural leader of the 'rural class'. With regard to the provision of agricultural inputs it becomes, at the same time, part of the 'urban class'.
>
> Plainly, in its own terms, Lipton's conception of class is untenable. Underscoring his difficulties is a second deficiency, a reductionist conception of politics. Beginning with a claimed identification of policies and plans that are made by and for urbanites, Lipton must then provide urban and rural classes to conform to his assumption that certain politics and interests must always and automatically represent certain classes.
> [*Corbridge, 1982: 101*]

It is in fact extremely unlikely that any political science study would lead to the identification of categories of political actors as broad, discrete and stable as Lipton's rural and urban classes-cum-interest groups.

Ashok Mitra's 'Terms of Trade and Class Relations'

It is an illustration of the weakness of the political analysis in the work of Lipton and Mitra that they operate with almost identical politico-economic models and yet, by adding different *assumptions* about political alliances, reach opposite conclusions about whether India is characterised by urban bias or rural bias. Lipton argues that the rural elite is persuaded to work in political alliance with the urban sector by the offer of input subsidies as compensation for policies which artificially lower the selling prices of agricultural products (see above). Mitra argues that there emerged in India in the 1960s a political alliance between the rural elite and the urban bourgeoisie in which the rural elite trade their command of the mass rural vote banks for policies which *increase* the market prices of agricultural products [*Mitra, 1977: Chapter 8*]. The conclusion of Mitra's very neatly structured book is that this shift in the terms of trade in favour of agriculture is a prime cause of the declining rate of growth in Indian industry since the mid-1960s, and descent into 'quasi-stagnation':

> Now for a summing up. There has been a perceptible decline in the rate of Indian industrial growth since 1965–66, and signs of a quasi-stagnation are becoming markedly evident. This development, we suggest, is causally related to the continuous movement in relative prices against industry and in favour of agriculture. As argued in Section II, the shifting terms of trade have been instrumental in eroding the level of real incomes of the majority of the population in both urban areas and in the countryside; the demand for mass consumption goods has levelled off as a result. At the other end, by far the major part of the income additionally generated in the economy during the past decade has flown into the hands of a small fraction of the community; a number of luxury consumer goods industries have sprung up to satisfy their relatively sophisticated requirements. This has in turn called for a substantial demand for fresh capital funds, which have been generally under strain. In the case of most of these new industries, investments have also been disproportionately large in relation to the size of the market because of the high degree of built-in indivisi-bilities. To cover overheads, producers have been forced to fix prices at a relatively high level, a practice which has further inhibited demand. What has thus emerged is a syndrome of high capital intensity – large indivisibilities – high cost – high price – low demand – low output in the industrial sector. [*Mitra, 1977: 163*]

Apart from their respective conclusions about whether India is to be charac-terised as urban or rural biased,[20] there are a few other differences between Lipton and Mitra in the substance of their arguments. Lipton does not admit of any fundamental class (= interest) cleavage within the urban sector. While the existence of urban poverty is accepted [*Lipton, 1977a: 54*], it is also claimed that a substantial fraction of the urban poor are 'really' rural because they come from and return to rural areas [*Lipton, 1977a: 226-7*]. More generally, it is suggested that the entire urban population benefits from at least some aspects of urban bias [*Lipton, 1977a: passim*]. Mitra by contrast operates explicitly with a four-fold sectoral-cum-class scheme: 'In the farm sector, the two classes exhausting the genus are the surplus-raising rich (and middle) peasants and the small and landless ones. Outside agriculture, the two major economic categories are the bourgeoisie and the working class.' [*Mitra, 1977: 99*]

Both Lipton and Mitra posit that the mass of the rural population not producing a significant marketed surplus are too 'illiterate, commercially weak and poorly organised' [*Mitra, 1977: 163*] to prevent the rural elite from representing their own (elite) interests as the interests of agriculture as a whole. However, while Mitra sees a major contradiction between the two rural classes, Lipton sees this contradiction as only partial, arguing that the entire rural population, including the landless and deficit farmers, ultimately stand to gain from high producer prices for agricultural products [*Lipton, 1977a: 42*]. As in the analysis of the urban sector, Mitra sees more intra-sectoral class contradiction than does Lipton (see also below).

Another difference between Lipton and Mitra is that in at least two senses 'the state' looms somewhat larger in the former's work. Mitra adheres broadly to the Marxian concept of the state as it features in *The Communist Manifesto*, i.e. as a 'committee of the bourgeoisie', with no autonomy or existence independent of the expression of class interests [*Mitra, 1977: 5 and 101*]. Lipton not only sees some autonomy for the state – a capacity to act in political independence of class interests [*Lipton, 1977a: 59*] – but also sees urban bias manifested both in economic policies and in the distribution of the investment, administrative and welfare services of the contemporary 'welfare state' (see above). Mitra, more faithful to the classical and Marxian traditions (see below), has nothing to say (in this book at least) about these latter dimensions of the contemporary state; he is concerned mainly with the analysis of input and output markets and economic policy, although he also bolsters his argument by reference to tax and credit policy [*Mitra, 1977: 110-11*].

Otherwise many of the differences between Lipton and Mitra in their treatment of rural-urban relations are matters of style stemming from differing ideological and normative stances. While Lipton sees his work as representing a break with existing analyses, Mitra locates himself within a well-established tradition running through Marxism from Adam Smith and Ricardo, and organises his book along these lines. Explicitly in the Marxian tradition, he makes *class* the central concept of his work where Lipton emphasises *sector*. Correspondingly, Mitra finds it important to discuss in detail the relation of class interest to political action – a discussion in which he incidentally does indicate reservations and embarrassment about inferring class political action from policy outcomes without any intervening study of politics itself [*Mitra, 1977: 92-6*] – while accepting without comment the unspoken classical assumption about the validity of the rural agricultural versus urban industrial divide. Lipton explicitly discusses and defends the rural-urban divide, but virtually assumes away the problem of relating the concepts of class and interest (see above). One might also note that Mitra explicitly sees the political alliances which he posits as but one of a number of possible responses to class conflicts over three sets of terms of trade: 'the terms of trade between agriculture and industry, between the rich peasantry on the one hand and small peasants and farm workers on the other and finally, between the industrial bourgeoisie and industrial labour' [*Mitra, 1977: 100*]. There is in Mitra's work a greater sense of the possibility of changes in class alliances [*Mitra, 1977: Chapter 7*] than one finds in Lipton's book, although in the application of Mitra's work to other countries there is at least a hint of an attempt to generalise his analysis to produce a counter-Liptonian thesis about 'rural-bias' on a world scale.[21]

M. J. Mamalakis: The Theory of Sectoral Clashes

While the work of both Lipton and Mitra has gained considerable currency in development studies, that of M. J. Mamalakis [*1969 and 1971*] is relatively unknown outside the ranks of the Latin American specialists to whom it is addressed. Although it appeared in print several years before Lipton's work and bears a close resemblance to it, Lipton was unaware of it. Mainly perhaps because his ideas were subjected to considerable debate and empirical testing by Latin American specialists and found wanting [*e.g. Barraza, 1969; Dominguez, 1971*] Mamalakis' ideas appear never to have spread beyond a relatively restricted group of scholars. The phenomena with which he was attempting to grapple — the causes and consequences of the policy of import-substituting industrialisation under heavy tariff protection pursued by most Latin American countries from the 1930s until the 1960s — remain however the subject of lively intellectual debate among Latin Americanists.[22] True to the Latin American scholarship in which his work originates, Mamalakis places more weight on international economic variables than do Lipton and Mitra.

Few would dispute Mamalakis' contention that government promotion of input-substituting industrialisation resulted in manufacturing industry replacing export primary production, either in the form of agriculture or mining, as the foremost and dominant economic sector in Latin America [*Mamalakis, 1969: 22*]. The mention of mining as one of the previously dominant sectors in Latin America is however an indication that Mamalakis does not operate with a simple rural agricultural-urban industrial duality. His basic unit of analysis is the industrial sector. Where Lipton found the primary motor of politics and the pattern of government resource allocation to lie in the rural-urban conflict, and Mitra in a class conflict model where urban and rural sectors were an important parameter for defining classes, Mamalakis finds it in the clash of industrial sectors. Yet in fact his politico-economic model is far less different from those of Lipton and Mitra than this statement at first seems to imply.

In the first place, Mamalakis identifies the policy of favouring industry as yet another stage in a long history of 'urban bias' in Latin America: 'The biggest obstacle to Latin American development has been the continuity of its defective allocation process, which persistently directed resource surpluses to the support of cities, services and consumption' [*Mamalakis, 1971: 108*]. He ultimately comes down to a model of urban privilege very like Lipton's. The main element of the urban-industrial complex which Mamalakis sees as suffering from discrimination — the capital goods sector — is so discriminated against that it barely exists [*1969: 19*].[23] This ultimate resort to an urban versus non-urban (agriculture and mining) divide is a contingent feature of

Mamalakis' work, and not intrinsic to his method. For his main aim is to demonstrate that clashes between industrial sectors, rather than between the class, functional or income groups which he sees as the central actors in the 'Ricardian, Marxist, Keynesian, neo-classical and structuralist' schools, are '*the* moving force behind growth as well as inflation' [*Mamalakis, 1969: 9*]. The actual specification of the sectors in conflict is said to be an empirical issue, and his four-sector model – mining, industry, agriculture and services – contingently derived to suit the typical Latin American situation [*Mamalakis, 1969: 17-19*]. One might note here that, since he provides no criteria for demarcating sectors, and implies various cross-cutting criteria – type of product, production for export or local consumption, and domestic or foreign and public or private ownership [*Mamalakis, 1969: 12*] – his 'theory' appears extremely 'elastic' [*Anderson, 1969: 47*]. It could easily be manipulated in such a way that falsification would become difficult.

While Mamalakis sets out by stating that he intends to demonstrate the usefulness of a model of sectoral rather than class conflict in the analysis of the economics and politics of growth, he soon introduces the notion of class differentiation within sectors. His 'classes' are in fact functional or income groups. Within each sector there is a group of government employees, of employers, white-collar workers and blue-collar workers [*Mamalakis, 1969: 19*]. By establishing a politico-economic model with four sectors and four classes within each sector, he presents us with a far wider range of potential political alliances than do Lipton and Mitra in their 2 x 2 models. Mamalakis does in fact attempt to specify the pattern of alliances between his sixteen different 'class' groups at various stages in recent Latin American history [*Mamalakis, 1969: 18-24*]. The details of his analyses are however beyond the scope of this article.

There is a great deal more which could be said about Mamalakis' work, both as description and critique, than available space permits (see *Redclift, this volume*). Hopefully, what has been said is adequate to indicate how he, Lipton and Mitra, starting from different concerns, intellectual traditions and ideological viewpoints, all end up with the proposition that the main dynamics of political and economic development in the Third World lie in national alliances between groups defined in both rural-urban sectoral and class terms.

CONCLUSION

This paper has attempted first to provide a critical survey of the work of a few recent theorists who have identified in the pattern of rural-urban relations the prime cause of slow economic growth and/or continuing mass poverty in the contemporary Third World. It has attempted secondly to reveal the extent of their debt to classical and Marxian political economy and the analytical problems to which this gives rise. Implicit in this critique is the belief that the rural-urban dichotomy has been asked to bear too heavy a burden. In terms of economic activities there is often more overlap between and differentiation within the two sectors than the theorists' models would imply. And the theorists have been too ready to assume and define away the complexities of actual patterns of political action by reducing politics to a set of conflicts between a few large social categories defined in an *a priori* fashion on the basis of their relationships in the processes of production and distribution.

These criticisms do not indicate any lack of sympathy with these theorists' project. For all its deficiencies of excessive simplification and generalisation, Lipton's [*1977a*] work, for example, does provide a solid foundation for understanding the prevalence of a certain pattern of policy-induced resource allocation throughout most of the Third World. And Robert Bates [*1981*] has recently built on this to develop a theory of 'urban bias' for tropical Africa which is considerably more plausible and less open to the charges of simplification and generalisation. Because Bates's method is so similar to Lipton's an extended exegesis would not be warranted here. The highlights of Bates's work are: a greater degree of attention to and competence in dealing with the political motivation for patterns of public resource allocation, leading to the recognition of the present existence and possible future growth of political coalitions other than the prevalent 'urban-biased' coalition [*Bates, 1981: 119-32*]; the analytical separation of the food and export crop sectors [*Bates, 1981: Chapters 1 to 3*]; and the incorporation into his analysis of factors specific to the tropical African situation, notably the fragility and recent origins of contemporary state systems [*Bates, 1981: passim*] and the evidence of an open land frontier in many places [*Bates, 1981: 54-60*].

Bates's book illustrates that it is premature to reject the possibility of developing models of sectoral relationships which go beyond the confines of particular countries and particular times.

NOTES

1. Mitra is consciously working in the Marxian tradition. Lipton devotes considerable attention to tracing the ideas of classical and neo-classical economists on rural-urban relations [*1977a: Chapter 4*].
2. Thus Adam Smith [*1776: Book 2, Chapter 3*] was willing to admit that some non-productive workers were essential.
3. See, for example, the discussion of the emergence of neo-classical economics in Deane, 1978: 94-102.
4. In the absence of any explicit discussion of this issue in the work of the classical political economists there are, naturally enough, ambiguities. For example, Steuart [*1767*], having devoted the whole of his first book to agriculture and population, deals in Book 2 with 'trade and industry', and virtually implies that they are separate sectors of the economy.
5. One might note that Smith specifically exempts 'China and Indostan' from this characterisation and suggests that the degree of 'urban bias' in Great Britain has tended to decrease because of the competition among capital for productive outlets [*Smith, 1776: Book 1, Chapter 10, Part 2*].
6. Smith, 1776: Book 3, Chapter 1.
7. Ibid. From the title of Smith's Book 1.
8. Smith, 1776: Book 1, Chapter 6.
9. On the erroneousness of the dominant, if not quite universal, Marxian expectation that small-scale family farming would be destroyed by industrialisation, see Goodman and Redclift, 1981: Chapter 1.
10. Note that Marx indicates very clearly his affiliation with the classical views in his footnote to the first sentence: 'Sir James Steuart is the economist who has handled this subject best.'
11. For some views of Hoselitz's work in relation to modernisation theory see *Economic Development and Cultural Change*, Vol.25, Supplement, 1977.

12. For critical comments on Lipton's work from a 'dependency' perspective see Seers, 1977: 9-14.
13. For an exchange between Michael Lipton and Dudley Seers on the validity of Lipton's city-country line, see Institute of Development Studies, 1977: 2-6, 17-18 and 24-7.
14. Claval [1980: 63 and 69] explains that spatial analysis has featured much more prominently in Francophone than in Anglophone social science.
15. See, for example, Moore (this volume) on Sri Lanka; and Radwan and Lee [1979: 179] on the UAR.
16. See, for example, Kothari, 1970: passim; and Moore, 1981, Chapter 8.
17. Thus Crissman [1981: 104] remarks that 'The Chinese have traditionally viewed towns and cities as integral though nodal parts of a predominantly rural social fabric rather than attributing to them a fundamentally different nature (as has happened in the post-feudal West).'
18. See Corbridge, 1982, who makes this point about the debate between Lipton and Terry Byres, a proponent of Mitra's views.
19. For a typical such review, see Van Arkadie, 1977.
20. One might note here that the data on rural-urban terms of trade which are important to both analyses are the subject of much debate. See, for example, Tyagi, 1979.
21. See Byres, 1977; and, for background, Corbridge, 1982; Byres, 1974; and Byres, 1979.
22. See, for example, Collier, 1979.
23. It is also implicit in his discussion that service sectors serving low income urban groups are the victims of industrial bias.

REFERENCES

Anderson, B., 1969, 'Commentary' (on Mamalakis, 1969), Latin American Research Review, Vol.4, No.3.
Balogh, T., 1966, The Economics of Poverty, London: Weidenfeld and Nicolson.
Barraza, L., 1969, 'The Relevance of Sectoral Clashes to the Mexican Economy', Latin American Research Review, Vol.4, No.3.
Bates, R.H., 1981, Markets and States in Tropical Africa, Berkeley: University of California Press.
Byres, T., 1974, 'Land Reform, Industrialisation and the Marketed Surplus in India', in Lehmann, D. (ed.), Agrarian Reform and Agrarian Reformism, London: Faber and Faber.
Byres, T., 1977, 'Agrarian Transition and the Agrarian Question', Journal of Peasant Studies, Vol.4, No.3.
Byres, T., 1979, 'Of Neo-Populist Pipe-Dreams: Daedalus in the Third World and the Myth of Urban Bias', Journal of Peasant Studies, Vol.6, No.2.
Claval, P., 1980, 'Centre-Periphery and Space: Models of Political Geography', in Gottman, J. (ed.), Centre and Periphery – Spatial Variations in Politics, London: Sage Publications.
Collier, D. (ed.), 1979, The New Authoritarianism in Latin America, Princeton, N.J.: Princeton University Press.
Corbridge, S., 1982, 'Urban Bias, Rural Bias and Industrialisation: An Appraisal of the Work of Michael Lipton and Terry Byres', in Harriss, J. (ed.), Rural Development Theories of Peasant Economy and Agrarian Change, London: Hutchinson.
Crissman, L.W., 1981, 'The Structure of Local and Regional Systems', in E.M. Ahern and H. Gates (eds) The Anthropology of Chinese Society, Stanford: Stanford University Press.
Deane, P., 1978, The Evolution of Economic Ideas, Cambridge: Cambridge University Press.
Dominguez, J.I., 1971, 'Sectoral Clashes in Cuban Politics and Development', Latin American Research Review, Vol.6, No.3.
Dumont, R., 1966, False Start in Africa, London: André Deutsch.
Goodman, D. and Redclift, M., 1981, From Peasant to Proletarian. Capitalist Development and Agrarian Transitions, Oxford: Basil Blackwell.
Hart, J., 1977, Review of M. Lipton's 'Why Poor People Stay Poor', People, Vol.4, No.2.
Harvey, D., 1973, Social Justice and the City, London: Edward Arnold.
Harvey, D., 1982, Limits to Capital, Oxford: Basil Blackwell.
Ho, S.P.S., 1982, 'Economic Development and Rural Industry in South Korea and Taiwan', World Development, Vol.10, No.11.

Institute of Development Studies, 1977, *'Urban Bias'* – *Seers Versus Lipton*, Discussion Paper No.116, Brighton: The Institute.

Kothari, R., 1970, *Politics in India*, Boston: Little, Brown and Co.

Kriedte, P. *et al.*, 1981, *Industrialization Before Industrialization*, Cambridge: Cambridge University Press.

Lipton, M., 1968, 'Strategy for Agriculture: Urban Bias and Rural Planning' in Streeten, P. and Lipton, M. (eds), *The Crisis of Indian Planning*, Oxford: Oxford University Press.

Lipton, M., 1972, *Transfer of Resources from Agriculture to Non-Agricultural Activities: the Case of India*. Communication Series No.109, Brighton: Institute of Development Studies.

Lipton, M., 1977a, *Why Poor People Stay Poor. Urban Bias in World Development*, London: Temple Smith.

Lipton, M., 1977b, 'Urban Bias: Generalisation versus Particularity', in Institute of Development Studies, *'Urban Bias'* – *Seers Versus Lipton*, Discussion Paper No.116, Brighton: The Institute.

Mamalakis, M. J., 1969, 'The Theory of Sectoral Clashes', *Latin American Research Review*, Vol.4, No.3.

Mamalakis, M. J., 1971, 'The Theory of Sectoral Clashes and Coalition Revisited', *Latin American Research Review*, Vol.6, No.3.

Marx, K., 1867, *Capital, Volume 1*, reference to the 1887 English edition, reprinted 1965, London: Lawrence and Wishart.

Mitra, A., 1977, *Terms of Trade and Class Relations*, London: Frank Cass.

Mitrany, D., 1961, *Marx Against the Peasant*, London: Collier Macmillan.

Moore, M. P., 1981, *The State and the Peasantry in Sri Lanka*, Brighton: D. Phil. thesis, University of Sussex.

Newby, H., 1978, 'The Rural Sociology of Advanced Capitalist Societies', in Newby, H. (ed.), *International Perspectives in Rural Sociology*, Chichester: John Wiley.

Newby, H., 1980, 'Rural Sociology', *Current Sociology*, Vol.28, No.1.

Nisbet, K., 1967, *The Sociological Tradition*, London: Heinemann.

Radwan, S. and Lee, E., 1979, 'The State and Agrarian Change: A Case Study of Egypt, 1952–77', in Ghai, D. *et al.*, (eds), *Agrarian Systems and Rural Development*, London: Macmillan.

Ricardo, D., 1817, *Principles of Political Economy and Taxation* (Reprinted with an Introduction by R. M. Hartwell, Harmondsworth: Penguin Books, 1971).

Roll, E., 1973, *A History of Economic Thought*, London: Faber and Faber.

Schickele, R., 1968, *Agrarian Revolution and Economic Progress* – *A Primer for Development*, New York: Praeger.

Seers, D., 1977, 'Indian Bias?' in Institute of Development Studies, *'Urban Bias'* – *Seers Versus Lipton*, Discussion Paper No.116, Brighton: The Institute.

Singer, H. W., 1977, 'Reflections on Sociological Aspects of Economic Growth Based on the Work of Bert Hoselitz', *Economic Development and Cultural Change*, Vol.25, Supplement.

Smith, A., 1776, *The Wealth of Nations* (Reprinted with an Introduction by A. S. Skinner, Harmondsworth: Penguin Books, 1970).

Steuart, Sir James, 1767, *An Enquiry into the Principles of Political Oeconomy* (Reprinted in two volumes with an Introduction by A. S. Skinner, Edinburgh: Oliver and Boyd, 1966).

Tyagi, D. S., 1979, 'Farm Prices and Class Bias in India', *Economic and Political Weekly*, Vol.14, No.39.

Van Arkadie, B., 1977, 'Review Article. Town Versus Country?' *Development and Change*, Vol.8, No.3.

Relative Agricultural Prices and the Urban Bias Model: A Comparative Analysis of Tanzania and Fiji

by Frank Ellis*

The paper critically examines agricultural price aspects of the urban bias model, especially the links between class interests, government policies, and the trend of real agricultural prices. The paper contains an analysis of the principal factors both economic and political underlying agriculture's terms of trade in two contrasting countries, Tanzania and Fiji. Both case studies, in different ways, raise doubts about the generality of urban bias propositions as they relate to agricultural prices. They also suggest important weaknesses in the model's interpretation of the politics of farm prices.

INTRODUCTION

This paper sets out to examine two facets of the urban bias debate, and to do so in detail for two case-study countries, Tanzania and Fiji. The two aspects to be explored are trends in relative prices between agriculture and the rest of the economy, and the relationships of class interest to government policy which appear to push real agricultural prices in one direction or the other. By focusing on these selected features of the urban bias thesis, and subjecting them to the scrutiny of empirical evidence from two rather different countries, it is hoped to advance the critical assessment of the robustness and explanatory power of the model put forward by Michael Lipton.[1]

The manipulation of prices to the disadvantage of agricultural producers, both historically and across countries, is one of the central tenets of the urban bias thesis. The way in which this topic is conceptualised in the book *Why Poor People Stay Poor* may be summarised by reference to selected quotations from that work exemplifying the main propositions which are put forward. These quotations also provide a useful starting point for considering some of the difficulties which arise in the application of urban bias concepts to empirical work in individual countries:

> Government policy on urban-rural terms of trade forces him (the big farmer) to accept low prices, which his cheap inputs and other artificial advantages *vis-à-vis* small farmers dispose him to bear with equanimity. [*Lipton, 1977: 97-8*]

* School of Development Studies, University of East Anglia. This paper was written while the author was on secondment to the Fiji Employment and Development Mission in 1982–3. I am indebted to John Cameron, my colleague on that project and at East Anglia, for detailed comments on earlier drafts of the paper and for helpful discussions on conceptual aspects of the material. I am also grateful to Michael Lipton and to John Harriss for discussions on the penultimate version of the paper.

the impact of private monopoly and public power has substantially and increasingly made agricultural output cheaper relative to other output. [*Lipton, 1977: 187*]

a transfer of 15-20 per cent of income among sectors (by price twists) will dwarf any *transfer* via tax effects. [*Lipton, 1977: 270*] (Author's italics)

It is above all by cheapening farm outputs that both private and public powers transfer savings capacity from agriculture to the rest of the economy. [*Lipton, 1977: 293*]

The deliberate raising of non-farm prices, relative to the prices of farm goods, is directed at structural transformation of poor economies through industrialisation, first by forced savings transfer, second by price incentive. [*Lipton, 1977: 307*]

Nor need we decide if the terms of trade have 'moved against' agriculture .... This is an arbitrary exercise, because its outcome depends on when 'previously' is. Moreover, even if a 'normal' year, with average climate and no price twists, could be found, any subsequent trend in agriculture's terms of trade could not be interpreted without more information. [*Lipton, 1977: 288*]

The main propositions about biased agricultural prices which may be derived from these quotations and more generally in the book seem to be (a) that artificially depressed agricultural prices are an integral part of 'urban bias' as a whole, not only being of significance on their own but also lending support to other components such as unbalanced savings and investment patterns, unequal income and consumption patterns, and uneven burdens of taxation (see also Lipton [*1977: 145*]); (b) that the chief agents of artificially depressed agricultural prices (as far as urban bias is concerned) are governments followed closely by the exercise of private monopoly power; (c) that agricultural landlords and big farmers are prepared to accept low prices because they have been co-opted into a single urban class by being made the sole beneficiaries of subsidy policies on agricultural inputs; (d) that the chief motivation for biased pricing is the generation of capital to invest in industrialization; (e) that terms of trade analysis is an inadequate vehicle for the empirical substantiation of urban bias in agricultural pricing due to problems of interpreting trends and correctly identifying causalities; (f) that the most appropriate empirical test of the existence of urban bias in agricultural pricing is to compare domestic farm/non-farm price relativities with those prevailing at the border (i.e. with world price relativities for the same baskets of commodities) [*Lipton, 1977: 288-307*].

Stated in this fashion the logic of agricultural price aspects of the urban bias model appears reasonably straightforward. However, both the distillation of this interpretation and its application to case-study material involves a number of actual or potential ambiguities which remain to be resolved. The main outstanding difficulties are summarised briefly as follows.

First, the urban bias argument tends to weave in and out at will between the farm/non-farm and rural/urban distinctions, such that whether the critical comparison is a *spatial* one or an *intersectoral* one is left uncertain. While doubtless there are some Third World countries for which these two distinctions are so close as to allow them to be treated as synonymous for empirical purposes, there are others with diverse rural service and cottage industries where such imprecision could be quite misleading.

Second, the expression 'price twists' is never actually defined in *Why Poor People Stay Poor* but appears for the first time, without comment or explanation, rather more than half-way through the book [*Lipton, 1977: 247*]. Since up to that point frequent reference is made to the 'urban-rural terms of trade' (for example, in the first quotation cited above), the reader might be forgiven for becoming confused about which of the two concepts is considered central to the thesis. At times it is the unfavourable movement of relative agricultural prices which dominates the argument; at others (notably the penultimate chapter on price twists) it is the comparison with an alternative, more equitable or more efficient, relative price (or set of prices) which is the critical focus of attention.

Third, the politics of urban bias are undoubtedly controversial, not just with respect to the hypothesised response of large farmers to low agricultural prices but also regarding the general conscription of agriculturalists other than poor peasants and landless labourers into a single urban class sharing common interests [*Griffin, 1977; Byres, 1979; Corbridge, 1982*]. Where relative prices are concerned the argument rests on the simultaneous fulfilment of so many contingent conditions that it is difficult to envisage their being met except in extraordinary circumstances. Big farmers must be so large as to guarantee their lack of any community of interest with small farmers (a sharply dualistic farm and rural social structure); they must also by virtue of farm size and surplus production be virtually the sole recipients of subsidised agricultural inputs; and their gains from subsidised inputs plus other alleged perks of their urban allegiances must be presumed greater than the losses they incur by accepting artificially depressed output prices.[2] In situations where these conditions (especially the first) are not met it seems quite plausible that the direction of causality would be reversed, i.e. that in the absence of a constituency of larger farmers prepared to advance the interests of the farm sector as a whole, the plight of small farmers would be even more serious than it is.[3]

Fourth, the price arguments of the urban bias model are to an important degree based on situations where the marketed output of the agricultural sector predominantly consists of food grains and other production for domestic urban markets. It is this which permits the inference to be drawn that low agricultural prices (for which read 'food prices') artificially raise the real incomes of urban dwellers (by reducing the real cost of their food purchases) and hence also helps to moderate the wage levels of industrial labour. It is also this supposition which leads to the relative neglect of the potential significance of export price movements (external terms of trade) for domestic intersectoral price relativities.[4] There are a great many Third World countries (especially in Africa, Central America, the Caribbean and the Pacific) where the marketed surplus of the agricultural sector predominantly consists of export crops, food crop production being mainly consumed as means of subsistence in the rural economy. Where this is the case, not only do export prices become a factor of major importance in relative intersectoral prices but also the automatic association of rural loss with urban gain in intersectoral income comparisons is broken.[5]

Fifth, it is difficult to accept in the way it is formulated the case put forward (refer to last quotation cited above) for neglecting the evidence of empirical analyses of intersectoral terms of trade. While it can be readily acknowledged that great care is required both in the construction of terms of trade indices and in investigating and distinguishing the different causes of terms of trade movements, these are no more susceptible to 'arbitrary' interpretation than any other empirical investigation in development studies.[6] The alternative 'price twists' approach itself presents severe difficulties of verification. ('I am not happy about individual items, for it is hard to assess the total effect on farmers of these different sorts of price twists, but dangerous to isolate them.' [*Lipton, 1977: 304*]) Moreover, empirical investigation of the *changing* links between state power, class interests and relative agricultural prices in individual countries (surely desirable in the context of a supposedly comprehensive thesis about rural-urban relations) inevitably requires selectivity in the time-series variables to be researched due both to the intrinsic complexity of the topic and to the need to explore underlying causalities in detail. Analysis of trends in real agricultural prices and incomes from farm sales, which is what the terms of trade is all about, provides just such a selective focus around which dynamic relationships of political economy can be constructed.

The analysis of this paper attempts to push as clear a path as possible through these considerations. This means making specific choices with respect to points which are ambiguous or in contention. The approach adopted here has six main attributes: (i) the price relationships examined are farm/non-farm, not rural/urban, (ii) farm prices are examined at the producer (farm-gate) level, (iii) time-series analysis of the price and income terms of trade of agricultural producers is complemented and extended by reference to the border prices of export crops and to the share of producers in the final sales value of their output, (iv) special attention is given to the institutional structures, policies and mechanisms particular to each country which clearly have a direct influence on relative agricultural producer price levels, (v) the politics of farm price levels are reconsidered in the light of the case-study experience of different kinds of farm interest groups and their relative impact on observed trends, (vi) the limitations of relative price analysis (whether of the terms of trade or price twists kind) for explaining trends of farm and non-farm household incomes are recognised at the outset, and where possible data on sectoral income trends are examined separately from relative price trends.

The two countries examined here each possess characteristics which make them potentially illuminating case-studies of the merits of the urban bias model. For Tanzania, this is partly because over a considerable period the country possessed an international reputation for 'rural bias', and is cited by Lipton as one of the possible exceptions to the general applicability of his model [*Lipton, 1977: 74*]. Fiji is interesting due to its contrasts both with the kind of economy which apparently stimulated the formulation of the urban bias model (India, Pakistan, Bangladesh) and with Tanzania (a small island, open economy as against a large, continental, semi-closed one). Both case-study countries are distinguished by the dominance of export crops in the aggregate marketed surplus of agriculture (Fiji even more so than Tanzania) and by the relatively minor significance of large capitalist farmers and land-owners in their contemporary agrarian structures.

TANZANIA

Tanzania as a Case-Study: Background

The departure point for most studies of the contemporary political economy of Tanzania has tended to be the adoption in 1967 of the major declaration of intent on development strategy known as the Arusha Declaration [*Nyerere, 1968: 231-50*]. It is this and a closely related document [*Nyerere, 1968: 337-66*] which between them most concisely articulated the government's intention to follow a rural-based 'socialist' development strategy. Whether or not 1967 is treated as a genuine turning point in the long-term political economy of Tanzania (and there are many who would argue in retrospect that this was not the case[7]), it certainly set in train a process in which private capital and the market were rapidly circumscribed; and the state came to exercise comprehensive control over the relevant variables in the rural-urban equation, with the single obvious exception of trends in the external prices of export crops [*Hyden, 1980: 131-40; Ellis, 1983*]. Hence from the late 1960s onwards the Tanzanian state was potentially in a very strong position to pursue an active rural-centred strategy. This position was further strengthened from 1974 onwards by the decision to resettle the previously scattered rural population into nuclear villages, thus further integrating small farmers into the administrative orbit of the state and further limiting the scope for non-state transactions.

Features of the Tanzanian agricultural economy relevant to the subsequent analysis are (i) the predominance of small-farm agriculture in the production of a marketed surplus, larger-scale agriculture being restricted to a single foreign-owned tea estate and state-owned operations in sisal, sugar and a proportion of wheat production; (ii) the associated widespread participation of small farmers in the production of major export crops; (iii) the confinement of all peasant crops of any quantitative or strategic significance to sale through state marketing channels at producer prices set by the state in advance of each crop season; and (iv) the dissolution between 1973 and 1976 of the former cooperative marketing system [*Ellis, 1982a: 264*], the organisation of which tended to be dominated by the 'larger' and 'more commercially-orientated' farmers.

Also of contextual relevance here is the balance between urban and rural populations, shown in the 1978 Census to be 2.2 million urban dwellers (13 per cent) and 14.9 million rural dwellers (87 per cent). In 1978 there were 3 million rural households in Tanzania distributed over 8,000 designated villages. Detailed accounts of the evolution of state policy towards agricultural production including villagisation are contained in a number of sources [*Coulson, 1977, 1982; Hyden, 1980*], and on the implementation of agricultural price and marketing policy in Kriesel *et al.* [*1970*] and Ellis [*1982a, 1983*].

The Terms of Trade of Agriculture in Tanzania in the 1970s

Evidence on the trend of agriculture's terms of trade in Tanzania between 1970 and 1980 is summarised in Table 1. The methodology as well as source data of this exercise is described in detail in Ellis [1982a]. The coverage of the

TABLE 1

TANZANIA: ANALYSIS OF THE PRICE AND INCOME TERMS OF TRADE OF SMALLHOLDER CROP PRODUCERS, 1970–1980

Year[1]	Price Terms of Trade[2] 1970 = 100.0	Income Terms of Trade[3] 1970 = 100.0	Output Index[4] 1970 = 100.0
1970	100.0	100.0	100.0
1971	91.7	105.1	114.6
1972	88.4	98.2	111.1
1973	81.9	95.3	116.4
1974	66.6	68.9	103.5
1975	59.8	63.5	106.2
1976	89.3	79.5	89.0
1977	111.5	103.6	92.9
1978	85.7	87.3	101.9
1979	76.2	78.1	102.5
1980	64.1	61.1	95.3

1. Refers to crop seasons 1969/70 to 1979/80.
2. Weighted average producer prices deflated by modified National Consumer Price Index. Weights are the share of each crop in total producer income (producer price x quantity marketed), and are calculated for each year separately.
3. Index of gross producer income (producer price x quantity marketed) deflated by modified National Consumer Price Index.
4. Income index divided by price index.

Source: Ellis [1982a: 281-3 and Appendix Tables 1-3]

analysis is nineteen smallholder crops, all of which came under state price and marketing arrangements in the course of the 1970s and which between them encompass most of the marketed crop production of the Tanzanian peasant economy (estate tea, sugar and sisal are excluded).

The analysis shows a very substantial decline in both the price and income terms of trade of peasant crop producers in Tanzania over the 1970s. Between the beginning and end of the decade the price terms of trade fell by 36 per cent and the income terms of trade by 39 per cent. The volume index of marketed agricultural production remained virtually stagnant at around its 1970 level for most of the decade, having slipped back sharply from an earlier growth trend which lasted through until 1973.

These findings merit further explanation both as to the pattern of annual changes in prices and incomes shown in Table 1, and as to the composition of the trends between different categories of crops. First it should be stressed that the results are robust as concerns the base-year used and the sensitivity of the findings to alternative deflators (always a potential source of difficulty in terms of trade analysis). By 1970 real agricultural prices had already been declining for at least three years [*ILO, 1978: 188-90 and Appendix II*], so that the adoption of 1970 as a base-year would tend to understate rather than exaggerate the steepness of the downward trend from the late 1960s onwards. The deflator used is the National Consumer Price Index for Tanzania, modified slightly to exclude items of no pertinence for peasant living standards [*Ellis, 1982a: 278 n.13*].[8]

Secondly, the main reason for the strong upward fluctuation in both real prices and incomes in 1976 and 1977 was the unprecedented international coffee price boom of those two years [*Ellis and Hanak, 1981*]. This exemplifies an important feature of the composition of the total farm-gate value of production marketed through official channels in Tanzania in the 1970s. Coffee alone accounted for 35 per cent of total crop income at the producer level over the observation period of this analysis and all the export crops taken together accounted for 78 per cent. Hence the overall intersectoral terms of trade is heavily weighted by the real producer price trends of export crops, domestic food crops being grown predominantly as means of subsistence for the large proportion of the population living in the rural economy and being much less important in the marketed agricultural surplus. This is a major contrast to the typical case informing much of the urban bias thesis.

Thirdly, the overall terms of trade trend contains some important distinctions in the periodisation of the time-series and in the experience of different commodity groups. Real agricultural prices declined most sharply between 1970 and 1975, when they fell by 40 per cent, followed by the steep temporary rise already noted, and the reassertion of the downward trend thereafter. More recent evidence shows that this renewed decline continued beyond the end of the observation period discussed here, almost certainly taking the real price index below its 1975 level in 1981 [*ILO, 1981: 295, 451*].

Export and domestic crop real prices moved in parallel up to 1974 after which they diverged sharply with the impact of the coffee price boom removed from the comparison. While export crop real prices continued to decline after 1974, albeit at a slower rate, domestic crops were accorded significant real price increases in the sub-period 1974–77. This followed a serious food crisis in Tanzania in 1973 and 1974 which provoked the government at least temporarily to place heavy emphasis on attractive food crop prices to farmers. However, this gain was short-lived, and real producer prices of food crops were rapidly eroded by an acceleration of domestic inflation from 1978 onwards. By the end of the decade producer prices of domestic food crops were still 16 per cent below their 1970 level in real terms and prices of export crops were 43 per cent lower.

Surplus Transfers and Intersectoral Income Comparisons

Further details of the Tanzania case are contained in other papers by this author [*Ellis, 1981, 1982a, 1982b*]. Here, attention is directed to three additional aspects of relevance to assessing the explanatory power of the urban bias thesis. These are the trend in the real border prices of export crops (external terms of trade), the mechanism and quantitative significance of surplus transfers out of the peasant economy, and the comparison of farm and non-farm household income trends over this period.

The potential significance of external price trends for internal price relativities in a Tanzania-type economy is already implicit in the high proportion of total farm-gate value attributed to export crops. The main feature is that while real producer prices of export crops declined by 43 per cent, their weighted real unit export value increased by 5 per cent.[9]

The divergence between these two price trends reveals the principal mechanism of surplus transfer which characterised peasant-state relations in Tanzania during the 1970s. This took the form not of deliberately raising industrial prices relative to the sales prices of agricultural output (the chief mechanism suggested in the urban bias model for effecting such transfers [Lipton, 1977: 16, 79, 128-9, 296]) but of widening the gap between the producer prices and sales prices of crops marketed through state channels. The deterioration in the producer share of the sales value of agricultural crops between 1970 and 1980 is summarised in Table 2. This shows that for fourteen

TABLE 2

TANZANIA: EVOLUTION OF THE PRODUCER SHARE OF THE FINAL SALES VALUE OF
AGRICULTURAL CROPS, 1970–1980

Year[1]	Sales T Shs m	Producer Value T Shs m	%
1970	1,047	695	66.4
1971	1,236	773	62.5
1972	1,248	776	62.2
1973	1,430	842	58.9
1974	1,650	772	46.8
1975	1,815	909	50.1
1976	2,195	1,286	58.6
1977	3,868	1,765	45.6
1978	3,642	1,583	43.5
1979	3,634	1,542	42.4
1980	4,188	1,741	41.6
Total	25,954	12,683	48.9

1. Refers to crop seasons 1969/70 to 1979/80.

Source: Ellis [1983]

crops marketed through state channels the producer share of sales value declined from over 66 per cent in 1970 to 42 per cent in 1980. The figures are extracted from a more comprehensive exercise detailing the way in which parastatal crop marketing agencies acted as a syphon for the transfer of financial resources from the peasantry to the state during the 1970s [Ellis, 1983]. The main findings of that exercise are briefly summarised as follows:

1. The gross resource transfer was equivalent to an average tax of 27 per cent on the aggregate crop income which would have accrued to growers had they maintained their previous share of the final sales value of their output.[10]
2. Roughly half this estimated surplus transfer flowed directly to central government in the form of increased central taxation (export and sales taxes), and half flowed into, and was absorbed by, the parastatal marketing authorities. Research into the latter proportion revealed that it was predominantly associated with declining efficiency (rising real unit costs) in crop marketing and a rapid increase in payroll costs due to the expansion in employment of permanent personnel. More generally, surplus transfers out of agriculture in Tanzania in the 1970s were associated far more closely with the recurrent maintenance of a proliferating, unproductive state and parastatal bureaucracy than with productive accumulation.

Direct comparisons between real farm incomes and real non-farm incomes in Tanzania over this period are problematic due to various unresolved difficulties with the validity of macro-economic data series and alternative deflators [*Ellis, 1981: 28-31; ILO, 1981: 422-60*]. However, one dimension is clear and unambiguous: average real non-farm wages and salaries declined at least as steeply, and possibly by even more, than the income terms of trade of peasant crop producers between 1970 and 1980. The comparative figures are a 39 per cent fall in the income terms of trade of crop producers (Table 1) and a 48 per cent fall in real non-agricultural wage and salary incomes [*ILO, 1981: 451*].

The reasons why this comparison is insufficient on its own are, first: that the income terms of trade give only partial insight into the trend in average total farm incomes (subsistence consumption and non-crop farm activity should be taken into account and total values require converting to a household basis) and, second: that there are large and steeply divergent discrepancies between real non-farm output and real non-farm incomes in Tanzanian macro-economic data. The ILO report [*1981: 428-34*] constructs an argument to suggest that real average farm incomes on balance increased by 8 per cent as compared to the 48 per cent decline in real non-farm incomes mentioned above. However, this result depends on the single critical assumption, unsupported by empirical evidence, that farm household real subsistence food consumption increased by 20 per cent over this period.

This is not the place to engage in an extended debate on these comparisons. Suffice it to say that on the alternative, probably more realistic, assumption that real rural household subsistence consumption no more than remained static in this period, then average real farm incomes would have declined, though not (due to the significance of subsistence in total farm income) by as much as the income terms of trade decline. The main conclusion remains that average non-farm incomes were subject to a steep real decline over this period, and that the magnitude of their fall was probably greater than that of farm incomes, given the capability of farmers at least to maintain the level of the subsistence component of their income.

Implications for the Urban Bias Model

In many of its particulars the Tanzanian experience of the 1970s would appear to fit the urban bias model rather well. The intensification of the 'price twist' against small farm export crops, the steep increase in the level of real surplus transfers out of the agricultural sector, the appropriation and consumption of that surplus by a non-farm bureaucratic class: all these seem to accord closely with the tenor of the urban bias argument.

Yet there remain important aspects of events in Tanzania which do not *quite* conform with urban bias logic, which diverge from certain urban bias suppositions, and which consequently give rise to doubts about whether the model is useful for explaining the Tanzanian case. These are associated with the *political economy* of the urban bias model rather than its purely economic attributes. In particular they are concerned with the politics of farm prices, i.e. the presence or absence of specific class interests which might explain the motivation for squeezing the farm sector by artificially holding down producer prices (especially of export crops).

It is relevant first to stress again how closely the stated intentions of the Tanzanian government corresponded to the prescription for overcoming urban bias, as discussed in the final chapter of *Why Poor People Stay Poor [1977: 328-52]*. State power was firmly in the hands of a leadership accorded international recognition for its commitment to rural orientation and concern for the poor. Urban capitalists and rich farmers alike were virtually eliminated as economic or political forces capable of standing in the way of strategic intentions. The state apparatus was decentralised into small towns and villages in the early 1970s precisely with the intention of diminishing centralised political power and prestige *[Nyerere, 1972]*. Likewise, civil service postings were regularly rotated across regional and district centres, both giving higher level personnel wide experience of conditions in different parts of the rural economy and preventing the entrenchment of key individuals in favoured urban locations. Villagisation established a structure of participation and democracy at the village level which on the face of it gave rural dwellers great scope for expressing their interests and entering the planning process at grass roots level.[11] Urban wages were kept down (no 'labour aristocracy' here), industrial prices were controlled, agricultural marketing agencies were devolved to the main locations of the crops they serviced.

Yet in this period the prices and cash incomes of peasant crop producers deteriorated so far as to cause the incipient disengagement of peasant agriculturalists from the monetary economy *[Hyden, 1980; Ellis, 1981]*. Surplus extraction from the peasantry dramatically accelerated and by the end of the decade represented an additional tax burden of 37 per cent on the value of marketed output *[Ellis, 1983]*. This transfer was not deliberately generated for purposes of urban growth or industrial accumulation,[12] but occurred as a result of the increasing needs of central government for recurrent revenues and the insatiable appetite of often rural-located parastatal marketing agencies for greater resources.

It is suggested here that one major factor in this turn of events was the elimination of 'larger' farmers as a potential political force in opposition to government policies. With the more 'progressive', the more commercially conscious, and the more articulate farmers either forced to maintain a low profile of choosing to leave farming altogether [Hyden, 1980: 105-51], the mass of poor peasant farmers lost their most effective spokesmen in defence of farming interests as a whole. This reverses the urban bias proposition that large farmers become accomplices of the urban elite in deliberately holding farm prices down. In Tanzania, by contrast, it was the prior elimination (and therefore relative absence) of a class of large farmers which robbed the agricultural sector of its political capacity to resist the deterioration of its real prices and incomes.

The lack of a class of large capitalist farmers also violates a closely related urban bias proposition, which is that the surplus producing capacity of large farmers, when they are brought into the 'urban class alliance', allows the urban classes to get away with squeezing agriculture without causing food (or other) consumption shortages in towns. In Tanzania it is doubtful whether the category of 'larger' farmers was ever sufficiently large to generate the marketed surplus required to sustain the non-farm population. On the contrary, the non-farm sector always depended critically on the surplus production of small farmers to sustain and increase consumption levels (especially through capacity to import determined by foreign exchange generated from export crop sales). In this light the actions of the state class (see below) in lowering real farm prices artificially was not part of a premeditated design to tap agriculture for a sustainable contribution to non-farm growth (the urban bias interpretation), but was economically irrational and ultimately self-defeating [Boesen, 1979; Coulson, 1975]. The outcome was an economic crisis which in the early 1980s virtually brought the entire non-farm economy to a standstill.

It is concluded from these considerations that a peasant-state dichotomy might provide a more helpful framework for interpreting the political economy of farm prices in Tanzania than the rural-urban dichotomy of urban bias. The peasant-state dichotomy features strongly in the Tanzanian literature [Shivji, 1973; 1976; Boesen et al., 1977; Boesen, 1979; Coulson, 1975; 1977; 1982; Bernstein, 1981; Hyden, 1980]. These contributions are theoretically varied and informed by diverse ideological positions. However, they share in common the attempt, absent in the urban bias approach, to identify the objective economic basis underlying major surplus transfers between different social groups, and to examine the implications of those transfers for the dynamics of the political economy. What distinguishes the state class of this approach from the alliance of classes in the urban bias model is the recognition that its lack of roots in the productive economy may result in involuntary behaviour of the class as a whole which differs greatly from the declared intentions of individuals within it [Shivji, 1973; 1976]. Thus, in Tanzania, the 'sincere egalitarian rhetoric' [Lipton, 1977: 14] of government leaders and civil servants co-existed with the objective necessity for a parasitic and expanding state class to secure ever greater resources from the productive, but politically weakened, peasant class.

The peasant-state approach permitted some researchers to predict the 'scissors crisis' of the Tanzanian state some years before the onset of economic collapse (see, for example Boesen [1979: 143]). It seems doubtful that the urban bias model could have achieved such accuracy of prediction due to its requirement of a conscious motivation for surplus transfers ('directed at structural transformation ... through industrialisation' as cited earlier) and its assumption that a marketed surplus would continue to be forthcoming from large farmers even when agriculture as a whole was being squeezed. Finally, there is the statistical evidence that non-farm household incomes in Tanzania fell probably even more steeply than the income terms of trade of crop producers over this historical period. In squeezing agriculture, the 'non-farm classes' of Tanzania ultimately squeezed themselves, a phenomenon more plausibly explained by the involuntary dictates of state class expansion than by conscious decision of urban-biased politicians and civil servants.

FIJI

Fiji as a Case-Study: Background[13]

As a case-study of rural-urban relationships, Fiji differs from Tanzania in some important ways. Fiji is a small-island capitalist economy. It is a highly open economy with virtually no foreign exchange controls and, by comparative international standards, very few import controls. Its total population in 1976 was 588,000 persons, of which 37 per cent lived in urban areas and 63 per cent in rural areas. It is a middle-income country by GDP criteria, having a per capita income of US$1,800 in 1980. The country obtained formal independence from Britain in 1970, and has subsequently maintained a stable multi-party system of government with elections every five years since 1972.

The twin pillars of Fiji as an open economy are sugar and tourism. During the 1970s sugar exports contributed, on average, 75 per cent of total export earnings. The sugar industry has also in recent years constituted approximately 16 per cent of GDP at factor cost and has provided employment for 22 per cent of the labour force. Sugar production is structured on a small-farm basis, consisting of 21,500 leasehold family farmers with farm sizes mainly in the range of 4 to 6 hectares. The procurement of sugar cane, its processing and marketing are undertaken by a single parastatal enterprise, the Fiji Sugar Corporation. Tourism is much less important than sugar in national income and employment but in the early 1970s was the main focal point of inflows of foreign capital and has been the second largest source of gross foreign exchange earnings.

The population of Fiji is composed of two major ethnic groups: the descendants of Indian indentured labour which was transported to Fiji to work in sugar plantations (Fiji-Indians), and the indigenous Melanesian population (Fijians). The former have constituted a higher proportion of the total population than the latter since the 1940s. Historically, the main economic base of the Fiji-Indian population has been sugar production, following the restructuring of the sugar industry on a small-farm basis after the termination of indenture in 1916. The main economic base of the indigenous Fijian population has been subsistence agriculture in nuclear villages, taking place in a context which emphasises the obligations of kinship within an extended clan system and a hierarchy of chiefs.[14]

The contemporary politics of Fiji reflect these historical antecedents [*Norton, 1977*]. The two main political parties are distinguished more by the ethnic basis of their support than by the articulation of different economic or political ideologies. However, since independence the material basis of this ethnic division has become increasingly blurred. A growing number of indigenous Fijians have become smallholder sugar growers, the Fijian village economy has become increasingly drawn into market relations, and both ethnic groups are fairly evenly represented in urban sector occupations (especially in government).

A unique feature of Fiji is its land ownership structure. Only 8 per cent of the entire land area is owned under private freehold title, a further 10 per cent being held by the state (still referred to as 'Crown Land'), and the remaining 82 per cent being owned in perpetuity by indigenous Fijian clans and administered for them by a statutory authority, the Native Land Trust Board (NLTB). The majority of Fiji-Indian small farmers are leasehold tenants either of Crown Land or NLTB land, and commercial small farming by Fijians also tends to take place on a leasehold basis, even if the land is technically owned by the same clan as the farmer, since most legal contracts (for example, bank loans) require leasehold titles. This land ownership structure has acted as a powerful brake on potential processes of rural differentiation [*Anderson, 1974*].

State intervention in Fiji agriculture is fairly important though it does not approach the comprehensive system of controls observed in Tanzania. With the exception of copra since 1975, the government does not intervene directly in agricultural price formation. The marketing of domestic food crops is undertaken by the same type of heterogeneous private marketing structure found in many other countries. The marketing of export crops is undertaken or facilitated by statutory authorities (the Fiji Sugar Corporation, the National Marketing Authority, the Coconut Board), but producer prices typically follow market trends in these cases.[15] The role of the state has been confined mainly to agricultural research and extension, and the execution of externally-funded agricultural development projects.

The Terms of Trade of Agriculture in Fiji in the 1970s

Evidence on the intersectoral terms of trade in Fiji is summarised in Table 3. This follows the same methodology as that utilised for Tanzania: the price terms of trade is a weighted average index of producer prices of agricultural crops deflated by the Consumer Price Index; the income terms of trade is the index of gross producer crop income (price x quantity) deflated by the same cost-of-living index. The number of crops included in the analysis – six – is considerably fewer than in the Tanzania exercise, but then in terms of quantitatively significant marketed output the agricultural economy is less diverse, especially on the export crop side. Sugar production alone constitutes such a large proportion of the total value of marketed agricultural production in Fiji that the inclusion of additional minor crops would make negligible difference to the aggregate results in this kind of analysis.[16]

The contrast between the data of Table 3 and those of Table 1 could hardly

TABLE 3

FIJI: ANALYSIS OF THE PRICE AND INCOME TERMS OF TRADE OF SMALLHOLDER
CROP PRODUCERS, 1970–1981

Year	Price Terms of Trade[1] 1970 = 100.0	Income Terms of Trade[2] 1970 = 100.0	Output Index[3] 1970 = 100.0
1970	100.0	100.0	100.0
1971	95.0	114.9	120.9
1972	104.7	85.8	91.1
1973	102.9	101.9	99.0
1974	178.7	123.5	69.1
1975	215.8	145.3	92.0
1976	158.8	187.6	96.8
1977	159.4	152.2	102.6
1978	145.4	174.3	116.0
1979	133.9	217.3	162.3
1980	166.6	223.9	134.5
1981	114.8	179.1	156.0

1. Weighted average producer prices deflated by the Consumer Price Index. Weights are the share
   of each crop in total producer income (producer price x quantity marketed), and are calculated
   for each year separately.
2. Index of gross producer income (producer price x quantity marketed) deflated by the Consumer
   Price Index.
3. Income index divided by price index.

Source: Primary data collected by the author from Fiji Sugar Corporation, Coconut Board,
   Ministry of Agriculture and Fisheries, and Bureau of Statistics.

be more extreme. The price terms of trade of agricultural producers in Fiji
remained between 35 per cent and 115 per cent above its level of the early 1970s
throughout the period from 1975 to 1980. The income terms of trade rose,
erratically but continuously, to a peak of 124 per cent above its 1970 level in
1980, before declining to 79 per cent above its 1970 level in 1981. The volume
index of marketed agricultural production increased substantially between the
first and second halves of the decade, and in 1981 stood 56 per cent above
its 1970 level.

The crops included in this analysis are sugar, copra, rice, cassava, taro and
yaqona (piper methysticum, a root-crop beverage consumed in substantial
quantities by both ethnic populations). Taro and cassava are the main domestic
food crops consumed by the indigenous Fijian population, while rice is an
important food crop, especially of the Fiji-Indian population, in which Fiji
is only about 50 per cent self-sufficient. The marketed output of sugar, copra
and rice is known with a high degree of accuracy due to government regulatory
activities in these areas. The marketed output trends of cassava, *yaqona* and
taro are more difficult to derive, and have been pitched on the conservative
side, taking into account the growth of the urban population in the 1970s,
the absence of any sustained shortages of domestic food crops and the existence
of exported surpluses of cassava and taro in some years.[17]

A disaggregation of the price terms of trade, between sugar, copra and domestic crops, is given in Table 4. Unlike the Tanzania case, the external prices of export crops have a direct impact on the evolution of the rural-urban

TABLE 4

FIJI: TRENDS OF REAL PRICES FOR MAJOR CROP CATEGORIES, 1970–1981

| | *Indices of Real Producer Prices* $1970 = 100.0$[1] | | |
Year	Sugar	Copra	Domestic Crops[2]
1970	100.0	100.0	100.0
1971	97.8	74.2	97.7
1972	111.7	39.8	102.2
1973	99.0	74.3	140.6
1974	182.4	204.9	114.2
1975	247.7	68.4	129.1
1976	170.2	65.5	125.4
1977	175.9	72.1	126.7
1978	155.0	67.8	120.8
1979	137.3	127.7	109.8
1980	176.9	73.7	122.3
1981	118.6	63.7	109.2

1. Indices in money terms deflated by the Consumer Price Index.
2. Weighted index of producer prices of rice, cassava, *dalo* (taro) and *yaqona* (piper methysticum). In the case of the root crops the prices underlying this index are calculated from the average retail prices for each crop collected by the Bureau of Statistics for the purpose of compiling the CPI. In the case of cassava and *dalo* it is assumed that the producer price was 65 per cent of the retail price in all years. For *yaqona* it is assumed that the producer price was 60 per cent of the retail price in 1970, moving up to 65 per cent of the retail price in equal steps by 1975, and then remaining at 65 per cent thereafter. See also Note 17 for further details on these data.

Source: As for Table 3 above.

terms of trade in Fiji. This is illustrated by the sharp contrast between sugar and copra in Table 4. Fiji experienced highly favourable external conditions for its sugar exports from 1974 to 1980. There were two international price booms, in 1975 and 1980 respectively, and in addition 40 per cent of total sugar output became covered by Lomé Convention arrangements after 1973 at favourable and stable price levels.[18] International sugar price levels fell sharply in 1981. This pulled the real grower price of sugar down to only 19 per cent above its 1970 level in 1981, and the overall price terms of trade down to 15 per cent above its 1970 level. In contrast to sugar, copra prices were generally unfavourable during the 1970s. There were two price booms again (1974 and 1979) but these were shorter lived than those of sugar, were embedded in real prices which stagnated between 30 per cent and 40 per cent below the level of the late 1960s, and there was no equivalent of the Sugar Protocol of the Lomé Convention to raise the average prices received. The real prices of domestic food crops increased sharply in the first half of the 1970s, after which they remained about 20 per cent above their 1970 level, albeit with some fluctuations, for the rest of the decade.

As in the case of Tanzania, the aggregate findings are not especially sensitive to the base-year chosen for analysis. This is clear from Table 3: whether the base-year was taken as 1970 or any combination of averages up to 1973 would not significantly affect the results of the analysis.

Producer Shares and Intersectoral Income Comparisons

A central feature of the Fiji case-study is the contrasting treatment of export crops as compared to Tanzania. The grower share of the proceeds of sugar and molasses sales had already been increased from a proportion which fluctuated between 50 and 60 per cent in the 1960s to a fixed 65 per cent in 1970 following a commission of enquiry chaired by Lord Denning [*Government of Fiji, 1970*]. Since then the grower share was raised again in 1975 to 70 per cent, and in 1980 to even higher proportions for output in excess of specified targets.[19] The average grower share reached 71.4 per cent in 1981. In spite of its progressively shrinking gross margin (35 per cent down to 28.6 per cent) the Fiji Sugar Corporation had not by 1981 experienced a loss in its milling and marketing operations. Contrast this with the experience of the Tanzanian export crop parastatals, the average gross marketing margin of which increased from 30 per cent to 68 per cent of gross sales value, while their cumulative losses amounted to T Shs 2 billion by 1980 [*Ellis, 1983*]. Export taxes on sugar remained very moderate in Fiji in the 1970s (ranging from 2 per cent to 4 per cent in different years) and were abolished in 1982 with the downswing in world prices. Copra prices were subsidised by the state from mid 1975, the average subsidy between 1975 and 1982 representing 16 per cent of gross crop income received by growers.

Non-agricultural wage and salary incomes in Fiji also increased in real terms during the 1970s, but not as dramatically or as erratically as the income terms of trade of farmers as shown in Table 3 above. Average real wages and salaries increased by 40 per cent up to 1977, after which they have remained more or less static in real terms following the introduction of national negotiating machinery which has linked wage increases to the rate of inflation.[20] This compares with the 124 per cent real increase of the income terms of trade of agriculture up to 1980, but the latter is strongly subject to cyclical variation according to world sugar prices and in 1981 experienced a large fall. Obviously there are intra-sectoral variations in this comparison both for agricultural producers and for non-agricultural wage and salary earners, but these are not such as to detract from the general thrust of the findings.

The outcome of these various trends is that rural-urban household income differentials, in any case not large in Fiji, did not in general widen in the period 1970 to 1981. Indeed, in the case of the sugar growers they clearly moved in favour of the small-farm sugar economy over much of the decade. This conclusion is supported by a wealth of partial and indirect evidence: the results of household income surveys in rural and in urban areas; census data revealing a low rate of increase in permanent rural-to-urban migration; and village surveys showing both that the age structure of village populations changed

little during the 1970s, and that there has been significant return migration
to villages of people who have worked for variable periods as wage earners
in the non-farm economy.[21]

Implications for the Urban Bias Model

Urban bias as defined by Lipton is hardly present in Fiji. On the contrary,
the emphasis of most urban policy (for, indeed, the organs of the state are
unequivocally located in urban areas) has been directed at elevating the
material living conditions of farmers and keeping in check the growth of urban
incomes. The rising share of growers in sugar export receipts, the subsidisation
of copra prices, the attempt to provide a purchaser of last resort for root crops,
heavily subsidised credit for agricultural borrowers[22] and the implementation
of several successful smallholder agricultural development projects all suggest
a state which tends to favour the maintenance of a vigorous small-farm
agricultural sector.

A weak explanation of this situation resides in the structure of the economy.
The significance of agricultural export crops, especially sugar, in the foreign
exchange and balance of payments of a highly open economy means that
agriculture could only be squeezed at considerable peril to the entire economy.
However, this is not sufficient. There are numerous countries where export
crops are treated as the prime target for surplus expropriation (witness
Tanzania).

More relevant is the conjunction of interests in control of the Fiji state,
and the constituencies from which the different groups in power derive their
support. Fijian government leaders continue to have their roots in the traditional rural social structure. Their electoral support derives little from the
advocacy of different modern economic ideologies and much from their
position as heads of ancient clan lineages [*Nayacakalou, 1975*]. As the Fijian
village economy becomes more drawn into the nexus of the market, so the
continued credibility of this traditional power depends greatly on the chiefs
being seen to foster improved standards of living in the villages and for Fijians.
Fiji-Indian government leaders (and opposition party politicians) also have
strong links to the rural economy [*Ali, 1980*] since a great number of them
have strong ties with the sugar economy (indeed, many of them are sugar
growers).[23] Moreover, sugar growers are a strong political force in their own
right through various grower organisations, and through the wide range of
non-agricultural occupations in the sugar zones which are critically dependent
on the health of the sugar economy for their survival. This 'peasant power'
is likely to be strengthened still further in the future by draft legislation which
creates a Sugar Growers Council to which all growers will automatically
belong, and which increases the participation of growers in decisions affecting
their welfare.[24]

The convergence of these predominantly rural based interests has probably
been strengthened rather than weakened by developments of the 1970s. That
an increasing number of Fijians have become small-farm sugar growers has
already been mentioned, and this has elevated the interest of Fijian leaders
in a vigorous sugar economy at the grower level. It has also become apparent

that Fiji, due to its distance from overseas markets and its relatively high wages, is unlikely to industrialise much on the basis of foreign capital, and what little industrialisation does take place is likely to be heavily concentrated in agro-processing industries.[25] Economic diversification has been most successful in rural sector activities, not in urban ones. In short, Fiji, a small capitalist economy, appears likely to remain committed in the foreseeable future to a rural, small-farm path of development.

COMPARATIVE LESSONS OF THE TANZANIA AND FIJI EXPERIENCE

The striking contrasts between the experiences of small farmers in Tanzania and Fiji during the 1970s yield some interesting conclusions about rural-urban relations, not just in the context of Lipton's urban bias thesis but also more generally.

Tanzania and Fiji have in common a rural production structure character-ised more by the equality of access to land and to agricultural income than by a grossly unequal ownership structure in agriculture. In Tanzania this resulted from the sharp curtailment of previous processes of rural differentiation by the whole galaxy of state interventions and takeovers which occurred from the mid 1960s onwards. In Fiji it resulted from decisions taken early in the colonial era to preserve most of the land area for the indigenous inhabitants under customary land rights, and also from the rather curious set of events in the 1920s when a foreign corporation converted its sugar plantations into leasehold small farms of a uniform size of 4 hectares and forbade any individual from holding more than one lease [*Anderson, 1974; Ward, 1980*].[26] Both countries thus differ substantially from the 'typical' agricultural ownership structure envisaged in the urban bias model (mainly drawn on Indian material), but then the search for generalisation of this kind may itself be a folly.

Tanzania and Fiji also have in common an acute dependence on agricultural export crops for the generation of foreign exchange and, since neither country possesses a substantial non-farm population requiring really large domestic flows of food crops, export crops in both are the chief source of external cash income to the peasant economy. Again, these conditions differ from those presupposed in the urban bias model which tends to assume a populous, large urban market-type economy in which the key relationships of the rural-urban equation are the supply and price levels of the marketed surplus of food. The external terms of trade, which scarcely receives a mention in the urban bias thesis, is potentially a critical factor for relative agricultural prices in economies like Tanzania and Fiji.[27]

This is where the similarities stop. In the observation period to which this analysis refers the impact on the rural economy of state action diverges greatly between the two case-studies. In Tanzania, which ostensibly adopted 'socialist' policies virtually along model anti-urban bias lines, the intersectoral terms of trade was turned heavily against peasant crop producers (a decline of 36 per cent and 39 per cent in the price and income terms of trade respectively), an enormous gulf was opened up between the procurement and sales prices of agricultural output, a substantial surplus transfer equivalent to an implicit tax of 27 per cent on peasant crop output was transferred from peasant farmers to the state, and marketed production declined from its peak and then stagnated.

In Fiji, a small capitalist economy pursuing only moderate intervention in agricultural markets and little intervention elsewhere in economic life, the intersectoral terms of trade moved strongly in favour of peasant crop producers (a rise, to 1980, of 67 per cent and 124 per cent in the price and income terms of trade respectively, though this is subject to much greater annual fluctuation than in the Tanzanian case), the margin between the procurement and sales prices of agricultural crops was narrowed (not only, as it happens, in the major case of sugar cited earlier), the state moved to subsidise a major crop in trouble from adverse external price trends, and marketed production rose substantially between the beginning and end of the decade.

There are three main observations which can be drawn from these similarities and contrasts. First, it is clear that in so far as real agricultural prices are concerned a genuinely peasant-orientated Tanzania could have followed the same path as Fiji over this period. The responsiveness of peasant agriculturalists in Tanzania to relative prices is strongly proven [*Ellis, 1982a*]; the intersectoral terms of trade would have risen by at least 5 per cent over the period if producer prices of export crops had simply been permitted to rise in line with their world market prices; and other external factors were no more disadvantageous for Tanzania than for Fiji during the 1970s (though admittedly Tanzania would have started from a much lower base).

Secondly, the urban bias model provides only a partial and not entirely convincing explanation of the failure of Tanzania to do this. The 'official' state ideology was one of strong rural bias and a large proportion of the state and parastatal apparatus was diffused the length and breadth of rural Tanzania. The failure was more pertinently associated with (i) the needs of a rapidly expanding state apparatus for recurrent resources in the context of an economy with a very low level of development of its productive forces, (ii) the failure to make an unambiguous choice between mobilisation of the rural population towards collective production and reliance on the monetary motivation of individual peasant agriculturalists, thus achieving neither path successfully, and (iii) the total neglect of peasant participation in matters affecting peasant welfare, in the crucial agencies where such participation might have helped to control the profligate expansion of bureaucracy.

The Tanzania story of the 1970s casts severe doubts on the policy implications of the urban bias approach. In the absence of a properly constructed analysis of class interests and the state (in place of a naive belief in the neutrality and potential fair-mindedness of government officials) the advocacy of state-led rural bias is fraught with perils.[28] A peasant state will require peasant farmers, not bureaucrats, either to be directly in charge of the state, or at least in the political position to exert considerable pressure on state action.

The third point follows from the second. The Fiji experience raises the question of whether the peasant state might not more likely be a capitalist rather than a bureaucratic or socialist state. Peasant production is a petty capitalist form of production, its driving force is individual motivation and the market, not collective production and social distribution. The strength of the small farmers' position in Fiji originated from the representation they directly possessed in the political structure of a pluralist state. This may appear a historical curiosity of such minor significance in the global scheme of things as not to warrant serious consideration. However, rather closer to home, it might be useful to reflect on the influence of French, German or Italian peasants on the political adoption and subsequent defence of the European Common Agricultural Policy. Defenders and sympathisers of the merits of the peasant or small-farm economy will need to go far beyond the mixed-up and ambivalent political economy of urban bias to attain their peasant utopia.

CONCLUSION

The central defect of the urban bias argument to emerge from the analysis of this paper, and one already stressed by several reviewers, is the uprooting of all those interest groups which might be expected to exercise political leverage within the state on the part of agriculture (richer peasants, capitalist farmers, resident agricultural landowners) and their indiscriminate conscription into the single urban class. This device is necessary for the urban bias model in order to sidestep the awkward reality of intra-agricultural class differentiation, but in so doing it incorrectly divorces the political objectives of various rural classes from the material basis of their interests in agricultural production and agricultural land ownership. Behind this lies an unpreparedness to confront the really central political issues implied by championing the peasants, which are about intra-agricultural choices of modes of production and land ownership, not about rural-urban struggles.

Neither is the urban bias model a general theory. Rather it is one amongst several attempts in development studies to generalise the experience of the Third World by weaving 'global theory' out of selected distinctive features observed in perhaps a handful of countries. This kind of 'global theory' is seldom useful for understanding the detail of particular problems in individual countries, is frequently falsified by research into topics which do not fit the generalisation, and is no substitute for the rigorous logic of established bodies of social scientific theory. This is not a rejection of innovative work in true theory, but the rich and incredibly diverse set of historical and contemporary experiences found in Third World countries is poorly served by grand attempts at descriptive oversimplification as exemplified by the urban bias model.

NOTES

1. This paper addresses itself to the full articulation of the urban bias model as set out in Lipton [*1977*]. Except where matters directly pertinent to agricultural prices are concerned I have tried to avoid repeating points made in reviews which followed the book's publication [*Griffin, 1977; Van Arkadie, 1978; Seers, 1977; Byres, 1979; Corbridge, 1982*].
2. If this were not the case then large farmers must be assumed to act as irrational economic agents.
3. This is an alternative proposition about the politics of farm prices which is of particular interest for the case of Tanzania described below.
4. Prices of agricultural export crops are virtually ignored in *Why Poor People Stay Poor* except for a brief mention towards the end of Chapter 13 where it is stated that: 'Many a poor country has a large share of world markets for an item like tea or jute, with limited demand, so that greater production for export could drive prices right down' [*1977: 322*]. However, this perception is not followed through into the domain of intersectoral price relativities, in part due to an erroneous belief that export crops are almost always produced by foreign

estates or large farmers, and in part because the global generalisation that there is 'no long-run trend in international prices against poor countries' exports as a whole' [*1977: 322*] is much too readily accepted as applying to all agricultural export situations.

5. This is because the incomes of *rural* households become more heavily influenced by export sales than by the prices paid to them for their sales to the urban population, and the real incomes of *urban* households may be more heavily influenced by the prices of imported foodstuffs than by purchases from their own rural sector. In any case the link between intersectoral price relativities and incomes for urban households is rather tenuous, depending on the significance of domestic foods in the urban consumption basket, on the share of wages in urban value added, and on the balance of non-food purchases between imported and domestic manufacturers.

6. For a competent approach to the resolution of base-year and other time-series problems in terms of trade analysis, see Rahman [*1981*].

7. Both Coulson [*1977*] and Hyden [*1980*] treat the Arusha Declaration as part of a continuum in the state approach to the peasant economy rather than a radical departure from previous developments.

8. There are significant conceptual weaknesses in other procedures which have been suggested for modifying the NCPI. The inappropriateness of excluding the food category of the NCPI [*ILO, 1978: 256*] when it is producer rather than retail prices of agricultural crops which require deflating is discussed in Ellis [*1981: 44-5*] and Ellis [*1982b: 70*].

9. The magnitude of this real increase rises to 16 per cent if the full National Consumer Price Index rather than its modified version is used as the deflator [*Ellis, 1983*].

10. This is over and above pre-existing levels of taxation on agricultural sales up to the base-year of the observation period of this analysis.

11. The framework for this was set out in the Villages and Ujamaa Villages (Registration, Designation and Administration) Act passed in July 1975. This Act was later amended in 1979 to allow village governments to raise revenues, to make village by-laws, and to fine village members who failed to comply with such by-laws.

12. It is not sufficient as a counter-argument here to place undue emphasis on the proportion of development expenditure which was assigned to industrial rather than agricultural projects in this period. For one thing, a genuine effort was made to locate industrial projects outside the major urban centres; for another, the source of funds for most industrial investment was external aid donors, *not* internal 'saving' from the agricultural sector.

13. The source of much of the basic data cited in following paragraphs is Government of Fiji, Bureau of Statistics, *Current Economic Statistics*, Suva, quarterly. The development of this analysis of the rural-urban terms of trade in Fiji depends to a considerable degree on original research, using primary source material, undertaken between September 1982 and March 1983 as part of the Fiji Employment Development Mission. This work remains unpublished at the time of writing.

14. The term 'clan' is used to describe patrilineal descent groups called *mataqali* in Fijian. Much fuller accounts of the Fijian social system and chiefly structure are contained in numerous sources, both specifically on that topic [*Nayacakalou, 1975*] and in more general works on the population and economy of the islands [*Belshaw, 1964; Ward, 1965; Spate, 1959*]. Historical accounts of Fiji's Indian migrants and of the origin of the small-farm sugar production system are given in Gillion [*1962 and 1977*], Anderson [*1974*] and Moynagh [*1981*].

15. For a brief period in the mid 1970s the National Marketing Authority acted as a purchaser of last resort for domestic root crops, but this scheme collapsed because producer prices rose of their own accord to levels which the NMA could not possibly meet without incurring large losses given its overhead costs.

16. The average share of sugar in the total producer value of the crops included in this analysis was 79 per cent.

17. The baseline for estimated marketed output trends for root crops is the per capita consumption (excluding subsistence) of these crops obtained from the computer tapes of the 1977 Household Income and Expenditure Survey. This is used to estimate total marketed output in 1977 as discussed in the Bureau of Statistics publication *Fiji National Accounts Studies, Part II: Sources and Methods* (July 1982). For *yaqona*, marketed output is assumed to have grown at a constant annual rate of 6 per cent reflecting the rapid increase in its consumption by the Fiji-Indian population during the 1970s. For cassava and taro the growth rate is

assumed at 3 per cent per annum. In both cases it is possible that marketed output growth was in reality greater than this, given a growth rate of the urban population of over 4 per cent per annum between 1966 and 1976, and the rapid commercialisation of village agriculture which took place during this period. Other sources of relevance here are Casley [*1969*], Rotherfield and Kumar [*1980*] and Government of Fiji [*1982*].

18. The Fiji quota under the Sugar Protocol of the EEC/ACP Lomé Convention is 172,000 tonnes. The prices for this quota have hitherto been fixed at the raw sugar equivalent of EEC target prices for sugar beet farmers negotiated annually under the Common Agricultural Policy.

19. The growers' share after 1980 was 70 per cent on sugar production up to 325,000 tonnes, 72.5 per cent on production between 325,000 and 350,000 tonnes, and 75 per cent on production above 350,000 tonnes.

20. This refers to the Tripartite Forum, a negotiating machinery established in 1976 consisting of representatives from trade unions, employers and the government.

21. This evidence has been collected and analysed as part of the work of the Fiji Employment and Development Mission, working in Fiji from September 1982 to April 1984.

22. Agricultural loans from the Fiji Development Bank are at half the annual rate of interest of normal commercial borrowings in Fiji (in 1983, 5.5 per cent against 11 per cent).

23. One of the most important of these is the Kisan Sangh, which played a central role in the political development of the Fiji-Indian population [*Ali, 1980*].

24. This draft legislation exists at the time of writing as The Sugar Industry Bill, 1982. It is designed to improve grower representation by bringing into one forum interests which were previously advanced in a fragmentary way by rival grower unions.

25. The small size of the domestic market is obviously a critical factor contributing to the relatively weak ability of Fiji to attract foreign capital, in spite of the stability of its political system and openness to international capital flows.

26. There does exist a potential problem in Fiji concerning the availability of land for lease by Fiji-Indians to the extent that Fijian clan owners decide not to lease (or not to renew expiring leases) to aspiring non-Fijian tenants. However, hitherto this problem has remained more hypothetical than substantive.

27. The reason a certain amount of emphasis is placed on this point is that in the 1980s external market conditions appear likely to be very much more unfavourable for agricultural exports than in the 1970s. Hence in Fiji, for example, the terms of trade could move against agriculture on the basis of declining real sugar prices alone.

28. This is revealed particularly sharply by the analysis of Hyden [*1980*] where the rural ideology of the Tanzanian state is interpreted as a necessary strategy forced on the ruling class by the need to 'capture' a recalcitrant peasantry and bend its will to the modernisation and development of the economy.

REFERENCES

Ali, A., 1980, *Plantation to Politics: Studies on Fiji Indians*, Suva: University of the South Pacific/Fiji Times.

Anderson, A. G., 1974, *Indo-Fijian Smallfarming: Profiles of a Peasantry*, Auckland: Auckland University Press/Oxford University Press.

Belshaw, C. S., 1964, *Under the Ivi Tree: Society and Economic Growth in Rural Fiji*, London: Routledge and Kegan Paul.

Bernstein, H., 1981, 'The State and Peasantry in Tanzania', *Review of African Political Economy*, No. 21, pp. 44-62.

Boesen, J., 1979, 'Tanzania: From Ujamaa to Villagisation', in Mwansau, B. U. and Pratt, C. (eds), *Towards Socialism in Tanzania*, Dar-es-Salaam: Tanzania Publishing House.

Boesen, J., Storgaard, M. and Moody, T., 1977, *Ujamaa: Socialism from Above*, Uppsala: Scandinavian Institute of African Studies.

Byres, T., 1979, 'Of Neo-Populist Pipe-Dreams: Daedalus in the Third World and the Myth of Urban Bias', *Journal of Peasant Studies*, Vol. 4, No. 3.

Casley, D. J. L., 1969, *Report on the Census of Agriculture 1968*, Suva: Government Printer, Council Paper No. 28 of 1969.

Cliffe, L. and Saul, J.S. (eds), 1972, *Socialism in Tanzania: An Interdisciplinary Reader*, Nairobi: East African Publishing House.

Cliffe, L., Lawrence, P., Luttrell, W., Migot-Adholla, S. and Saul, J.S. (eds), 1975, *Rural Cooperation in Tanzania*, Dar-es-Salaam: Tanzania Publishing House.

Corbridge, S., 1982, 'Urban Bias, Rural Bias and Industrialisation: An Appraisal of the Work of Michael Lipton and Terry Byres', in Harriss, J. (ed.), *Rural Development: Theories of Peasant Economy and Agrarian Change*, London: Hutchinson.

Coulson, A., 1975, 'Peasants and Bureaucrats', *Review of African Political Economy*, No. 3, pp. 53-8.

Coulson, A., 1977, 'Agricultural Policies in Mainland Tanzania', *Review of African Political Economy*, No. 10, pp. 74-96.

Coulson, A., 1982, *Tanzania: A Political Economy*, Oxford University Press.

Ellis, F., 1981, 'Agricultural Pricing Policy in Tanzania, 1970–1979: Implications for Agricultural Output, Rural Incomes and Crop Marketing Costs', *ERB Paper*, 80.2, University of Dar-es-Salaam. Also available as *Development Studies Discussion Paper*, No. 84, University of East Anglia.

Ellis, F., 1982a, 'Agricultural Price Policy in Tanzania', *World Development*, Vol. 10, No. 4, pp. 263-83.

Ellis, F., 1982b, 'Prices and the Transformation of Peasant Agriculture: the Tanzanian Case', *IDS Bulletin*, Vol. 13, No. 4, pp. 66-72.

Ellis, F., 1983, 'Agricultural Marketing and Peasant-State Transfers in Tanzania', *Journal of Peasant Studies*, Vol. 10, No. 4.

Ellis, F. and Hanak, E., 1981, 'An Economic Analysis of the Coffee Industry in Tanzania 1969/70–1978/79: Towards a Higher and More Stable Producer Price', *ERB Paper*, 80.4, University of Dar-es-Salaam.

France, P., 1969, *Charter of the Land: Custom and Colonisation in Fiji*, Melbourne: Oxford University Press.

Gillion, K.L., 1962, *Fiji's Indian Migrants*, Melbourne: Oxford University Press.

Gillion, K.L., 1977, *The Fiji Indians: Challenge to European Dominance 1920–1946*, Canberra: ANU Press.

Government of Fiji, 1970, *The Award of the Rt Hon Lord Denning in the Sugar Cane Contract Dispute 1969*, Suva: Government Printer.

Government of Fiji, Bureau of Statistics, quarterly, *Current Economic Statistics*, Suva.

Government of Fiji, Bureau of Statistics, 1982, *Household Income and Expenditure Survey*, Suva: Government Printer.

Griffin, K., 1977, 'Review of Lipton's *Why Poor People Stay Poor*', *Journal of Development Studies*, Vol. 14, No. 1.

Hyden, G., 1980, *Beyond Ujamaa in Tanzania: Underdevelopment and an Uncaptured Peasantry*, London: Heinemann.

International Labour Office, Jobs and Skills Programme for Africa (JASPA), 1978, *Towards Self-Reliance: Development Employment and Equity Issues in Tanzania*, Addis Ababa: ILO.

International Labour Office, Jobs and Skills Programme for Africa (JASPA), 1981, *Basic Needs in Danger*, Addis Ababa: ILO.

Kriesel, H.C., Laurent, C.K., Halpern, C. and Larzelere, H.E., 1970, *Agricultural Marketing in Tanzania: Background, Research and Policy Proposals*, Michigan State University, Dept of Agricultural Economics.

Lipton, M., 1977, *Why Poor People Stay Poor: Urban Bias in World Development*, London: Maurice Temple Smith.

Mitra, A., 1977, *Terms of Trade and Class Relations*, London: Frank Cass.

Moynagh, M., 1981, *Brown or White? A History of the Fiji Sugar Industry 1873–1973*, Canberra: ANU, Pacific Research Monograph No. 5.

Mwansasu, B.U. and Pratt C. (eds), *Towards Socialism in Tanzania*, Dar-es-Salaam: Tanzania Publishing House.

Nayacakalou, R.R., 1975, *Leadership in Fiji*, Melbourne: Oxford University Press.

Norton, R., 1977, *Race and Politics in Fiji*, University of Queensland Press.

Nyerere, J.K., 1968, *Freedom and Socialism*, Dar-es-Salaam: Oxford University Press.

Nyerere, J.K., 1972, *Decentralisation*, Dar-es-Salaam: Government Printer.

Rahman, A., 1981, 'Variations in Terms of Exchange and Their Impact on Farm Households in Bangladesh', *Journal of Development Studies*, Vol. 17, No. 4.

Rothfield, R. and Kumar, B., 1980, *Report on the Census of Agriculture 1978*, Suva: Government Printer, Parliamentary Paper No. 28 of 1980.

Saul, J. S., 1979, 'Tanzania's Transition to Socialism', Chapter 10 in his *The State and Revolution in Eastern Africa*, London: Heinemann, pp. 249-92.

Seers, D., 1977, 'Indian Bias?' in *Urban Bias – Seers Versus Lipton*, Brighton: Institute of Development Studies, Discussion Paper No. 116.

Shivji, I. G., 1973, 'Tanzania: the Silent Class Struggle', in *The Silent Class Struggle*, Dar-es-Salaam: Tanzania Publishing House, Tanzanian Studies No. 2.

Shivji, I. G., 1976, *Class Struggles in Tanzania*, Dar-es-Salaam: Tanzania Publishing House.

Spate, O. H. K., 1959, *The Fijian People: Economic Problems and Prospects*, Legislative Council of Fiji, Council Paper No. 13 of 1959, Suva: Government Printer.

Van Arkadie, B., 1978, 'Review Article: Town Versus Country', *Development and Change*, Vol. 8, No. 3.

Ward, R. G., 1965, *Land Use and Population in Fiji*, London: HMSO.

Ward, R. G., 1980, 'Plus Ca Change ... Plantations, Tenants, Proletarians or Peasants in Fiji', Chapter 7 in Jennings, J. N. and Linge, G. J. R. (eds), *Of Space and Time*, Canberra: ANU.

Urban Bias, Rural Bias or State Bias? Urban-Rural Relations in Post-Revolutionary China

The authors aim to evaluate the relevance of 'urban bias' and 'rural bias' to the Chinese case. They present empirical evidence on the nature and extent of differentiation in rural-urban living standards, examine the political basis of relevant economic policies and investigate the relationship between these policies: both the changes in labour productivity in each sector and the inter-sectoral savings transfers. Both 'urban' and 'rural bias' hypotheses illuminate certain dimensions of Chinese development strategy. But the realities of rural-urban relations have been complex, and analysis must be supplemented by a focus on the divide between state and society, and the question of 'state bias'.

Some writers argue that socialist strategies of development, including the Chinese, have been examples of strong 'urban bias'. Others believe China has pursued a 'rural-biased' strategy. This article investigates the applicability of both these analytical categories, and suggests that the realities of rural-urban relations in post-revolutionary China are more complex than either of these simple characterisations allows.

Our analysis proceeds as follows. Since the central concern of poor people is their standard of living, we begin, in Section I, by examining the evidence on this, the most fundamental aspect of urban-rural differentiation. Section II investigates the ideological and political forces behind the economic policies which influence the outcomes presented in Section I. Section III examines these policies and their outcome in respect to labour productivity changes in each sector and inter-sectoral savings transfers.

URBAN-RURAL DIFFERENCES IN INCOME AND STANDARD OF LIVING

Statistical Problems

Over the past few years a flood of statistical material has been published in China. This enables a much better understanding of China's economic problems than before 1976. However, it must be remembered that historical data dealing with the years from 1957 to the late 1970s are based largely on guesswork, since the statistical apparatus was in disarray for much of this period.

* Jesus College, Cambridge. Peter Nolan wishes to thank the Social Science Research Council for financial support in the preparation of this paper, the grant being administered by the Department of Applied Economics, Cambridge.
** Institute of Development Studies, University of Sussex.

During the Great Leap Forward in the late 1950s massive falsification of data occurred, over and above that normally associated with administratively planned economies [*Aird, 1982: 209-10*]. In the Cultural Revolution the very idea of statistical expertise came under attack. According to Sun Yefang, 'in those chaotic years, nearly all statistical organs at different levels throughout the country were disbanded, the staff were transferred and large quantities of materials were burned' [*Sun, 1981*].

Defining 'urban' and 'rural' is a problem in all countries. In China, as elsewhere, the principal difficulty is with respect to people living in suburbs. China's cities have a large number of people who are under the administration of the city, but who work in agriculture; and in large numbers of suburban families, some work in agriculture and others have non-agricultural occupations. Obtaining accurate and consistent data is a massive problem. Although China has attempted to construct clear criteria to demarcate 'urban' from 'rural', the criteria have not been easy to implement, not merely because the statistical system was in disarray for most of the period from the late 1950s to late 1970s but also because of practical complexities of residence and occupation [*Orleans, 1982*]. China's current official series on 'urban' and 'rural' population appear to be trying to include only the non-agricultural 'urban' population [*SSB, 1982: 507*], but considerable guesswork is likely to have been involved. One of the leading Western demographers of China writes: 'Chinese demographers – and I would say the Chinese government – do not have precise statistics on urban population and do not hesitate to use approximations' [*Orleans, 1982: 288*].

A further complication, specific to China, is the fact that a lot of data relevant to this essay relate to 'commune members' on the one hand and 'staff and workers' on the other. Most 'commune members' live in the 'rural' areas, but many live in the suburban areas of municipalities. Most commune workers work in agriculture, but not all of them do. Most 'staff and workers' work in cities, but some work in villages. Rather than attempt to manipulate data with an often already shaky foundation, we have opted to use the data as they are, accepting that this involves categories that are not always precisely comparable.

Comparing average income and expenditure in urban and rural areas of poor economies is fraught with difficulties because the nature of economic activity is different in the two sectors [*Nolan, 1979*]. Urban workers in regular employment often have access to fringe benefits that may not be reflected in reported earnings figures, and peasants often have extremely varied sources of income about which it may be hard to get information (information on income from the 'private plot' in China is a notable example of this). Even if accurate figures on average household income could be obtained, data on family size are needed for these to be translated into comparable figures on average income per capita, and there is reason to think average family size is not the same in urban and rural areas. Translating reported figures on average income per capita into comparable figures reflecting the real value of income in each sector is a further problem. First, there may be differences between the price at which the peasants' self-produced and self-consumed items are valued and the price paid in urban markets. In the 1950s in China farm gate prices seem to have been on average below those in urban retail outlets [*Nolan, 1979*], but since then the differential has been reversed. Secondly, city life may involve urban workers in extra expenditures which provide no extra utility — notably transport costs, but also a portion of outlays on rent, electricity and water charges, and even some material items such as alarm clocks and work-clothes. Moreover, to compare the real value of consumption in the two sectors, evidence is needed in respect to savings behaviour and inter-sectoral income transfers. Some attempts were made in China in the 1950s to allow for these things, and Chinese writers argued that the net effect was to considerably reduce the urban-rural gap (see, for example, the data for Hubei province in Table 1).

If it is difficult to make meaningful comparisons of the real value of income and consumption in town and countryside at a point in time, it becomes a Herculean task to assess changes over time. Estimates in value terms of changes

TABLE 1

CALCULATION OF DIFFERENTIAL IN REAL VALUE OF INCOME BETWEEN PEASANTS
AND STAFF AND WORKERS, HUBEI PROVINCE, 1956
(Unit: Yuan per capita)

			Yuan
Peasants:			
	(i)	Gross income	112.67
		Production expenditure, taxation, savings	(28.03)
	(ii)	Income for spending on material and cultural livelihood	84.64
Staff and workers:			
	(iii)	Total income, including wage and non-wage income	168.68
		Money sent back to support relatives	(9.90)
		Money deposited in banks or saved in ready cash	(8.40)
	(iv)	Income for spending on material and cultural livelihood (net income)	150.38
		Deduction on account of differential in price of consumer goods [1]	(35.1)
		Deduction on account of extra urban expenditure (rent, water and electricity charges, transportation costs)	(9.48)
	(v)	Real value of income used for consumption.	105.8

Ratio of: (ii) to (iii) = 1:1.99
            (ii) to (iv) = 1:1.77
            (ii) to (v) = 1:1.25

Note: 1. Rural consumer goods' general price level is only 76.66 per cent of the level in urban markets.

Source: 'On the basis of the expansion of output, our province's people's livelihood has magnificently improved,' *HBRB*, 11 August 1957.

in the urban-rural gap must be treated with great caution, and the available data on physical consumption of different items is probably more useful in analysing the urban-rural 'gap' (see below).

Intra-sectoral Differentials

Though the urban-rural dimension is useful for thinking about some development issues, in analysing income distribution and related problems, it should be remembered that China, no less than other economies, has important intra-sectoral differentials. Within the rural production team (the lowest level of collective ownership, work organisation and income distribution prior to the recent reforms)[1] considerable inequalities existed in households' average per capita income from the collective, mainly on account of variations in the worker-dependent ratio [*Nolan, 1983b: 1437-8*]. At a broader level, rural inequalities reflect spatial differences in average peasant income. The Chinese authorities have hardly interfered at all to extract 'differential rent' income from better located peasants and they have prevented intra-rural migration which might have helped to erode these differences. The most they have done (pre-1976) is to push richer areas into high marginal reinvestment rates and set upper limits to collective income distribution. Even then, substantial income differences existed, as the data for Guangdong province in Table 2 suggest. After 1976 upper limits to peasant income were removed and better located areas, mostly close to cities, experienced large increases in income so that the absolute gap between their average incomes and those of well located areas rose substantially [*Nolan, 1983a*].

TABLE 2

AVERAGE PER CAPITA DISTRIBUTED INCOME IN PRODUCTION TEAMS IN
GUANGDONG PROVINCE, 1975

Av.p.c. Distributed Income (*yuan*)	Number of Production Teams Surveyed (10,000)	Proportion of Total (%)
<40	5.02	17.2
41-50	4.96	16.9
51-100	15.83	54.0
101-150	2.79	9.5
>150	0.72	2.4
Total	29.32	100.0

Source: Nolan [*1983a: 44*]

Within urban areas earnings vary for a number of reasons. In the state sector each occupation has different wage ranks [*Korzec and Whyte, 1981: 251*]. During the Cultural Revolution decade there was a tendency for wage earners to be clustered in the middle ranks of each occupational wage scale, but little information is available on the proportion of wage earners in different ranks.

Since liberation, a considerable gap has existed between average wages in the urban state and collective sectors − in 1980, for example, average wages of staff and workers in state-owned units (containing 77 per cent of the total number of staff and workers) were 29 per cent above those in urban collective-owned units [*SSB, 1982: 107 and 433*]. Within both state and collective units average wages vary between different sectors. In 1980 in both state- and collective-owned units average annual wages were highest in 'construction and exploration of resources' (923 *yuan* and 714 *yuan* respectively) and lowest in 'agriculture, forestry, water conservancy and meteorology' (636 *yuan* and 489 *yuan* respectively) [*SSB, 1982: 433*]. In addition, the worker-dependant ratio varies between households. Unsurprisingly, recent survey data show quite a wide range in average per capita incomes of staff and worker families (Table 3).

TABLE 3

INCOME DISTRIBUTION AMONG STAFF AND WORKERS, 1981

Av.p.c. Monthly Income (*yuan*)	No. of House-holds	Av.Monthly Income (*yuan* p.c.)	Av.No.of Persons per Household	Av.No.of Employees per Household	Av.Monthly Earnings per Employee (*yuan*)
<20	179	18.89	5.60	1.63	64.9
20-24	476	24.95	5.22	1.96	66.4
25-34	2772	33.25	4.66	2.18	71.1
35-49	3685	44.72	4.00	2.43	73.6
50-59	1037	58.68	3.70	2.79	77.8
>59	566	72.93	3.20	2.69	86.8
Total/Av.	8715	41.70	4.24	2.39	74.0

Note: From a national sample survey in 46 cities and towns.

Source: SSB [*1982: 438*]

Urban-rural Differences in Income and Consumption

Insufficient evidence is available to enable a clear account to be given of changes in the urban-rural gap in the real value of income and consumption from the 1950s to the 1980s. Some of the most relevant pieces of information are given in Table 4. The broad picture they suggest is this. From 1952 to 1957 both money and real wages rose quickly in the cities. Peasant incomes in current prices rose less rapidly; moreover, part of the increase was on account of the rise in the value of self-produced self-consumed items (see below), so that peasants' average real incomes certainly rose more slowly than those of urban workers. During these five years the absolute gap in average per capita consumption at current prices widened considerably.

From 1957 to the late 1970s China's urban workers experienced a fall in money wages at the same time that their cost of living index reportedly rose

TABLE 4
INCOME AND CONSUMPTION IN TOWN AND COUNTRYSIDE

	Average Annual Wage of Staff and Workers in State-owned Units (Current Yuan)	Cost of Living Index of Staff and Workers	Real Wage Index for Staff and Workers in State-owned Units	Av. p.c. Income of Staff and Workers (Current Yuan)	Real Spendable Income for Staff and Workers in State-owned Units (Index)	Peasants' av. p.c. Income (Index: Current Prices)	Peasants' av. p.c. Income Distributed by Collective (Current Yuan) of which: ready cash	Peasants' av. p.c. Income (Collective plus Non-Collective) (Current Yuan)	Peasants' Real Income p.c. (Index)	Peasants' Av. p.c. Consumption of: (i) Peasants Current Yuan	(i) Peasants Index (At "Comparable" prices)	(ii) Non-agricultural Population Current Yuan	(ii) Non-agricultural Population Index (At "Comparable" prices)
	(i)	(ii)	(iii)	(iv)	(v)	(vi)	(vii)	(viii)	(ix)	(x)	(xi)	(xii)	(xiii)
1952	446[1]	100[1]	100	-	-	100[4]	-	-	-	62[2]	100[2]	148[2]	100[2]
1957	637[1]	109.6[1]	130	254[2](a)	-	127.9[4]	40.5[5](14.2)[6]	-	-	79[2]	117.1[2]	205[2]	126.3[2]
1962	592[1]	-	-	-	-	-	46.1[5]	-	-	-	-	-	-
1964	661[1]	-	-	243[2](a)	-	-	47.5[5]	-	-	-	-	-	-
1965	652[1]	120.3[1]	122	-	-	-	52.3[5](14.5)[6]	-	-	100[2]	124.8[2]	237[2]	136.8[2]
1970	609[1]	-	-	-	-	-	59.5[5]	-	-	-	-	-	-
1975	613[1]	-	-	-	-	-	63.2[5](12.4)[6]	-	-	-	-	-	-
1978	644[1]	125.3[1]	115	316[1](a)	100[3]	-	74.0[5](19.0)[6]	134[1](b)	100[3]	132[2]	157.5[2]	383[2]	212.9[2]
1980	803[1]	-	-	-	-	-	-	-	-	173[2]	184.4[2]	468[2]	227.6[2]
1981	812[1]	140.7[1]	129	463[1](a) -500[2](a)	-	-	101.3[1]	223[1](b)	167.4[3]	-	-	-	-
1982	-	-	-	-	138.3[3]	-	-	-	-	-	-	-	-

Note: (a) from sample surveys giving monthly income figures
(b) sample survey data
(c) "By comparable price we mean that when comparing the indicators, in value terms, of different periods, the changes in price are deducted to show exactly the change in quantity", (SSB, 1982 : 510)

Sources: (1) SSB, 1982 : 11, 202, 429, 435-436
(2) Chinese Economic Yearbook, 1983 : Section Viii, p.28
(3) Beijing Review: 16 May 1983
(4) SSB, 1974 : 174
(5) Chinese Agriculture Yearbook, 1981 : 45
(6) An outline..., 1982 : 202

by more than 14 per cent, resulting in a substantial fall in their average real wages. However, because of the tight controls on rural-urban migration that operated for much of this period [*Orleans, 1982*], increases in urban employment apparently came about to a considerable extent through increasing the number of wage earners per family, largely via an increase in the proportion of married women in paid employment [*Emerson, 1982: 241*]. Consequently, the average number of dependents per worker in urban families fell significantly.[2] As a result, average urban incomes per capita, even in real terms, may have risen over these years. Indeed, the data on average per capita consumption for the non-agricultural population suggest a rise of more than 60 per cent in real terms over the two decades.

In current prices, the value of peasant income from the collective almost doubled from 1957 to 1978. However, a large part of the increase simply reflected an increase in the current value of in-kind distribution on account of the rise in agricultural purchase prices (used to calculate the value of collective income). Over the two decades average collective cash distribution per capita rose by only a small sum (Table 4, column (vii)). Information on private sideline income in this period is negligible. Given the degree of official disapproval from the mid-sixties to the mid-seventies it is probable that its contribution to peasant income was less than in 1952-7. The reported figures for real average per capita peasant consumption show a rise of about one-third over these two decades – a much lower rate of advance than was recorded for the non-agricultural population. Indeed, in absolute terms the gap in the average per capita consumption between peasants and the non-agricultural population widened from 126 *yuan* in 1957 to 251 *yuan* in 1978.

After 1978 both rural and urban incomes in current prices rose extremely quickly. However, this was also a period of considerable inflation by modern Chinese standards, and calculation of changes in real incomes is difficult. The Chinese data report that both urban and rural dwellers achieved important progress in real average incomes, but that for the first time in China's post-revolutionary history, peasants' real incomes rose more rapidly than urban workers'.

We turn now from the highly problematic data on the urban-rural gap in value terms, to the less ambiguous data on material consumption (Tables 5-6). Throughout the post-Liberation decades the gap in average grain consumption per capita has been small, though data from the 1950s show that the proportion of 'fine' grains (i.e. wheat and rice) was higher in the cities [*Nolan, 1981: Chapter 3*] and it is only since 1978 that the rural proportion seems to have risen perceptibly. In 1952–7 average urban consumption levels of basic goods other than grain were reportedly several times higher than in the villages (Table 5) and the gap in non-basic foodstuffs was often even wider [*Nolan, 1981: Chapter 3*]. Purchases of 'luxury' consumer goods were at a very low level in both sectors, but average per capita consumption levels of these goods were vastly higher in towns than in the countryside.

From the late 1950s to the late 1970s, average consumption of basic commodities increased slowly, and in some cases even declined (notably vegetable oil). In absolute terms, such growth in average per capita consumption of these items as occurred was greater in the urban than in the rural areas,

TABLE 5
AVERAGE CONSUMPTION IN CHINA'S CITIES AND TOWNS, AND VILLAGES

Item	Grain[1]		Vegetable oil		Pork		Sugar		Cotton Cloth[8]		Bicycles		Sewing Machines		Radios		Watches	
Unit	kgs.p.c.		kgs.p.c.		kgs.p.c.		kgs.p.c.		metres p.c.		no./10,000 people		no./10,000 people		no./10,000 people		no./10,000 people	
Year	Cities/Towns	Villages	Cities/Towns	Villages	Cities/Towns	Villages	Cities/Towns	Villages	Cities/Towns	Villages	Cities/Towns	Villages	Cities/Towns	Villages	Cities/Towns	Villages	Cities/Towns	Villages
1952	241	192	5.1	1.7	10.1[2]	5.5[2]	3.0	0.6	12.1	4.6	44.9	0.4	13.5	0.1	2.7	neg.	55.5	neg.
1957	196	205	5.2	1.9	9.0	4.4	3.7	1.1	10.0	5.8	50.4	4.2	19.4	1.1	21.8	0.2	107.6	neg.
1962	184	161	2.5	0.8	4.3[3]	2.3[3]	n.a.	n.a.	5.8	2.9	n.a.	n.a.	n.a.	n.a.	n.a.	n.a.	n.a.	n.a.
1965	218	177	5.0	1.1	10.0[4]	4.5[4]	3.7	1.2	11.6	4.8	89.8	11.7	47.5	5.6	52.9	3.5	148.4	2.2
1970	209	185	4.4	1.1	11.9[5]	5.4[5]	4.5	1.5	15.6	6.4	166.6	17.5	110.3	11.1	75.8	15.8	181.9	2.8
1975	217	187	4.8	1.2	13.6[6]	5.9[6]	5.9	1.5	15.1	5.9	246.0	27.6	132.7	14.8	287.2	39.7	513.8	11.7
1977	223	188	4.6	1.0	14.0	5.7	9.3[7]	2.2[7]	15.0	6.1	n.a.	n.a.	n.a.	n.a.	n.a.	n.a.	n.a.	n.a.
1979	219	203	5.5	1.3	13.7	7.8	9.6	2.4	16.8	7.0	301.8	60.1	176.7	32.9	444.3	117.4	815.0	84.1

Notes: 1. This relates to 'traded grain'. Average per capita grain ration of people's commune members was reportedly as follows (unit:kgs., unhusked): 1957 = 203, 1975 = 207, 1977 = 208, 1979 = 244.

2. 1953.

3. Average for 2nd Five Year Plan (1958-62).

4. Average for the 'three years of readjustment' (1963-65).

5. Average for 3rd Five Year Plan (1966-70).

6. Average for 4th Five Year Plan (1971-75).

7. 1978.

8. Includes mosquito net cloth, curtain cloth, cotton clothing, cloth used for shoes and hats, cloth used for livelihood by units, publicly used cloth in organs and groups, and since 1963 it has included chemical fibre cloth and blended synthetic and natural fibre cloth.

n.a. = not available   neg. = negligible.

Source: <u>An outline ...</u>, 1982:207-11.

TABLE 6

CONSUMPTION IN TOWN AND COUNTRYSIDE, 1978–1981[1]

Item	Unit	Peasants 1978	Peasants 1981	Staff & Workers 1981
Av.p.c. consumption of:				
Grain	kgs.	174[2](248)	180[2](256)	145
of which: wheat & rice	kgs.	87[2](123)	121[2](173)	n.a.
Vegetables	kgs.	142	124	152
Edible oil	kgs.	2.0	3.1	4.8
Meat[3]	kgs.	5.8	9.4	20.5
Eggs	kgs.	0.80	1.25	5.2
Fish and shrimps	kgs.	0.84	1.28	7.3
Sugar	kgs.	0.73	1.10	2.9
Liquor	kgs.	1.2	2.3	4.4
Clothes[4]	yuan	14.7	23.6	67.2
Stocks per 100 people of:				
Bicycles	no.	5.4	8.1	32.1[5]
Sewing machines	no.	3.5	5.0	16.6[5]
Radio sets	no.	3.0	7.7	23.7[5]
Wrist-watches	no.	4.8	10.0	56.8[5]
TV sets	no.	negl.	0.16	13.6[5]
Housing space p.c.	sq.mtrs.	8.4(1979)	10.2	5.3

Notes: 1. All these data are from sample surveys, except for the housing figure.

2. Unhusked figures in brackets. The unhusked figures are rough estimates only.

3. Pork, beef, mutton, poultry.

4. The structure of clothing consumption is so different in each sector that it was thought more useful to include a figure for the total value of clothes purchases.

5. Derived from 'per household' figures. Average size of staff and workers' households was reported as 4.24 persons in 1981 [*SSB, 1982: 438*].

Source: SSB [*1982: Section 11*]

so that the absolute gap was reportedly wider in the late 1970s than in the 1950s. Overall supply of a small range of 'luxury' consumer durables grew rapidly from the low base of the 1950s. By the late 1970s the urban-rural gap in average per capita purchases of these items was extremely wide.

In the post-Mao period average consumption levels of a wide range of agricultural and non-agricultural consumer goods has increased at an unprecedented rate. It is quite likely that the rate of growth has in many cases been faster on average in the countryside than in the towns. However, as Table 6 shows, the reported gap in 1981 was still very wide for an extensive array of items.

China's post-revolutionary government inherited massive inequalities in health and education between town and countryside. During the 1950s, although tremendous progress was made in both sectors, relative to their share of population, the urban areas benefited much more than the countryside. For example, the cities' share of the rapidly expanding number of hospital beds was still around 75 per cent in 1957, the same figure as in 1949 (Table 7).[3] However, in the following two decades the stress shifted sharply: from 1957 to 1975 the number of urban hospital beds reportedly rose almost twofold

TABLE 7

DISTRIBUTION OF HOSPITAL BEDS (% IN BRACKETS)

	All China		Cities		Villages	
Year	Total	People per bed	Total	People per bed	Total	People per bed
1949	80,000	6771	60,000 (74.8)	961	20,000 (25.2)	24,200
1952	160,000	3593	121,000 (75.7)	592	39,000 (24.3)	12,897
1957	295,000	2912	221,000 (74.9)	450	74,000 (25.1)	7,392
1965	766,000	947	458,000 (59.8)	222	308,000 (40.2)	2,025
1975	1598,000	576	637,000 (39.9)	175	961,000 (60.1)	841
1979	1932,000	503	740,000 (38.3)	174	1192,000 (61.7)	707

Source: Chinese Economic Yearbook, 1982 : Section VI, 3 and 26.

while the numbers in the villages rose by almost twelvefold, producing a dramatic fall in the number of peasants per rural hospital bed. However, the initial gap in the welfare levels in town and countryside was so great that in the late 1970s the gap was still considerable. Across the whole of China, in 1979 there still were over 700 people per hospital bed in the villages compared to less than 200 in the towns (Table 7).

Turning to education, despite considerable efforts made during the Cultural Revolution decade to raise rural standards [Pepper, 1980], the gap was still wide. For example, in Sichuan province in 1982 the reported figures for pupils per teacher were:

Rural areas: Middle schools = 33.9
                      Primary schools = 20.8
Cities and towns: Middle schools = 20.0
                      Primary schools = 11.6

The reported enrolment rates among Sichuan's school-age children in 1982 were 99.0 per cent in the cities and 90.7 per cent in the villages, though the drop-out rate in the villages was such that at the completion of primary school education only 70.6 per cent were reported to be still attending school. The proportion of primary school graduates going on to middle school in Sichuan in 1982 was over 85 per cent in the cities (excluding county towns), compared to only 40 per cent in the villages [Nolan, 1983c].

Having examined the evidence on income and standard of living in town and countryside, we now turn to look at the political and ideological issues that helped shape the policies that influenced the socio-economic outcomes outlined in this section.

THE IDEOLOGY AND POLITICS OF RURAL-URBAN RELATIONS

Ideological Analysis: Consensus and Conflict

CCP ideology inherited the modern Chinese radical view of rural-urban relations, integrated into a Marxist analysis of antagonistic class contradictions, both domestic and international. From this perspective, rural-urban relations embody three forms of exploitation: first, politico-administrative-military cities (*cheng*) populated by corrupt bureaucrats and their clientele, battening on the surplus exacted from the peasantry through taxation; second, commercial cities (*shi*) populated by merchants and usurers who exploited the peasantry through trade and financial manipulation (the usual Chinese word for 'cities', *chengshi*, combines both these ideas); third, the foreign-dominated 'treaty port' cities, which were bridgeheads of imperialist exploitation. It was the task of the revolution to eliminate these forms of urban dominance and exploitation.

According to official ideology, rural-urban relations in the period of socialist transition would have two main characteristics: (i) the cities would lead the countryside, with 'industry leading agriculture' economically and 'workers leading peasants' politically. The CCP has thus maintained the Marxist-Leninist distinction between the peasantry and the industrial working class; (ii) rural-urban relations would change from exploitative to mutually supportive as the cities changed from centres of consumption and extraction to centres of production and social progress [*Liu Shaoqi et al., 1949*]. Over the longer term, as relations of production were homogenised between urban and rural areas, any residual 'non-antagonistic' differences between city and countryside would gradually disappear. In the transitional period, however, rural-urban inequalities would unavoidably persist.

These have been analysed in terms of the much-debated concept of 'bourgeois right' which originates in Marx's *Critique of the Gotha Programme*. When applied to the problem of inequality between peasant and worker, the idea of 'bourgeois right', according to the Chinese, implies that the correct way to move towards greater equality is to raise rural labour productivity and incomes rather than lowering urban incomes. Proposals to the contrary have been dismissed as 'harmful absolute egalitarianism'. Official spokesmen have used the highly ambiguous 'socialist principle of (income) distribution' ('to each according to his work') to argue that higher incomes for urban workers were fair, given their higher productivity [*Mao Tse-tung (Mao Zedong), 1957: 402*]. Other justifications have rested on arguments that urban work requires greater skills than rural, or that industrial work was more 'tense', unpleasant or time-consuming than agricultural.

Arguments of this type, even if one were to accept their basic plausibility, fail to clarify the legitimate *extent* of rural-urban inequalities: for instance, officials argue that urban incomes should only be 'somewhat' greater than rural, while their own statistics show levels of urban productivity to be *vastly* greater. Moreover, much of the extra productivity of urban workers is due to their greater use of machinery rather than harder work or higher skills. How does one measure the economic contribution of 'unproductive' workers in state administration? Official analysts of rural-urban differentials have been reluctant to grasp these particular political nettles: rather they often seem to be grasping at ideological straws.

Despite basic elements of ideological agreement, CCP leaders of competing political persuasions have adopted different perspectives on rural-urban questions. Radical 'Maoist' spokesmen have voiced populist, rural-orientated themes, stressing the continued influence of pre-revolutionary rural-urban antagonisms and the need for more thorough-going redistributive measures. Their 'pragmatic' opponents have emphasised the complementarity of city and countryside and their inevitable 'growing together'. The former group pointed to class differentiation *within* sectors: in the cities, between 'proletarians' and 'revisionist' bureaucrats/'bourgeois intellectuals' and in the countryside between 'poor and lower-middle peasants' and their enemies, former landlords and old and new rich peasants. The latter group saw each sector as relatively homogeneous: in the cities, a 'working class' including both mental and manual 'labourers', and in the countryside undifferentiated 'commune members'. As we shall see later, these ideological differences have had a considerable effect on policies in different phases of post-revolutionary history.

But to understand the dynamics of rural-urban policies, we need to penetrate beneath ideology to the structural realities of the Chinese post-revolutionary state. One of the strengths of Lipton's analysis [1977] is that he asks questions about the social and political character of the state: he identifies three characteristics of an 'urban-biased' state. First, many state officials are 'cosmopolitans' who define their aspirations in terms of international metropoles, usually the United States and Western Europe. Second, state officials tend to be, or become, urbanites themselves and their actions reflect urban interests. Third, state policy reflects the dominant influence of organised and articulate urban interests; the rural population, especially the poor, are likely to be 'pressure-less'.

In investigating the applicability of these political theses to the Chinese case, we shall divide our analysis into two sections: first, an examination of the socio-political character of the Chinese state itself; second, of the relationship of this state to society and the play of political interests.

The Socio-Political Character of the Chinese State

1. *State as nation-state.* Let us first focus on the state as an external actor, i.e. as the institutional embodiment of the nation in a world of nation-states. To what extent has the Chinese state been dependent on, or penetrated by, external forces and how has this affected policies on rural-urban issues?

Broadly speaking, we can identify two periods of significant foreign influence. In the mid 1950s, Soviet influence on planning priorities was considerable and probably strengthened the industrial/urban orientation of the First Five Year Plan (FYP). Lampton, for example [1974: 14] suggests that the urban orientation of the Soviet health system was transmitted to China through influential Soviet advisers in the fledgling Ministry of Health. Soviet influence over new governmental institutions during this crucial formative stage of state construction left a lasting imprint, long after the advisers had gone home and despite Maoist claims that China had turned its back on Soviet-style 'revisionism'.

The second period of foreign influence began with the 'open-door' policies of the post-Mao leadership after 1976. These policies have admitted certain pressures, familiar in other Third World contexts, which act to reinforce the power of urban elites and bias resource allocations towards the cities. First, growing links with Western countries and Japan have strengthened the position of urban intermediary elites, whose power rests on their ability to handle external links. Second, the international demonstration effect has had a profound impact at all levels. Many cadres and professionals have become entranced with advanced Western technology and a frenetic technology-buying spree during 1977–9 led to wasteful importation of resources primarily destined for the urban and industrial sectors. Moreover, the general population, especially in the cities where the foreign presence is most evident, have become increasingly attuned to Western consumption patterns, imported through tourism, returned travellers, films and advertising. This creates pressures for urban-orientated resource allocation (for example, importing colour TV plants from Japan for predominantly urban use). In contrast to the 'metropolitan' orientations highlighted by dependency theorists, however, the Chinese state has generally been effective in asserting national priorities and evading external dependence.

Internally, the state has acted to enforce a 'national interest' *vis-à-vis* partial interests within the country. It is fashionable (and, to varying degrees, proper) to dismiss 'national interest' as a cloak for sectional power, whether of the state itself or certain dominant classes. The Chinese socialist state, however, emerged from a context of prolonged anti-imperialist struggle, a great deal of its support resting on nationalist sentiments which transcended sectional antagonisms. To this extent the state's strategic actions have reflected 'national' priorities, overriding differential interests, whether class or urban-rural. CCP leaders have consistently defined the central developmental imperative as rapid structural change to establish a basis for national power and prosperity. This helps explain the paradox that the First FYP was a period of pronounced urban-industrial policy bias, at a time when the *rural* character of the post-revolutionary state was at its strongest.

In short, urban-orientated policies need not reflect urban-dominated politics; 'nationalist' priorities exert independent influence in certain key transitional periods. This may be particularly important in revolutionary socialist countries which face acute international hostility, particularly at their inception. But the policy impact of nationalism decreases as the experience of anti-imperialist struggle recedes into the past and the intensity of international hostility declines. Politics becomes denationalised, in reality if not in rhetoric; the 'national interest' is increasingly manipulated to serve the interests of the state itself or of dominant classes. To understand development policy in this later stage, we must concentrate on the socio-political character of the state itself and on the overall interplay of social interests in the political arena.

2. The 'state-in-itself'. The early post-revolutionary Chinese state[4] had a far greater rural character than its Soviet predecessor. The vast majority of the 4.5 million party members in 1949 were of peasant origin and many of them became officials in the post-revolutionary state machine. These 'old cadres' have remained a crucial force at least until the late 1970s and their political sympathies have often been instinctively 'ruralist'.

But during the three decades since Liberation, the Chinese state underwent a double transition in its socio-political character. First, there is evidence of an urbanisation of the state. The 1950s saw a major effort to recruit urbanites into the party and government bureaucracy, notably from among industrial workers and intelligentsia. By 1957, 13.7 per cent of party members were workers, 14.8 per cent intellectuals and 66.8 per cent peasants [*Lewis, 1963: 108*]. In 1959 4.4 per cent of urban dwellers were party members, compared with only 2.2 per cent of the general population [*White, 1983: 30-2*]. Though precise statistics are lacking, this pattern of representation continued over the next two decades and has probably intensified over recent years with the pensioning off of 'old cadres' and increased recruitment of intelligentsia into party and government.

Second, there has been a process of 'desocialisation' whereby state personnel become detached from their social origins and take on a new social identity based on their position in the hierarchy of politico-administrative power [*Kraus, 1983*]. To this extent, state personnel become a distinct social group with their own material basis and social ideology. To the extent that this bureaucratic apparatus is situated in urban areas, this process embodies an 'urbanisation' of the state. But one should not see this in simple bipolar terms, since the state machine is distributed along an administrative central-place hierarchy from the capital down to 'administrative villages' (small rural towns).

Throughout the post-revolutionary period, therefore, the Chinese state has been socio-politically ambiguous. In *ideological* terms, the urbanist themes of classic Marxism-Leninism have warred with the ruralist themes of Maoism. In a system based on ideological orthodoxy, the impact of these conflicting 'official' perspectives, on both policy and population, should not be under-estimated. In *political* terms, competing factions have espoused conflicting ideological perspectives. In such a concentrated and hierarchical system of power, the question of which group of leaders holds power at any one time exerts decisive influence over policy. In *personnel* terms, the party and government remain socially ambiguous. The majority of party members are still peasants and many party and government cadres are from rural backgrounds with rural connections. In *institutional* terms, there are differences between the three main organisational pillars of the Chinese state: the party, government and armed forces. On one side, the government is perhaps the most fully urbanised structure, in terms of location, personnel and political orientation. On the other side, the People's Liberation Army (PLA) has remained more consistently ruralist, reflecting the facts that it has primarily recruited from among the peasantry and a large section of its officer corps are of rural origins. As for the Party, though it masquerades as an institution transcending competing institutions and social forces, it does in fact embody them to a considerable degree; as the pervasive institution, it is in turn pervaded.

Each major institution is further differentiated internally, with implications for policies on rural-urban questions. Different government agencies and party sections have their own distinctive 'organisational ideologies' and, as Oksenberg argues [*1982: 173*], 'inter-agency conflict is at least as much at the heart of Chinese politics as factional struggles'. For example, the big industrial ministries and, in certain periods, the Ministries of Health and Education have exerted claims on resources which favour the interests of urban groups. By contrast, the Party's Rural Work Department and, within the government, bureaux of grain and agriculture have 'gone to bat' for peasant interests.

In territorial terms, moreover, officials from agricultural localities have pressured for greater resources for agriculture and redistribution away from richer, more industrialised provinces [*Lardy, 1978; Paine, 1981*]. There have also been clashes between different principles of territorial organisation: between urban-centred 'economic regions' based on large cities and delineated by 'natural' links of marketing and communications, and administratively defined units (notably provinces, counties and special districts) where rural questions are more important and bureaucratic imperatives more definite [*Lewis, 1971*]. The spokesmen of each system view themselves as defending their respective rural hinterlands against the other, but they appear to be merely different forms of urban dominance.

In sum, despite a secular trend towards urbanisation of the state's orientations and interests, it has retained important elements of its revolutionary rural character. However, these divergent social forces have to a considerable degree been transformed or transcended by state interests based on the institutional materiality of state structures. As such, the rural-urban cleavage is subordinate to that between state and (both rural and urban) society.

The State and 'Pressure Politics'

The 'totalitarian' model is often used to analyse Chinese politics, implying total dominance of state over society. While this model captures important political realities, notably the pervasive ideological orthodoxy and hierarchical politico-administrative controls, it is a one-dimensional image which misses certain crucial political processes. While on first acquaintance with Chinese politics one is struck by the ubiquity of political controls and the overweening strength of the state, deeper analysis reveals a contrasting picture of weakness — the limits of state power, its frequent inability or unwillingness to take key decisions and its susceptibility to countervailing social forces.

How does one understand this contradictory juxtaposition of seeming strength and apparent weakness, of authoritarianism combined with sometimes acute sensitivity to social interests? On the one hand, the complex network of political, administrative and coercive controls gives the state a high degree of 'autonomy', an ability to transcend conflicting interests in civil society and to define and implement a *raison d'état*, either in its own or in the 'national' interest. Yet the state is politically circumscribed in several ways. First, as we have seen, it contains people from different social groups and reflects their diverse interests internally. Second, certain social groups and institutions can maintain areas of 'social space' which give them varying degrees of autonomy *vis-à-vis* the state. For example, politico-administrative controls are weaker outside the cities and rural collectives have enjoyed a good deal of autonomy, particularly in periods of intra-party conflict. The government machine proper ends at the county level and the party network is weak in many villages. Third, the state's own legitimacy rests on proven developmental success; thus to validate itself, it depends on the active co-operation of society. Without adequate peasant marketings the state's industrialisation programme would founder; it depends on urban elites to manage that programme. This co-operation must be constantly renewed. Fourth, the very pervasiveness of controls and the lack of formal channels for interest articulation builds up a steam of unresolved problems and discontent. To avoid explosions, like the Cultural Revolution, this steam must be drawn off by political or economic means. While some of these factors apply equally to both city and countryside, there is a basic sectoral difference: in the countryside the state faces problems stemming from its lack of control, while in the cities problems often stem from the very pervasiveness of control.

These factors imply that the state is susceptible to pressures from social interests. Unlike Western 'interest groups', these are usually not expressed in organised form. Indeed, the state takes pains to prevent independent organisations through proscription and pre-emption (setting up pliable 'mass organisations'). One of the rural-urban differences argued by Lipton − the degree of organisation of urban over rural interests − is less relevant in such a context. Even so, an organisational gap does exist to some extent; peasants have complained throughout the past three decades about the lack of effective organised channels to express their grievances. To counter any simplistic picture of a scattered, unorganised peasantry, however, it is important to remember that the countryside is highly organised (in communes, brigades and teams) and that these institutions have proven to be two-edged swords: not merely 'transmission belts' to enforce state demands but also agencies of peasant power, resistance and evasion.

Urban interests, notably staff and workers in the state sector, are organised in trade unions. State control over the unions has generally been tight. The major exception to this was the wage reform of 1956 when the large rise in urban wages was clearly connected with a rise in the degree of trade union independence [*Harper, 1969*]. The inauguration of the 'rational low wage policy' for urban workers in the following year was accompanied by a reassertion of state control over the unions. This was an 'incomes policy' of an extraordinary kind, one that could only be implemented in the absence of independent trade unions.

This incomes policy was one aspect of a wider attempt by the CCP leadership during the Maoist period to counter the power of an urban coalition which had emerged during the First Five Year Plan. It was composed of three major groups − government cadres, professional intelligentsia, and workers in state industry − divided on certain issues, but united in their common desire to increase the flow of resources to urban areas, to improve wages, employment, housing, education and health facilities, and cultural amenities. Their interests have influenced the policies of certain bureaucratic agencies, notably the industrial ministries, welfare agencies and departments responsible for science and technology. Lampton [*1974*] has identified the influence of this coalition on health policy, arguing that 'allocation has generally favoured the urban, heavy industrial, and elite sectors of the society', except during periods of Maoist counter-pressure. A similar case could be made in the field of educational policy.

But 'ruralist' elements within the Party have not been the only counterweight to the mounting power of urban interests. The pressure of the rural interest has limited the scope of state power and urban prerogatives. The cities are islands in a rural sea: as of 1981, 86 per cent of the population still lived in the countryside; 72 per cent of the labour force worked in agriculture; agriculture contributed 42 per cent of national income and (in 1980) 48.2 per cent of China's exports were farm or processed farm products. Without securing at least the compliance and better still the active co-operation of the agricultural population, the developmental efforts of the Chinese state and minimal levels of urban living standards are inconceivable. The 'rural factor' loomed large in *all* major policy deliberations, directly or indirectly, as both constraint and impetus.

But the power of rural interests does not stem merely from their 'objective' importance. Chinese farmers have taken political actions which are redolent of traditional Chinese state-peasant relations. On the one hand, they have used 'negative' methods, such as go-slows, statistical misreporting and surreptitious 'strikes', practices often winked at or even organised by rural cadres. On the other hand, they have used more active methods to voice their discontent, particularly during periods when state controls have loosened or the economic situation has deteriorated. During the 'three hard years' after the Great Leap Forward, there were sporadic outbreaks of rural violence and small peasant revolts. Peasants have also reacted strongly to widening rural-urban differentials. During the mid 1950s, for example, millions of peasants flooded into the cities, drawn by rising industrial wages [*Fang and Huang, 1957; Rao Wen, 1957*]. Many peasants complained: 'The industrial workers don't do much work and get a lot to eat, while the peasants do a lot of work and don't get much to eat. The Party only takes care of the industrial workers and doesn't take care of the peasants' [*NFRB, 25 October 1957*].

Stringent administrative controls were introduced in 1955 to stem this 'blind inflow' of peasants. For example, all citizens wishing to move to the urban areas were required to have certificates of employment or acceptance from a school, or an official document of approval from an urban agency of population control before they were allowed to reside legally in the city. However, many rural emigrants continued to evade state controls and at least 14 million peasants got through the net on a temporary or permanent basis in the 1960s and early 1970s. Compared to the mid 1950s, however, the level of rural emigration was very much reduced. But urban controls alone could not have withstood rural pressure without complementary measures, such as the increased emphasis on agricultural modernisation and rural welfare and strict urban wage restraints. In a sense, China's cities in the 1960s and 1970s were like social fortresses, the migration controls forming a wall against rural incursion. This seems to have concentrated the minds of state officials, Maoist or not, and imparted a certain rural orientation to policy. Much of the development strategy of the 1960s and 1970s rested on this implicit bargain between state and peasantry.

However, in spite of greater official emphasis on rural development, peasant discontent built up steadily during the 1970s over a familiar set of issues: pricing policy, planning priorities (notably the pressure to produce grain), enforced high rates of accumulation in rural collectives, political and administrative interference and economic levies by higher level collectives (notably the commune), constraints on richer areas realising their productivity gains, constraints on private production and exchange, and overly egalitarian remuneration systems. With the death of Mao, these pressures created a political wave which helped to sweep away Maoist leaders and carry Dengist leaders to shore.

It would be inaccurate, therefore, to characterise Chinese interest politics in terms of a simple contrast between an articulate, well-organised and thus powerful urban population and a silent, inert, 'pressureless' rural population. Chinese peasants are neither unorganised nor inert; they are not captives of the state nor do they lack resources for asserting their interests. It is important to add, moreover, that both urban and rural interests are internally differentiated: in the cities between 'reds' and 'experts', professionals and manual workers, workers in state and non-state sectors; in the countryside between richer and poorer areas, collective units and households (see above). Certain political coalitions cut across the rural-urban divide, but a detailed exploration of these patterns would take us beyond the scope of this paper.

There is an important relationship between these pressure politics and the policy dynamics of the past three decades. The distributive impact of an emerging coalition of urban interests was visible in the mid 1950s but the strength of rural response was clearly important in setting the context first for the Great Leap Forward and later for the policies on rural development and urban incomes pursued during the next two decades. Though powerful urban institutional and social interests have continued to lay claims to a dominant share of state allocations, the state has been forced to act as broker between both urban and rural interests. The policy ambiguity of the Maoist period reflected this process and the developmental failure of Maoist policies provoked discontent. Eventually outright opposition among both rural and urban interests created a strong political impetus for (and heavy burden on) the post-Mao leadership.

Our findings in this section about the nature of the Chinese state and pressure politics provide a context for our discussion of the economic determinants of incomes and standards of living in each sector which we deal with in the next section.

SOME ECONOMIC INFLUENCES ON THE URBAN-RURAL DIFFERENTIAL

In an economy lacking free movement of labour within and between sectors and in which the state possesses enormous control over the economic process, methods of analysing income determination appropriate to free market settings lose much relevance. In a planned economy, the main influences on average real income in each sector are (i) changes in real net value of output per worker in that sector, and (ii) and the influence of workers in that sector on the state's policy governing the distribution of changes in output per worker (a) between consumption and accumulation in that sector, and (b) between one sector and the other. Points (i) and (ii) naturally are deeply interrelated. The political influences have already been discussed. In this section we summarise the picture in respect to the dimensions of, changes in, and factors influencing output per worker in each sector, and in respect to inter-sectoral savings transfers.

Real Output per Worker in the Countryside

Already by the early 1950s China appeared to have run up against a barrier in respect to arable area. Indeed, reported figures show an absolute decline in the arable area from the 1950s through to the late 1970s.[5]

The numbers of rural workers increased enormously due to tight controls on migration to cities, 'rustication' of large numbers of urban dwellers in the 1960s and 1970s [Orleans, 1982], and high natural rates of population increase in the villages (until the 1970s): the number of workers in the rural areas reportedly rose from 182 million in 1952 to 306 million in 1979 [SSB, 1982: 105]. The number of labour days worked per year by each worker probably increased as the Party raised the pressure in the 1960s and 1970s to participate in winter mass construction campaigns [Rawski, 1979: 109-13]. The collectives found serious difficulty in ensuring diligent and skilful work for the collective before the reforms of post 1978. For a variety of reasons (notably too high a marginal reinvestment rate constraining growth of personal income from the collective) collective labour was 'supervised' rather than 'self-motivated', leading to serious managerial diseconomies of scale and, therefore, to relatively low effectiveness of collective labour, shown in sharp perspective by the dramatic improvement in this respect post 1978 [Nolan, 1983b].

The application of modern inputs in agriculture has proceeded rapidly, though this was from a negligible base. Tractor-ploughed area rose from 2.4 per cent of the total arable area in 1957 to 42.4 per cent in 1979, and application of chemical fertilisers (nutrient weight) per hectare rose from 3.3 kgs in 1957 to 109.2 kgs in 1979 [Nolan, 1983b: 1398]. However, the share of state investment going to agriculture has been small,[6] and it is estimated that over 75 per cent of agricultural capital construction from 1949 to 1979 was financed by peasants themselves [Nolan, 1983b: 1401].

A big change after the early 1960s was the growth of commune- and brigade-run enterprises. By 1980 such enterprises employed only 9.6 per cent of the total rural workforce [SSB, 1982: 105 and 192], and commune-run industry accounted for only 5.6 per cent of China's total industrial output [SSB, 1982: 212]. However, the share of commune and brigade-run enterprises in gross income was important (14.7 per cent in 1974, 29.9 per cent in 1979) [An Outline ..., 1982: 169] and their labour productivity much above that in agriculture.[7]

The outcome of these changes in the rural economy was as follows. Output per hectare, from an already quite high level under 'traditional' technique, performed creditably – grain output per sown hectare, for example, rose from 1.46 tons in 1957 to 2.53 tons in 1978 [SSB, 1982: 6]. However, the capital cost needed to achieve this was relatively high: the capital-output ratio (agricultural fixed assets, excluding land, compared to the gross value of agricultural output) is reported to have risen from 0.29 in 1957 to 0.67 in 1978 [*An Outline ..., 1982: 119*]. Real gross output per worker hardly rose from the late fifties to mid-1970s (Table 8). Moreover, the degree of static inefficiency in the rural economy was considerable, as is partially indicated by the rapid

TABLE 8

OUTPUT PER WORKER IN CHINESE AGRICULTURE AND INDUSTRY

	Gross Value of Output per Worker (1970 Prices)		Net Value of Output per Worker (Current Prices)[3]	
	Agriculture[1]	State Industry[2]	Agriculture	Industry
1952	367	4167	196.3	923
1957	411	6336	220.1	1834
1965	373	8943	274.0	2763
1975	436	n.a.	335.0	2593
1978	497	11,085	n.a.	n.a.
1979	538	11,790	432.6	2858
1981	560	11,815	n.a.	n.a

Sources: (1) *An Outline ...*, 1982 : 29 and 85, and Nolan [*1983b: 270*]
　　　　(2) *SSB* [*1982: 270*]
　　　　(3) Yang and Li [*1981: 103-104*]

growth of real output per worker post 1975.[8] Until the late 1970s the possibilities for raising peasant real incomes without assistance from the urban sector was extremely limited due to the slow growth of real output per rural worker.

Real Output per Worker in Industry

After attaining a relatively high overall rate of accumulation during the First Five Year Plan, China thereafter mostly pushed the rate even higher.[9] For most of the 1960s and 1970s the industrial sector took around 60 per cent of total state investment, the proportion only dropping slightly in the early 1960s and late 1970s.[10] Within state industrial investment, 'heavy' industry took about 90 per cent of the total after the First Five Year Plan (when the share was already 85 per cent) and only fell much below 90 per cent in the late 1970s.[11] A further important feature of state investment on capital construction has been the extremely small share allocated to 'non-productive' investment:[12] this was squeezed from over one-third in the early 1950s to 10-15 per cent in the 1960s and 1970s, until it rose rapidly in the late 1970s, reaching more than 40 per cent in 1981 [*SSB, 1982: 313*]. While such a strategy might make sense over a short period such as the First FYP, pursued over the long term it implied a very crude view of the determinants of economic growth, paying too little attention to the dynamic feedback effects on growth of output of increases in real income and to static efficiency considerations in capital allocation.[13]

Absolute numbers employed in industry rose impressively, from a reported 14 million in 1957 to 43 million in 1975 [*Yang and Li, 1981: 104*]; total 'staff and workers' rose from 31.0 million in 1957 to 82.0 million in 1975 [*SSB, 1982: 107*]. However, the *structure* of employment was not transformed: industry's share of combined employment in agriculture and industry rose from 6.8 per cent in 1957 to only 12.7 per cent in 1975 to 15.1 per cent in 1979 [*Yang and Li, 1981: 104*]. In part this slow change in the structure of employment was a product of continued rapid population growth until the 1970s, but in part also it is to be explained by the stress given in state investment to the capital-intensive heavy industry sector.[14] The issue of workforce motivation in this context is more complex in industry even than in the countryside. It is likely that the stagnation in urban real wages after the First Five Year Plan proved a problem in obtaining effective work performance in the cities, which in turn helped to constrain the growth of output. Also, it is possible that the absence of strong incentive-orientated payment systems in factories from the 1950s to late 1970s was a barrier to improved performance.

A serious problem in obtaining rapid growth of industrial output from the late 1950s to the late 1970s was the sceptical approach towards foreign technology. (This was a problem in agriculture too, but probably not so severe.) 'Administratively planned' economies have serious difficulties in generating indigenous technical progress, so that access to foreign technology is especially important for them. While China was not completely cut off, her limited use of outside technology was a handicap in attaining a high growth of industrial output and probably helped to reinforce the emphasis on a high rate of accumulation as the main channel to growth of output: given that the quality of the capital stock was growing so slowly, more reliance, it could be argued, had to be placed on its quantitative expansion.

The outcome for industry was as follows. Capital per worker grew rapidly over the long term, rising more than ninefold from 1957 to 1978, while the number of industrial workers rose less than threefold.[15] The value of fixed assets per worker was vastly greater, and increasingly so, in industry than in agriculture.[16] Chinese data report an annual average real growth of industrial output of around 9-10 per cent (compound) from 1957 to 1979,[17] but at an increasing capital cost: in state industry gross value of industrial output per 100 *yuan* of fixed assets (original value) reportedly fell from 138 *yuan* in 1957 to 98 *yuan* in 1965 and still stood at only 105 *yuan* in 1975 [*Chinese Economic Yearbook, 1982: section VI, 18*].

The real gross value of output per worker reportedly almost doubled from the late 1950s to the late 1970s (Table 8). An already enormous absolute gap between agriculture and industry in the gross value of output per worker widened greatly from the 1950s to the late 1970s (Table 8). However, because industry has a higher consumption of material inputs per unit of output than agriculture, the gap in net value is much less than for gross value of output per worker (in current prices)[18] (Table 8). For a variety of reasons, it appears that industry became increasingly profligate in its use of material inputs, so that net industrial output per worker grew much more slowly than gross output and indeed stagnated from the mid sixties (Table 8).

In sum, industry generated a very large surplus per worker compared to agriculture, but found it hard to increase this from the mid 1960s onwards.

Inter-sectoral Savings Flows

A major potential influence on inter-sectoral savings flows is the inter-sectoral terms of trade. In the early 1950s the terms of trade between industrial and agricultural commodities had certainly moved sharply against agriculture in relation to the 1930s, but already by around 1957 they had returned to the 1930s position,[19] and there is no doubt that a major improvement (for agriculture) occurred between 1957 and 1975 (Table 9). Since 1975 a further sharp improvement for agriculture has occurred in the inter-sectoral terms of trade, though the improvement in the state's purchasing price for farm products post 1975 was, at least initially, offset to some degree by a fall in the free market price index (Table 9). Moreover, it has been made clear that no increase in the state's purchase price for farm output is to occur in the next few years. It seems likely that a major part of whatever long-term rise in peasant real incomes took place from the 1950s to the late 1970s, and at least part of the increase since then, is attributable to the transfer of purchasing power on account of the shift in the inter-sectoral terms of trade. In the cities, at least until the late 1970s, the state seemed to have been able to hold food prices stable, but at the cost of forgoing the profits it earned on food sales in the 1950s. From the early 1960s it subsidised urban food prices because of the rise in the price it paid to peasants for its food purchases.

A number of elements are involved in inter-sectoral savings flows at current prices. There has been a persistent import surplus for the rural sector (Table 10), which probably has been 'financed' by a net capital inflow to the countryside. Unpaid-for farm exports occurred through the agricultural tax. This was relatively severe initially, but remained fixed in absolute terms so that its share of farm income fell steadily.[20] Financial outflows have taken place through the banking system and myriad informal channels. In addition to peasant commodity purchases, commodity inflows have occurred in the form of state budgetary outlays on capital construction in agriculture.[21] Financial inflows have taken place through a variety of state budgetary and banking channels, through credit co-ops, as well as informal channels, such as money sent to rural relatives by urban workers. Producing a net figure for all these flows is extremely difficult for one year, yet alone over time.

Although peasant purchases from outside the villages appear to have exceeded sales, it is important to note that the state has massively dominated agricultural marketings through its obligatory quota and 'above quota' purchases.[22] Though it is impossible to guess the amount that peasants would have voluntarily sold to the state at the existing prices (assuming they could not have sold freely to the free market), it is possible that the total would have been less, and very likely that the structure of sales would have been oriented towards higher-value non-grain items than was in fact the case.[23]

TABLE 9

URBAN-RURAL TERMS OF TRADE

Item	1950	1952	1957	1965	1975	1978	1981
1. General index of purchase price for agricultural and sideline products	100	121.6	146.2	187.9	208.7	217.4	301.2
2. State commercial departments' list purchasing price index for agricultural and sideline commodities	100	121.6	146.2	185.1	n.a.	207.3	257.2
3. General retail list price index of industrial commodities sold in villages	100	109.7	112.1	118.4	109.6	109.8	111.9
4. Comprehensive index of relative prices in exchange of industrial and agricultural commodities $\frac{(1)}{(3)} \times 100$	100	110.8	130.4	158.7	190.4	198.0	269.2
5. Index of retail price of agricultural means of production sold through state commerce	100	108.2	110.8	114.7	100.0	100.1	103.2
6. Rural free market price index	n.a.	100	109	173	327 (1977)	222	212 (1979)

Notes: The index in line 1 includes the state list purchasing price ('quota price'?), the 'negotiated' purchasing price, and purchasing price of 'surplus farm and sideline products' ('above quota price'?). It clearly does *not* include either rural or urban free market prices. See SSB [*1982: 519*]. The divergence of the indices in lines 1 and 2 in the late 1970s and early 1980s results from an increasing proportion of the purchase of farm produce being made at 'negotiated' or 'above quota' prices. In 1980 and 1981 proportion of farm and sideline produce purchased in different ways was as follows (unit: 100 m. *yuan*): [*SSB, 1982: 347*].

	1980	1981
Purchases at:		
1. list price	542.2	555.6
2. increased price for over-purchase	151.0	200.0
3. negotiated price	80.0	110.0
4. market price (purchase from peasants by non-agricultural residents)	69.0	89.4
Total purchase of farm and sideline produce	842.2	955.0

Sources: (1)–(5): *Chinese Economic Yearbook [1982, Part VI: 23]*, and SSB [*1982: 412-14*]; Nolan [*1983c: 18*].

TABLE 10

INTERNAL BALANCE OF TRADE (100 MILLION *YUAN*, CURRENT PRICES)

	Village's Commodity Purchases	Purchase of
	of which: Capital Goods	Farm and Sideline
	Total for Agriculture	Produce[1]
1952	151.2	14.1	140.8
1957	235.8	32.6	217.5
1970	458.0	129.2	347.8
1975	664.2	224.7	478.6
1980	1189.7	346.0	842.2

Notes: 1. Including purchases at list price, at extra-quota price, at negotiated price and market price, by departments of domestic trade and foreign trade, industrial and other departments, and by non-agricultural residents from peasants.

Source: SSB [*1982: 333, 345 and 347*]

Another channel through which inter-sectoral transfers can occur is 'unequal exchange'. This is empirically even more elusive than the previous channels. Chinese economists now are generally agreed that serious 'unequal exchange' has existed throughout the post-Liberation period (and thus does today) in the sense that the 'price' of industrial commodities is much greater than their 'value' (in terms of embodied labour) and the 'price' of agricultural commodities is much below their 'value'. A simple manifestation of this is the huge contribution made to the state budget by profits and taxes from industrial sales to the peasants. However, precise measurement is another matter and there is a wide variety of views on how best to do this. For one careful effort at estimating the extent of rural-urban unequal exchange, see Chen [*1982*].

CONCLUSIONS

We cannot base our analysis of development strategy on any simple political model of 'urban bias'. There are two reasons for this. First, the political balance between urban and rural forces is not as clear-cut as the model proposes. It is true that development policy has been given an urbanist cast by urban-orientated ideological themes, the claims of urban institutional and social interests and the relative weakness of interest articulation and organisation among the rural population. On the other hand, the countervailing power of rural interests has been significant and the state itself, in terms of ideology, structure and personnel, has retained powerful ruralist elements.

This ambiguous political reality is reflected in our findings on the economic aspects of urban-rural relations. A number of our findings can be used to support the idea of 'urban bias' in China. First, throughout the post-revolutionary period, the standard of living has been higher in the cities than in the countryside, and the absolute gap in the real value of average income is probably even wider in the early 1980s than it was in the 1950s. Second, China has tightly controlled rural-urban migration, so that the urban-rural gap in living standards can hardly begin to be 'resolved' by market forces. Third, industry has taken the lion's share of state investment and it has reached a position of massive dominance within the gross value of output of agriculture and industry combined. Its share is reported as 41 per cent in 1952, at 1952 prices, and 69 per cent in 1981, at 1980 prices. Industrial activity occurs mainly in urban areas; despite big advances in 'rural' industry since the early 1960s, peoples' commune industry by 1981 still contributed only 6.2 per cent to the total gross value of industrial output. Fourth, the share of industrial output devoted to producing farm inputs is small. For example, in 1981, agricultural machinery, chemical fertiliser and farm chemicals together accounted for only about 4 per cent of the gross value of output in industry. Fifth, 'unequal exchange' has operated right through to the present day in commercial transactions between farm and countryside. Sixth, the urban sector has exercised tight control over farm marketings, the vast bulk passing obligatorily through state channels.

In addition to the above arguments, a strong case can be made for extending the notion of 'urban bias' to include the surrounding peasantry who benefit from relatively close proximity to large cities. This is a wider concept than simply 'suburban area peasants' who are formally under the cities' administration and, in more advanced provinces, such as Jiangsu or Guangdong, might include up to about one-third of the peasant population. The state has been reluctant to confiscate the differential rent income of such areas, and they have modernised much more rapidly than other parts of the countryside. Even under Mao their average standard of living was much above that of other peasants and after 1978 the absolute gap in income widened greatly [Nolan, 1983a].

A case can also be made for a 'rural bias' interpretation in China's development strategy. First, during the Cultural Revolution decade considerable advances were made in reducing the urban-rural gap in health and education, in part due to state policy in diverting resources from town to countryside, and in part due to collective endeavour in the communes. Second, the inter-sectoral terms of trade shifted strongly in favour of agriculture over the long term, rapidly so in the late 1970s. Third, instead of taxing increments to output the agricultural tax remained fixed in absolute terms from the 1950s to 1980s, so that it constituted a steadily falling proportion of total farm output. Fourth, there was probably a persistent commodity import 'surplus' for the farm sector over the long term, financed by a net financial inflow from the non-farm sector. Fifth, although the share of industrial output allocated to producing agricultural inputs has not been large, it increased after 1960; for example, the share of 'basic construction investment' allocated to agricultural machinery, chemical fertilisers and farm chemicals rose from 1.4 per cent in the First Five Year Plan to 5-6 per cent for most of the 1960s and 1970s [Wang, 1981: 577]. This fact, together with the rapid overall growth of industry, meant that the farm sector was able to modernise quickly after the early 1960s. Finally, the combination of a relative improvement in farm prices and lower material input costs per unit of output has meant that agriculture's share of the net value of output (at current prices) has stayed much higher than its share of the gross value of output: in 1952 its share of the combined net value of output of agriculture and industry was 83 per cent, and in 1981 it still stood at 49 per cent [*SSB, 1982: 20*].

Thus, depending on which aspects of the 'urban bias' thesis one wishes to stress, a plausible case can be made for or against it in the Chinese case. Furthermore, our analysis suggests that the political divide between city and country is less important than that between state and society, and that one ought to consider the degree to which state action transcends the sectional interests of both urban and rural population. This it may do in two ways. First, it may act in what it *perceives* as the wider interest of society as a whole. Thus the Chinese state pursued over a long period a high accumulation rate and priority allocation of investment to heavy industry. It considered that China would grow more rapidly if it had only limited access to foreign technology and relied on its own initiative. It thought for a long period that attempts to control population were undesirable. It tried to push forward relatively egalitarian methods of work organisation and income distribution. Taken together, these policies amounted to a strategy of high cost growth under which living standards of both peasants *and* workers grew slowly from the mid 1950s to the late 1970s. Yet in a country as poor as China, the first priority of urban *and* rural workers was growth of their standard of living. Second, there has been a strong tendency for the state to act in furtherance of its own interests as a distinct (yet internally heterogeneous) social force. In key areas of strategic choice, policies which are defensible, indeed vitally necessary, to promote economic efficiency, social equity and political democracy have been stifled or weakened by a state apparatus unable or unwilling to countenance change. This 'state bias' is of crucial importance in understanding Chinese development strategy and should be a central focus for future research.

NOTES

1. Between 1978 and 1983 massive changes occurred in China's agrarian system, involving abandonment of collective control of labour and collective income distribution. Land is still owned by the collective but is operated by individual households. Most small means of production and a portion of large ones have been sold off to households [see, for example, *Watson, 1983* and *Kojima, 1982*].

2. National sample survey data for staff and workers' households show the following:

	1957	*1964*	*1980*
Av. number of people per household	4.37	5.30	4.30
Av. number employed per household	1.33	1.56	2.35
Av. number of people supported by each employed person	3.29	3.40	1.83

Source: Chinese Economic Yearbook, 1982: Section VI, p. 25.

3. Although some peasants do use urban hospitals, the numbers are not large. In Sichuan in 1983, for example, one of the authors was informed that about 20 per cent of patients in city hospitals are peasants [*Nolan, 1983c*].

4. Throughout our analysis we shall use the term 'state' to include party, government and army since, in practice, these institutions have been parts of one relatively unified entity with a great deal of mutual interpenetration through personnel transfers and 'interlocking directorates'.

5. Available area: 1952 = 1619 m. *mou*, 1957 = 1677 m. *mou*, 1979 = 1492 m. *mou* [*An Outline of China's Agricultural Economy, 1982: 9*].

6. 'Agriculture, forestry, water conservancy and meteorology' accounted for the following proportion of state investment in capital construction: 1953-57 = 7.6%, 1958-62 = 11.4%, 1963-65 = 18.4%, 1966-70 = 11.4%, 1971-75 = 10.3%, 1976-80 = 11.0%, 1981 = 6.8% [*State Statistical Bureau, 1982: 300*]. Calculating agriculture's share of *total* investment in China is much more complex, and beyond the scope of this essay. However, when investment by people's communes themselves is included it is certain that the figures would rise above those given for state allocations. Careful calculations for the First Five Year Plan period, for example, show that when non-state investment is included, the proportion of gross fixed investment (at 1952 prices) allocated to agriculture was 19.8% [*Yeh, 1968: 521*].

7. Gross output per worker in commune- and brigade-run enterprises in 1980 was about 2000 *yuan* [*SSB, 1982: 192-3*] compared to only about 700 *yuan* in agriculture [*Chinese Agricultural Yearbook, 1982: 17,* and *An Outline ..., 1982: 85*].

8. 'Gross value of agricultural output' includes income from brigade- and team-run enterprises, but not from commune-run enterprises. If their output value was included it would probably improve these figures slightly. By 1980 the total income from commune-run enterprises was 33,220 m. *yuan* compared to 26,390 m. *yuan* from brigade-run enterprises [*SSB, 1982: 193*].

9. China's 'accumulation' rate as a proportion of national income is reported as follows: 1953-7 = 24.2%, 1958-62 = 30.8%, 1963-5 = 22.7%, 1966-78 = 31.2%, 1979 = 34.6%, 1980 = 31.6%, 1981 = 28.3% [*SSB, 1982: 21*]. 'Accumulation' is defined as 'that part of the national income which is used for expanded reproduction, non-productive construction and increase of productive and non-productive stock. Its material formation is the newly added fixed assets of material and non-material sectors (less depreciation of the total fixed assets) and the newly-acquired circulating fund in kind by the material sectors during the year' [*SSB, 1982: 509-10*].

10. Industry's share of total state investment in capital construction is reported as follows: 1953-7 = 45.5%, 1958-62 = 61.4%, 1963-5 = 52.1%, 1966-70 = 59.2%, 1971-5 = 58.2%, 1976-80 = 54.8%, 1981 = 50.3% [*SSB, 1982: 300-1*].

11. The share of 'heavy' industry in total state investment in capital construction is reported to be: 1953-7 = 85.0%, 1958-62 = 89.5%, 1963-5 = 92.2%, 1966-70 = 92.1%, 1971-5 = 89.5%, 1976-80 = 87.4%, 1981 = 80.2% [*SSB 1982: 302*]. 'Heavy' industry in Chinese statistics includes mining, lumber, processing raw materials, power and fuel industry, machine building industry, and industry producing agricultural means of production [*SSB, 1982: 514-15*].

12. 'Non-productive' investment includes 'residential quarters, public health centres, public utilities and other administrative organs catering to cultural and material needs of the people' [*SSB 1982: 517*]. The share of total investment in capital construction going to 'non-productive' sectors was reported to be: 1952 = 33.1%, 1957 = 24.0%, 1962 = 13.4%, 1965 = 15.3%, 1970 = 6.5%, 1975 = 14.3%, 1978 = 17.4%, 1981 = 41.3% [*SSB 1982: 313*].

13. For example, in 1981, for state industrial enterprises, the reported gross value of output per 100 *yuan* of fixed assets (original value) was 271 *yuan* in light industry and 61 *yuan* in heavy industry, while profits and taxes per 100 *yuan* of fixed assets (original value) were 64 *yuan* in light industry and 15 *yuan* in heavy industry [*SSB, 1982: 268*]. The reported gross value of output per worker is somewhat higher in light than heavy industry – in 1980 the figures in the state sector (at 1970 prices) were 17,976 *yuan* in light and 9,674 *yuan* in heavy, and in the collective sector (county level and above) the comparable figures were 7,466 *yuan* and 6,434 *yuan* [*SSB, 1982: 271-2*]. The reported net value of output per worker in 1975 (current prices) was 2,906 *yuan* for light industry and 2,398 *yuan* for heavy industry [*Yang and Li, 1981: 103-4*].

14. In 1980, staff and workers in different industrial sectors (state plus urban collective) were reported to be: heavy industry = 28.5 million, light industry = 18.3 million [*SSB, 1982: 108*].

15. Total fixed assets in state industry (original value) are reported to have increased as follows: 1952 = 14,920 million *yuan*, 1957 = 33,660 million *yuan*, 1978 = 319,340 million *yuan* [*SSB 1982:8*]. The number of industrial workers rose from 12.5 million in 1952, to 14.0 million in 1957, to 50.1 million in 1978 [*Yang and Li, 1981: 104*].

16. Fixed assets (original value) per worker in state industry in 1981 = 11,834 *yuan* [*SSB 1982: 8 and 106*]. Fixed assets per worker in agriculture in 1978 = approx 320 *yuan* [*SSB 1982: 105; An Outline ..., 1982: 119*].

17. At 'comparable' prices [*SSB 1982: 210*]. Net value of output (current prices) is reported to have grown at around 8-9% per annum (compound) from 1957 to 1979 [*Yang and Li, 1981: 103*].
18. Net value of output is obtained by deducting material outlays from the gross value of output. Material outlays in industry include raw materials, fuel, electricity, depreciation, and miscellaneous expenses. Material outlays in agriculture include the cost of seed, sprouting grains, fertilisers, insecticides, animal feed, fuel, and electricity; depreciation charges for agricultural machinery and equipment, and for draft animals and barns; and expenses of transport and communication [*Chen, 1967: 12*].
19. The price 'scissors' (index of purchase price of agricultural commodities divided by price of industrial commodities sold in the villages) reportedly changed as follows: 1930-6 = 100, 1950 = 75.9, 1952 = 82.1, 1957 = 96.9, 1965 = 110.6, 1978 = 140.4, 1979 = 171.3 [*Chen, 1982: 83*].
20. Agricultural taxes reportedly fell from 13.0% of basic accounting units' net income (9.5 per cent of gross income) in 1958 to 4.3 per cent of net income (2.9 per cent of gross income) in 1981 [*SSB, 1982: 199*]. 'Basic accounting units' mainly were production teams until the recent reforms.
21. In 1978 these apparently amounted to 6.1 per cent of the value of total agricultural sector commodity imports [*Ishikawa, 1982: 124*].
22. The state commercial departments' purchase of agricultural products as a proportion of the gross value of agricultural production was reported to be (%): 1952 = 18.6, 1957 = 29.2, 1965 = 46.5, 1970 = 43.8, 1975 = 32.2, 1978 = 31.5 [*Zhang Zhuoyuan, 1981: 72*].
23. Commercial departments' net grain requisition as a proportion of total grain output was reported to be (%): 1952 = 17.2, 1957 = 17.4, 1965 = 17.3, 1970 = 17.5, 1975 = 15.4, 1978 = 13.3 [*Zhang Zhuoyuan, 1981: 72*].

ABBREVIATIONS

HBRB	*Hubei Ribao* (Hubei Daily), Wuhan
JJGL	*Jingji Guanli* (Economic Management), Beijing
JPRS	Joint Publications Research Service, Washington D.C.
LD	*Laodong* (Labour), Beijing
NFRB	*Nanfang Ribao* (Southern Daily), Guangzhou
NYJJWT	*Nongye Jingji Wenti* (Problems in Agricultural Economy), Beijing
SSB	State Statistical Bureau, Beijing
TJGZ	*Tongji Gongzuo* (Statistical Work), Beijing
TJYJ	*Tongji Yanjiu* (Statistical Research), Beijing

REFERENCES

Aird, J. S., 1982, 'Recent demographic data from China: problems and prospects' in U.S. Congress Joint Economic Committee, 1982.
An Outline of China's Agricultural Economy, 1982, Beijing: Agriculture Publishing House.
Baum, Richard, 1971, 'The Cultural Revolution in the Countryside: Anatomy of a Limited Rebellion', in Robinson, T. (ed.), *The Cultural Revolution in China*.
Chen Jialiang, 1982, 'A thorough discussion of the scissors gap in the exchange of agricultural and industrial commodities', in *TJYJ*, Vol. 3, Beijing: Chinese Statistical Publishing House.
Chen, N. R., 1967, *Chinese Economic Statistics*, Edinburgh: Edinburgh University Press.
Chinese Agricultural Yearbook, 1980, 1981, Beijing: Agriculture Publishing House, translated in JPRS, 80270, 9 March 1982, *China Report, Agriculture,* No. 192.
Chinese Economic Yearbook, 1981, 1982, Beijing: Economic Management Magazine.
Chinese Economic Yearbook, 1982, 1983, Beijing: Economic Management Magazine.
Dong Fureng, 1982, 'Relationship between accumulation and consumption', in Xu Dixin *et al.*, 1982, pp. 79-101.
Eckstein, A., Galenson, W. and Liu, T. C. (eds), 1968, *Economic Trends in Communist China*, Edinburgh: Edinburgh University Press.

Emerson, J. P., 1982, 'The labour force of China, 1957–80', in U.S. Congress Joint Economic Committee, 1982.

Fang Lie and Huang Huaqiang, 1957, 'A Discussion About Some Problems Concerning the Peasants' Living Standards', *NFRB*, April 13.

First Five Year Plan for Development of the National Economy of the People's Republic of China in 1953–1957, 1956, Beijing: Foreign Languages Press.

Friedman, Edward, 1981, 'The original Chinese revolution remains in power', *Bulletin of Concerned Asian Scholars*, Vol. 13, No. 3, pp. 42-9.

Gurley, John G., 1975, 'Rural Development in China 1949–72 and the Lessons to be Learned from It', *World Development*, Vol. 3, Nos. 7/8, pp. 455-72.

Harper, Paul, 1969, 'The Party and the Unions in Communist China', *China Quarterly*, No. 37 (January–March), pp. 84-119.

Howe, C., 1973a, 'Labour organisation and incentives in industry, before and after the Cultural Revolution', in Schram, S. R., 1973.

Howe, C., 1973b, *Wage Patterns and Wage Policy in Modern China 1919–1972*, Cambridge: Cambridge University Press.

Ishikawa, S., 1967, 'Resource Flow between Agriculture and Industry – the Chinese Experience', *The Developing Economies*, No. 1 (March).

Ishikawa, S., 1982, 'China's food and agriculture: prospects and performance', in Reisch, E. M. (ed.), *Agricultura Sinica*.

Klatt, W., 1983, 'The staff of life: living standards in China, 1977–81', *China Quarterly*, No. 93 (March).

Kojima, R., 1982, 'China's new agricultural policy', *The Developing Economies*, Vol. 20, No. 4.

Korzec, M. and Whyte, M. K., 1981, 'Reading notes: the Chinese wage system', *China Quarterly*, No. 86.

Kraus, Richard, 1983, 'The Chinese State and its Bureaucrats', in Nee, V. and Mozingo, D. (eds), *State and Society in Contemporary China*, Ithaca: Cornell University Press, pp. 132-47.

Lampton, D. M., 1974, *Health, Conflict and the Chinese Political System*, Ann Arbor: University of Michigan, Michigan Papers in Chinese Studies No. 18.

Lampton, D. M., 1978, 'Development and Health Care: Is China's Medical Programme Exportable?', *World Development*, Vol. 6, No. 5.

Lampton, D. M., 1979, 'The New "Revolution" in China's Social Policy', *Problems of Communism*, No. 5-6 (September–December).

Lardy, N. R., 1978, *Economic Growth and Distribution in China*, Cambridge: Cambridge University Press.

Lewis, John W., 1963, *Leadership in Communist China*, Ithaca: Cornell University Press.

Lewis, John W., 1971, 'Commerce, Education, and Political Development in Tangshan 1956–69', in Lewis, J. W. (ed.), *The City in Communist China*, Stanford: Stanford University Press, pp. 153-79.

Liao Luyan, 1960, *The Whole Party and the Whole People Go in for Agriculture in a Big Way*, Beijing: Foreign Languages Press.

Lipton, M., 1977, *Why Poor People Stay Poor, Urban Bias in World Development*, London: Temple Smith.

Liu Shaoqi *et al.*, 1949, *New Democratic Urban Policy*, Tianjin.

Ma Hong and Sun Xiaoqing (eds), 1981, *Investigation of Questions on China's Economic Structure*, Beijing: People's Publishing House.

Mao Tse-tung (Mao Zedong), 1957, 'On the correct handling of contradictions among the people', in *Selected Works of Mao Tse-tung*, Vol. 5, Beijing: Foreign Languages Press, 1977.

Marx, Karl, 1972, *Critique of the Gotha Programme*, Beijing: Foreign Languages Press.

Mauger, P., 1983, 'Changing Policy and Practice in Chinese Rural Education', *China Quarterly*, No. 93 (March).

Nolan, Peter, 1979, 'Inequality of income between town and countryside in PRC in the mid-1950s', *World Development*, Vol. 7, pp. 447-65.

Nolan, Peter, 1981, *Rural Income in the People's Republic of China, 1952 to 1957, with Reference to Guangdong Province*, unpublished Ph.D. thesis, London University.

Nolan, Peter, 1983a, *Growth Processes and Distributional Change in a South Chinese Province*, London: Contemporary China Institute.

Nolan, Peter, 1983b, 'De-collectivisation of agriculture in China, 1979–82: a long-term perspective', *Economic and Political Weekly*, 6 August and 13 August.

Nolan, Peter, 1983c, 'Trip notes from research in Sichuan Province, July–August 1983', unpublished.

Nolan, Peter and White, Gordon, 1979, 'Socialist Development and rural inequality: the Chinese countryside in the 1970s', *Journal of Peasant Studies*, Vol. 7, No. 1 (October).

Oksenberg, Michel, 1968, 'Occupational Groups in Chinese Society and the Cultural Revolution', in *The Cultural Revolution: 1967 in Review*, Ann Arbor: University of Michigan, Michigan Papers in Chinese Studies No. 2, pp. 1-44.

Oksenberg, Michel, 1982, 'Economic Policy-making in China: Summer 1981', *China Quarterly*, No. 90 (June), pp. 165-94.

Orleans, L. A., 1982, 'China's urban population: concepts, conglomerations and concerns', in U.S. Congress Joint Economic Committee, 1982.

Paine, Suzanne, 1981, 'Spatial Aspects of Chinese Development: Issues, Outcomes and Policies 1949–79', *Journal of Development Studies*, Vol. 17, No. 2 (January), pp. 133-95.

Pepper, S., 1980, 'Chinese Education After Mao: Two Steps Forward, Two Steps Back and Begin Again', *China Quarterly*, No. 81 (March).

Rao Wen, 1957, 'Why is There a Difference in the Income Accruing to Simple and Complicated Work, Mental and Manual Labour?', *NFRB* October 22.

Rawski, T. G., 1979, *Economic Growth and Employment in China*, New York: OUP.

Reisch, E. M. (ed.), 1982, *Agricultura Sinica*, Berlin: Duncker and Humblot.

Schram, S. R. (ed.), 1973, *Authority, Participation and Cultural Change in China*, Cambridge: Cambridge University Press.

Skinner, G. W., 1964, 1965, 'Marketing and Social Structure in Rural China: Parts I, II and III', *Journal of Asian Studies*, Vol. XXIV, Nos. 1-3.

State Statistical Bureau, 1974, *Ten Great Years* (reprinted), Washington: Washington State College.

State Statistical Bureau, 1982, *Statistical Yearbook of China 1981*, Hong Kong: Economic Information Agency.

Sun Yefang, 1981, 'Strengthen statistical work, reform the statistical system', *JJGL*, No. 2.

United States Congress, Joint Economic Committee, 1982, *China Under the Four Modernisations*, Part 1, Washington D.C.: U.S. Government Printing Office.

Wang Haibo, 1981, 'The Relationship between Accumulation and Consumption', in Ma and Sun (eds), op. cit. (in Chinese).

Watson, A., 1983, 'Agriculture looks for "shoes that fit": the production responsibility system and its implications', *World Development*, Vol. II, No. 8.

White, Gordon, 1981, 'Higher Education and Social Redistribution in a Socialist Society: The Chinese Case', *World Development*, Vol. 9, pp. 149-66.

White, Gordon, 1982, 'Urban Employment and Labour Allocation Policies in Post-Mao China', *World Development*, Vol. 10, No. 8, pp. 613-32.

White, Gordon, 1983, 'The Postrevolutionary Chinese State', in Nee, V. and Mozingo, D. (eds), *State and Society in Contemporary China*, Ithaca: Cornell Univ. Press, pp. 27-52.

Xiang Qiyuan, 1982, 'Economic development and income distribution', in Xu Dixin *et al.*, 1982, pp. 102-29.

Xu Dixin *et al.*, 1982, *China's Search for Economic Growth: The Chinese Economy Since 1949*, Beijing: New World Press.

Xu Yi and Chen Baosen, 1981, 'On the Necessity and Possibility of Stabilising Prices', *Social Sciences and China*, Vol. 2, No. 3, pp. 121-38.

Xue Muqiao, 1981, *China's Socialist Economy*, Beijing: Foreign Languages Press.

Yang Jianbai and Li Xueceng, 1980, 'The Relations between Agriculture, Light Industry and Heavy Industry in China', *Social Sciences in China*, Vol. 1, No. 2 (June), pp. 182-212.

Yang Jianbai and Li Xueceng, 1981, 'The Structure of Agriculture, Heavy Industry and Light Industry', in Ma and Sun, op. cit.

Yang Shengming, 1981, 'The Structure of the People's Livelihood', in Ma and Sun, op. cit.

Yeh, K. C., 1968, 'Capital formation' in Eckstein *et al.* (eds), op. cit.

Zhang Liuzheng, 1980, 'Developing Agricultural Production, Improving the People's Living Standard', *NYJJWT*, No. 1.

Zhang Zhuoyuan, 1981, 'Establishing a rational economic structure; promoting socialist modernisation', in Ma and Sun, op. cit.

Zhao Xue, 1957, 'Who Leads Whom?', *NFRB* November 6.

'Generative' or 'Parasitic' Urbanism? Some Observations from the Recent History of a South Indian Market Town

by *Barbara Harriss and John Harriss**

Using data from sample surveys in a South Indian market town in 1973 and 1982–3, the paper examines the different views of Mellor and Lipton on the relations of small towns and their hinterlands, in the context of a growing agricultural economy. It is shown that the pattern of demand which has been generated by the 'green revolution' has not encouraged decentralised production, as in Mellor's model. It does appear, however, that a net transfer of resources from the countryside to the town, such as Lipton's model postulates, has been taking place, though the authors remain sceptical about this model as an explanation.

INTRODUCTION: ALTERNATIVE VIEWS OF RURAL-URBAN RELATIONS AND THE ROLE OF SMALL TOWNS

In his essay on *Urbanism and the City* David Harvey discusses the relationships between the formation of towns and cities, and the production, appropriation and distribution of social surplus product:

Capitalism ... has shown itself to be an inherently expansionary force ... expansion means a progressive penetration of market exchange, greater quantities of accumulated surplus, and a shift in the circulation of surplus value as new opportunities are explored, new technologies achieved and new resources and productive capacities are opened up. Urbanism ... plays an important role in this process ... The city functions as a generative centre around which an effective space is created out of which growing quantities of surplus product are extracted. *Overall economic growth presupposes both a willingness and an ability for those in the urban centre to put surplus value back into circulation in such a way that the city functions as a 'growth pole' for the surrounding economy.* (Authors' emphasis) [*Harvey, 1973: 248–50*]

* Nutrition Policy Unit, London School of Hygiene and Tropical Medicine; and School of Development Studies, University of East Anglia.

The authors are grateful to Professor John Mellor and Dr Peter Hazell of the International Food Policy Research Institute for making possible the re-survey of Arni in 1982–3, and to ESCOR of the Overseas Development Administration for funding. They are grateful also to Frank Ellis, Don Funnell, Satish Mishra and Mick Moore for comments made on an earlier draft.

But it is not always or necessarily the case that urban centres have these generative functions. Elsewhere Harvey explores the broad distinction between 'generative' and 'parasitic' cities first put forward by Hoselitz [*see Harvey, 1973: 233*]. Some cities (urban centres) contribute to the economic growth of their regions and may be described as 'generative', whereas others do not and are in this sense 'parasitic': 'a generative city will allocate a considerable amount of the surplus value accumulated within it to forms of investment that enlarge production. The investments may be in the city or in the surrounding rural area .... In this situation the city does return certain benefits to the rural area' [*Harvey, 1973: 233*]. From this allusion and from the logic of Harvey's argument it appears that under some conditions of the development of capitalism we might expect to find that 'those in the urban centre' *do not* put surplus value back into productive circulation so as to return benefits to the rural area.

In this paper we report on some of the results of an enquiry into the functions of a particular market town in South India in relation to its hinterland. We treat as a matter for empirical investigation the question of whether or not the town functions as a 'growth pole'. The question is of interest not only in itself. The answer to it will illuminate the whole process of economic development in the region, and the relations of 'town' and 'country' in that process. The context of our investigation is one in which there has been expansion of the agricultural economy as 'new opportunities are explored, new technologies achieved' − in this case because of the 'green revolution' [*B. Harriss, 1981; J. Harriss, 1982*].

The theoretical and practical interest of our enquiry is further amplified by comparison of two well-known general statements, by John Mellor and Michael Lipton, concerning the functions of small market towns in economic development, especially in India.

Mellor advocates a development strategy based on yield increasing and cost decreasing methods in agriculture and the linkage effects of such agricultural development. Under such a strategy, Mellor asserts, 'the market town could be the focal point for organisation and decision making' [*Mellor, 1976: 188*]. He notes that 'the market town approach has ... long been recognised as a means of taking jobs to the rural labour force (etc.)' yet, 'despite its intellectual appeal, the market town concept has, in general, failed because the basic strategy of growth did not provide the essential foundation for raising rural incomes.[1] With change in the strategy, the market town can become the corner stone of the development effort' [*Mellor, 1976: 188*].

The argument, in outline, is as follows. Increased agricultural production, based on cost decreasing technology, can make large net additions to national income. This income will accrue especially to larger cultivators, who tend to spend a large percentage of it on non-agricultural commodities. The consumer goods industries thus stimulated by rising rural incomes are likely to be relatively labour intensive, at least by comparison with the capital intensive producer goods industries which have been given priority under the existing Indian development strategy [*Mellor, 1976: chapter 5*]. Thus, increased agricultural production by the wealthier landowning classes generates demand for more non-agricultural production and so brings about increased employment.

The expanded employment of the lower-income labouring classes, who spend the bulk of their increased incomes on food, provides the demand for further increases in food production, so we see that there is an important complementarity between the objectives of increasing food production and increasing employment. The strategy calls for an industrial policy which conserves capital – so that as much as possible is made available for agricultural investment – and taps new sources of savings. Such an industrial policy would facilitate expansion of consumer goods production and encourage decentralised, small-scale industry. Mellor continues: 'rising rural incomes increase demand in rural areas and *thereby encourage decentralisation* (authors' emphasis) of production to those areas .... And the higher incomes in rural areas provide a larger pool for investment in local, small-scale industry' [*Mellor, 1976: 17*].

Mellor's argument is a programmatic one, and though it is based on considerable empirical analysis key parts of it appear to be more articles of faith than anything else. Admittedly Mellor emphasises that 'astute government policy' is necessary for the strategy to work. But even with this qualification the fairly critical assumption that increased incomes and increased demand in rural areas will encourage decentralisation of production is only very weakly supported empirically. Though Mellor concedes that the data are scanty, poor and old, he still argues that:

> Under small town and rural conditions (basic consumer goods like milk and tobacco products) are consumed in a form requiring much less capital intensity in their production. Thus, *if the structure of demand does not change drastically to conform to high income urban consumption patterns* (authors' emphasis), it may influence the choice of techniques as well as the scale (and location) of production of many of these goods. By means of both these factors, the demand structure associated with rising rural incomes can encourage a more decentralised and labour-using pattern of industrialisation [*Mellor, 1976: 175*].

Mellor lays out a programme under which small market towns would be 'growth centres', and he states some of the conditions for its fulfilment. It is relevant to ask, in relation to the region of our investigation, where agricultural development based on yield increasing and cost decreasing methods *is* taking place, how far those of Mellor's assumptions to which we have drawn attention are justified by experience. We recognise, though, that since several of the policies which are essential to Mellor's programme (such as that towards industry) have not been actively pursued in India, it would be unreasonable to anticipate that his whole scenario is being accomplished.

We may set alongside Mellor's statement Michael Lipton's analysis of the development process under conditions of 'urban bias', which he says 'stems from and benefits large towns of 10-20 000 people and more' [*Lipton, 1977: 58*]. Lipton's argument here is not presented in such a way that it is possible to spell out his assumptions and the connections that he makes in the way in which we have done for Mellor. There is indeed an intrinsic difficulty in examining a *sectoral* argument in micro-terms, and this is what Lipton flirts with here.

What Lipton means can perhaps best be deduced from his discussion of

Kautsky's views on 'Exploitation of the country by the town'. The essence of this is that 'as villages become more and more dependent on cash, and as rural moneylenders acquire urban interests and compete with urban lenders ... (a process takes place) in which spending that used to stay in the rural circuit, bidding up both demanded outputs and prices for rural people's products, moves into the urban circuit instead. Hence city dwellers − better off to begin with − find that both the volume of output that is demanded and the prices that they can command for it, improve, while the villagers' deteriorate' [*Lipton, 1977: 117*]. The process that Lipton writes of here is that which Harvey refers to when he speaks of the 'shift in the circulation of surplus value' that comes about with the development of capitalism. But whereas Harvey argues that 'overall economic growth presupposes ... (that) those in the urban centre ... put surplus value back into circulation in such a way that the city functions as a "growth centre" ', Lipton in effect suggests that they do *not*, with the result that the kind of economic growth which takes place tends to impoverish (especially) rural people. There are many problems with Lipton's argument. In this particular part of it, it is hard to see how the 'bias' in flows of money which he describes is better explained by his thesis of 'urban bias' (a broad statement about political alliances) than by Kautsky's (and Harvey's by implication) suggestions that it essentially results from increasing penetration of rural areas by the market economy.[2]

Lipton shares in a tradition which has viewed towns as being mainly exploitative and 'parasitic' in relation to their hinterlands, while Mellor's theory belongs with a range of models involving the conception that towns have 'generative' functions. The terms 'generative' and 'parasitic' are used here metaphorically, and the various analytical models which may be referred to in this way examine different aspects of urbanism. Both Mellor and Lipton offer us only partial accounts of rural-urban relations, and there may be circumstances in which *both* could be found to be substantiable empirically (or in which both would be falsified). They are most clearly contrasted with regard to the trends which may be set in motion by the expansion of commodity production in agriculture, and it is these which are the main focus of this paper. If the Lipton-Kautsky view is correct we should expect to observe a net transfer of financial resources from the countryside to the town, resulting from the dependence of agricultural producers upon urban inputs and urban finance; and also that these resources are employed in urban circuits of production and exchange. The flows of surplus value generated would not be such that the town would function as a 'growth pole'. If, on the other hand, the conditions of Mellor's scenario are fulfilled then we should expect to find that agricultural growth has generated demand for consumer goods and that this is encouraging decentralised production, financed at least in part from rural incomes.

CONTEXT AND METHOD

The market town we studied in 1973 and in 1982−3 was Arni, in the eastern part of North Arcot District in Tamil Nadu [*see papers in Farmer (ed.), 1977; and B. Harriss, 1976b*]. Its population of 38,664 in 1971 had increased by about

27 per cent to 49,284 in 1981. The town has its origins in the bazaar which grew up around a fort constructed in the Vijayanagara period, and it is still a minor administrative centre and a marketing centre especially for paddy and for groundnuts, the two crops which dominate the cropping systems of the local region. It is also one of the smaller centres of the handloom silk industry of Tamil Nadu. The concept of a 'typical' market town is as misleading as that for the 'typical village'. We would claim only that Arni shares many characteristics with other small towns in Tamil Nadu, and that if it is peculiar at all it is because of the existence of the silk industry – though it is quite common for small towns to have a particular industry as well as market functions.

In November and December of 1973 and 1982, and again in April 1983, we mapped and listed all the business and other activities of the built area of Arni (as opposed to the officially defined municipal area). We then drew, at each of the survey points, 6 per cent random samples of private and public sector production, trading and service units from our lists;[3] and we ourselves (with language assistance) interviewed the owners (or sometimes the managers) of each of the units in the samples. The interviews covered data on the history of the firms and backgrounds of the owners; sources of capital; value, geographical sources and destinations of inputs and of outputs; business expansion and investment; credit; and employment. We are well known in the town and have lived there for quite long periods in connection with this and other research. So our data are probably as reliable as it is possible to obtain in surveys of small businesses. We have data from the samples and from supplementary interviews on 89 units in 1973 and 118 in 1982–83, as well as additional information on other activities in the town.

Arni is situated in the most important paddy-producing part of North Arcot. In the District as a whole the introduction of high-yielding varieties of paddy and associated 'green revolution' inputs has met with greater success than almost anywhere else in the state. Official data show that rice production in North Arcot has increased by 5.5 per cent per annum since the introduction of HYVs in 1967. This is the highest growth rate (with Chingleput District) in Tamil Nadu, and it has been almost entirely due to yield increases. It is estimated that rice production increased by more than 50 per cent in the District in the period from 1973–74 and 1982–83 [*IFPRI, 1980: passim*]. Comparison of the results of our two surveys allows us to comment on some of the effects of this expansion of agricultural production at the level of a local urban centre, and to test the interpretations of Mellor and Lipton.

Our empirical material is marshalled to describe changes in economic activity in the town, and in the structure of its commodity flows. Examination of the commodity flows permits us to identify the present economic character of the town and its economic relationship to its immediate agricultural hinterland. Then we report changes in employment and wages before looking finally at three aspects of monetary flows and change over the decade: flows from private moneylending institutions, origins of capital invested in urban businesses, and destinations of accumulated profits.

THE ECONOMY OF THE TOWN 1973–83[4]

The principal economic activities (in terms both of the value of the business transacted and the numbers of people employed) of Arni remain rice milling/ paddy trading and the manufacture of silk saris. Other production activities are: welding and general engineering, artisanal tailoring, the manufacture of wooden furniture, pottery and tile making, artisanal goldsmithing, metal vesselsmithing, printing presses, bakeries and tyre retreading. Most of these activities, with the exception of pottery and goldsmithing, have expanded since 1973 but their financial value remains extremely small in relation to the two major production activities, and the numbers of people employed in them are not large. Several of them (like tailoring and goldsmithing) are made up largely of petty producers. These production activities supply basic consumer items to local markets, both urban and rural. While there has been expansion in welding and general engineering from 8 small units to 20 (much of the business being pumpset repair), there has been no development of the production of agricultural machinery or equipment, although one firm was about to go into the manufacturing of spare parts for electric pumpsets early in 1983. Even the servicing of tractors, trailers and power tillers is mostly carried out at other centres, especially in Vellore, the District capital. There are about 100 mechanical grain threshers in the region of Arni, and these are serviced in the town. But the expansion of the use of such machinery is reported as having stopped.

Amongst the service activities those of pawnbrokers, lawyers and doctors, and lorry and bus services are financially most important. Cycle hire and repair, barbers' shops, laundries and basic transport (carts and rickshaws) are also important in terms of the numbers of businesses involved. There has been a very marked expansion in the financial services supplied by the town. Both the numbers of pawnbrokers and the value of turnover of their businesses have increased (the latter by a factor of about five), while at the same time the numbers of commercial and cooperative banks operating in Arni has doubled, and 24 'finance corporations' have been set up in the last four years.

The most striking change in the trading activities of Arni is the increase in the number of cloth shops. There has been some expansion also in the number of provision shops and of general merchants, and a considerable expansion in the numbers of sellers of metal utensils.

There are also a small number of businesses in what are essentially 'new' items, which were rarely or never traded in 1973: bottled cold drinks, eggs (produced almost entirely on poultry farms near Chittor in Andhra Pradesh, *not* locally), fancy goods – especially modern cosmetics, ready-made clothes, a wide range of consumer plastics and steel furniture. It is important to note the origins and destinations of these commodities, in relation to the possibility suggested by Mellor that 'the demand structure associated with rising rural incomes (may) encourage a more decentralised and labour-using pattern of industrialisation'. Taking those items which have been listed here as having expanded considerably or as having recently entered into trade in Arni, we find that whereas only 14 per cent of our 1973 sample was made up by firms trading in them, in 1983 such firms made up 25 per cent of the sample. Table 1 shows

TABLE 1

ORIGINS OF PRODUCTION[1] OF 'NEW' AND 'EXPANDED' COMMODITIES (Rs '000)

Arni	Villages	Vellore	Madras	Cbe.	ODR	ODU	OSR	OSU	Total
				1983					
23	0.72	524.4	3647	4743.8	343	425.1	724.2	9733.9	20165.12
(0.1%)	—	(2.6)	(18.0)	(23.5)	(17)	(2.1)	(3.6)	(48.3)	
				(excluding petrol and oil)					
				1973					
—	—	143.9	1089.5	—	40	86.2	—	28	1387.6
		(10.4%)	(78.5%)		(2.9)	(6.2)		(2.0)	
				(excluding petrol and oil)					

ODR = 'Other Districts Rural'; ODU = 'Other Districts Urban'; OSR = 'Other States Rural';
OSU = 'Other States Urban'.

1. Care was taken in interviewing to distinguish between 'place of purchase' and 'place of production' of different items, though uncertainty remained in some cases.

that this expanded trade has brought about a considerable shift in Arni's trading pattern. It appears that these particular commodities are produced especially in Madras and Coimbatore (the first and second largest cities of Tamil Nadu) and in urban centres in other states (mainly Bombay and Calcutta, and also Bangalore and Hyderabad). There has in particular been a shift since 1973 towards trading in items which are produced in metropolitan cities outside the state. It is also noticeable that these items are being traded more extensively *within* Arni than the same items were ten years ago. Now 39 per cent of the sales of these items are to village consumers, compared with only 25 per cent in 1973. It is certain that the expansion of trade in these commodities is associated with rising rural incomes, as well as with the expansion of silk manufacturing and of public sector employment in the town. But it does *not* appear that the pattern of demand which has been created is encouraging fresh decentralised, labour intensive production.

The pattern of demand, as we observe it in those commodities in which trade has expanded, or the 'new' items which have entered into Arni's commerce, is apparently for 'big city' products, both in the sense that they are produced in big cities and that they correspond with urban fashion (like soft drinks, cosmetics and consumer plastics). The economy of Arni is altogether more open than Mellor's proposition would suggest. The condition which he introduces, that the structure of demand should not change 'to conform to high income urban consumption patterns', is not being satisfied, and there is little indication in Arni that the 'green revolution' has so far encouraged the creation of decentralised and labour intensive production. Interventions by the state to limit this development of demand for 'big city' products and to encourage decentralised production would be highly problematic in an essentially open market economy.

ECONOMIC GROWTH AND THE PRESENT STRUCTURE OF COMMODITY FLOWS

Our data show that over a period in which the population of the town grew by about 27 per cent, and the production of the most important crop grown in its hinterland by about 50 per cent, the value of commodity flows through the town grew by almost 400 per cent at constant prices (see Table 2). It is

TABLE 2

ESTIMATES OF THE VALUE OF COMMODITY FLOWS AT CONSTANT PRICES[1] (MILLION Rs)

	1973	1983	% growth
Total value of commodities	250.191	998.77	399
Agricultural products only	93.579	364.55	390
Silk manufacure only	25.761	213.07	827
Agricultural inputs		75.2	
Industrial/Workshop inputs	130.851	71.93	392
Consumer goods		274.02	

1. 1983 values deflated in relation to the All-India Index of Wholesale Prices for Major Commodity Groups.

clear that there has been a marked expansion in urban production, especially in the manufacture of silk saris, though this expansion is exaggerated by our data because our first survey in 1973 was made at a time of acute crisis for the industry, whereas the second was made in a period of boom. The silk industry has certainly contributed to an exceptionally large extent to the overall expansion of business activity in the town, though it is also clear that the productive transformation of, and trade in, agricultural commodities has made a substantial contribution too. The development of other activities (like pawn-broking and moneylending, and the wholesale and retail selling of cloth) must in large measure be the indirect result of the expansion in silk and in local agriculture. It is true that the expansion of public sector employment would have contributed to increased demand for consumer goods and services. The staff of the main post office in Arni, to give one example, has increased by 50 per cent. But it is implausible that this factor alone should have accounted for the level of expansion in turnover that we observe. An increase in *rural* effective demand must enter our explanation and is reported more fully below.

We can analyse the nature of the present private urban economy and its external linkages from a series of commodity flow tables. The first, Table 3, locates the origins of production of the goods which flow through or are transformed in Arni.

Grain amounts to 31 per cent of the flows of sampled firms. Grain flows originate mainly from the immediate rural hinterland of Arni, but increasingly

TABLE 3

ORIGINS OF PRODUCTION[1] OF GOODS, ARNI, 1982–83

(Rs '000)[2] (sample totals)

Origin	Grain	Non-grain agricultural products	Agricultural inputs	Industrial/ workshop inputs	Raw materials for silk industry	Consumer goods	Total
Arni	—	55		62		1,822	1,939
Local villages	17,528	258		190	45	31	18,052
Vellore		60	193	110		4,063	4,426
Madras			5,642	7,466	1,712	11,638	26,458
Coimbatore			170	328		5,458	5,956
Other districts (rural)	11,219	912	472	180		87	12,876
Other districts (urban)			92		4	773	869
Other states (rural)	7,790	1,803		8			9,601
Other states (urban)			2,546	376	24,066	9,343	36,331
Total	36,537	3,088	9,115	8,720	25,827	33,215	116,502

1. Refer to note 1, Table 1.
2. Rs value is inclusive of transport cost to point of purchase by firm located in Arni.

(and especially in times of drought) Arni is drawing paddy supplies from surplus districts at long distances both within Tamil Nadu and from the adjacent State of Andhra Pradesh. Non-grain agricultural projects (vegetables, flowers, jaggery (coarse sugar), eggs and wood) are of minor importance (2.6 per cent of flows) and are overwhelmingly non-local in origin. Raw materials for the silk industry comprise 22 per cent of flows and are also non-local in origin. Agricultural inputs make up 8 per cent of flows and are produced mainly in Madras, a pattern which also characterises the raw materials for workshop industry in Arni. Consumer goods amount to 28 per cent of flows and are produced in Madras and other metropolitan cities, Coimbatore, Vellore and in towns surrounding them. It would seem then that the locations of production of the agricultural goods comprising the economic base of the town are increasingly non-local and those of the other goods flowing through Arni are metropolitan or urban in origin.

The agricultural hinterland of Arni produces 15 per cent of commodities flowing through Arni. Paddy-rice predominates and local production of non-grain agricultural commodities is of minor importance.[5] Other rural regions in Tamil Nadu and in adjacent states supply 11 and 8 per cent of goods respectively: paddy from Thanjavur, South Arcot and Andhra Pradesh, and vegetables and silk thread from the region of Bangalore.

The local district capital of Vellore is responsible for the production of only 4 per cent of Arni's commodities: processed goods (especially milled rice) for the co-operative stores and jewellery. Of less quantitative importance are fertilizer and pesticides (made in Ranipet nearby), aluminium and brass vessels. The metropolis of Madras is the origin of 23 per cent of goods: in the main products of the petrochemical industries (fertilizer and pesticides, kerosene, petrol and diesel); but also a large variety of intermediate goods for small industries, workshops and services and a large range of consumer goods (notably jewellery, processed foods, drugs and liquor). The industrial city of Coimbatore and its urban-industrial satellites supply Arni with 5 per cent of its goods: domestic appliances, textiles and pumpsets. Other urban centres in Tamil Nadu supply Arni with aluminium and stainless steel goods, processed provisions and drugs. Urban and metropolitan centres in other states supply 32 per cent of goods, notably raw materials for the silk industry, fertiliser, pumpsets, rice mill spares, and consumer goods (shoes, electrical appliances, factory processed food, plastics, liquor, cloth – especially artificial fibres).

Apart from the silk and rice industries Arni itself produces very little. Of extremely minor importance are shoes, brass vessels and groundnut oil production.

It seems then that agricultural commodities comprise about a third of the direct supplies to Arni, while the products of metropolitan industries within and outside Tamil Nadu account for over one-half of the goods arriving in Arni.

Table 4 presents commodity flow accounts for the decade 1973–83. From this it is apparent that with the growing complexity of the urban economy more flows are intermediate rather than direct from origin of production to final destination. Comparison of locations of purchase with locations of production of goods flowing through Arni indicates the town's importance as a wholesale centre of consumer and intermediate goods manufactured in metropolitan centres. Comparison of flows in 1973 and 1983 indicates that flows to non-final destinations have increased from about 46 per cent in 1973 to 65 per cent of total flows a decade later. These flows consist of silk products sold to metropolitan wholesalers, paddy resold to rice mills within Arni and rice wholesaled to Coimbatore, Madras and their environs.

Whereas more than half the commodity flows from Arni in 1973 took the form of retail sales to final destinations, these were reduced to about a third a decade later. Despite this decline in relative importance retail sales have trebled in real terms and their rural-urban distribution is the best evidence we have of the multiplier effect of increases in agricultural incomes.

In 1973 per capita retail sales to residents of Arni approximated Rs 1900. Those for inhabitants of the modal market area (191,000) were approximately Rs 310. These figures, necessarily approximate, suggest that rural per capita effective demand for goods traded in Arni was about six times less than was urban effective demand. In 1983 per capita retail sales to residents of Arni approximated Rs 3444 in constant prices, while those to residents of the rural hinterland (estimated at 200,000) amounted to Rs 1039 in constant prices. While the real increase in urban effective demand is by a factor of 1.8, that of rural effective demand is apparently almost twice as great (3.4), reducing by half the rural-urban discrepancy in the value of purchases. Nevertheless,

TABLE 4

COMMODITY FLOW ACCOUNTS, ARNI (CONSTANT PRICES) (1973–83) (SAMPLE TOTALS)
(Rs '000)

1973[1] Region	Origin of purchase	Intermediate destination	Final destination	$O - D$[4]
Arni	1414.9	1452.2	4406.6	− 4443.9
Local villages	4083.8	779.6	3576.6	− 272.4
Vellore and region	3624.5	191.7	27.8	+ 3405
Other districts TN	3102.9	3130.2	1.0	− 28.3
Other states	1496.8	1227.4	—	+ 269.4
Gross Value Added	1288.6	—	—	
Error	—	104.2	104.2	
Total	15011.5	6885.3	8116.2	
1983[2]				
Arni	4982.2	10275.2	10379.4	− 15671.6
Local villages	8216.8	1992.9	12565.2	− 6341.3
Vellore and region	4292.6	391.2	16.4	+ 3885
Madras	8481.5	10305.8[3]	402.6	− 2226.9
Coimbatore and region	2050.1	13119.5	353.3	− 11422.7
Other districts (rural)	5269.8	1629.2	480.8	+ 3519.8
Other districts (urban)	312.6	3300.5[3]	—	− 2987.9
Other states (rural)	3652.3	391	—	+ 3261.3
Other states (urban)	15193.4	4341.5[3]	—	+ 10851.5
Gross Value Added	17133.2	—	—	
Total	69944.5	45746.8	24197.7	

1. Data for the groundnut and milk trades are included.

2. Data for groundnut and milk trades are excluded. Deflator of 0.457 used for constant prices.

3. These flows, largely silk products, may include some retail sales but these could not be distinguished from sales to non-final destinations.

4. Value at origin of purchase − value sold at intermediate destination and value sold to final destination.

rural per capita effective demand is still on average a third of its urban counterpart.[6]

Regional imbalances in commodity flows are suggestive of economic interdependence and integration. In 1973 a major surplus accrued to Vellore which received Rs 60 million more via goods purchased there and sold in Arni than was paid out on goods bought in Arni and sold in Vellore. The major transactional deficit region was Arni itself whose residents apparently bought Rs 50 million more than they received in income on private trading. A deficit of this sort would be reduced by flows which we have not summarised, notably income from public sector employment and loans from banks, money-lenders and pawnbrokers used for consumption. Such a deficit will also be reduced by the component of gross value added which is used for consumption.

The account for 1983 shows the existence of more and greater regional imbalances. Notably Arni, its rural hinterland and Coimbatore are in net deficit and rural districts within Tamil Nadu and other states and urban/metropolitan centres in other states are in net surplus. From these gross disequilibria we may conclude the development of greater spatio-economic interdependence.

The commodity flow accounts also show that the gross value added in trading, processing and servicing activities in Arni has increased in both absolute and relative terms. Whereas in 1973 it averaged 9 per cent, in 1983 it was apparently 24.5 per cent (averaging 40 per cent in manufacturing and 9 per cent in merchanting). Profit is an overwhelmingly large component of gross value added. This represents a net flow of resources into the town.

CHANGES IN RURAL-URBAN TRADING RELATIONS

Trading firms may be classified according to the degree to which the destinations of commodities transacted are urban. In 1973 the 76 retail firms fell roughly into four quartile groups according to the proportion of annual sales purchased by residents of Arni. These groups were differentiated in further respects (Table 5). Annual turnover was related to urban orientation. Firms most orientated to the town had greater total and average turnover and the largest requirements of starting capital, none of which originated in the agricultural sector. They also tended to be newer firms. We hypothesised then that a continuation of trends manifested in 1973 would result in an urban economy (decreasingly) linked by commodity flows to its surrounding rural hinterland: 'The dynamics of urban growth would then involve a decline in the relative importance of the transactional relationship with the agricultural hinterland which would become a provider of foodstuffs and only a residual economic market' [*B. Harriss, 1976b: 185*].

What actually seems to have happened is a more complex process than was foreseen. In 1983, as in 1973, those firms most orientated to urban final destinations retailed mostly goods with a high income elasticity. Their turnover was much greater than rurally orientated firms. They were also younger. But here the similarities with conditions a decade earlier end. In 1983, urban-orientated firms had smaller starting capital requirements than rurally orientated firms. They depended to a far greater extent on loans for initial and working capital than did urban-orientated firms a decade earlier.

TABLE 5

CHARACTERISTICS OF ENTERPRISES GROUPED BY RURAL-URBAN ORIENTATION

		Average annual output (constant prices) (Rs '000)	Initial capital (Rs '000)	Average starting date
1973				
Group	I	172	16	1962
	II	83	7.5	1955
	III	44	2.5	1949
	IV	34	5.3	1947
1983				
Group	I	237.6	5	1970
	II	257.7	12	1967
	III	125.7	10.5	1968
	IV	143.9	13.4	1962

Note: Group I = enterprises in which 75 per cent or more of turnover by value goes to Arni
Group II = enterprises in which 50-74 per cent of turnover by value goes to Arni
Group III = enterprises in which 25-49 per cent of turnover by value goes to Arni
Group IV = enterprises in which less that 25 per cent of turnover by value goes to Arni

We may observe a new phase of urbanisation with the establishment of a large number of small consumer goods shops, unrelated directly to agriculture. Thirty-eight per cent of firms surveyed in 1983 had set up within the last decade. There appears to be a high turnover of firms. The small-scale urban economy has been rejuvenated in a process of replacement rather than via the expansion of the bulk of firms existing in 1973. Firms which were large in 1973 remain large now.

HISTORY OF CHANGE: LABOUR AND EMPLOYMENT

The growth in the physical volume and the value of business transacted in the town has been associated with a comparable increase in employment, though most of this increase has again been made up by employment in the silk industry. Because so many more weavers are employed now than in 1973 a much greater proportion of the total number employed in Arni businesses lives in villages. The number of weavers has roughly tripled. The much greater increase in the value of the output of the industry is because more valuable saris with elaborate borders are now being produced. If we exclude weavers, total male employment increased by 92 per cent, employment for male residents of Arni increased by 175 per cent and employment for men living in surrounding villages increased by over 300 per cent. Employment of women (all from Arni itself and peripheral villages) also increased by over 300 per cent. The expansion of business turnover in Arni has, therefore, increased urban employment for people living in the surrounding rural area to a greater extent than for people resident in the town itself.

While employment in the town economy has undergone this marked expansion, however, the real value of wages has generally remained constant or has even declined, though there is of course variation between specific occupations (see Table 6). Over the same period, as data reported above show,

TABLE 6

WAGES (PER MONTH) 1973–83 (Rs)

	1973	1983	1983 deflated to 1973 prices	
			(a)	(b)
Average wage for all employees in sample	116	222	113	101
Weavers	120-150	230-250	116-127	105-114
Twisting factory workers				
(M)	65	160	81	73
(F)	50	140	71	64
Rice mill gumaster	100	225	114	103
Retail shop gumaster	75-100	150-200	76-101	68-91

deflators (a) using general consumer price index for agricultural labour in Tamil Nadu.
(b) using general consumer price index for industrial workers in Tamil Nadu.

gross value added, of which profit is the main component, has *increased* by 15 per cent. Owners of businesses have therefore tended to gain whereas the conditions of livelihood for wage workers have apparently not changed.

HISTORY OF CHANGE: FINANCIAL INSTITUTIONS AND PATTERNS OF INVESTMENT

The commodity flows involved in the greatly expanded business activity of Arni suggest that the economy as a whole is becoming more interdependent and integrated, and they show that expanded agricultural production and higher (*aggregate*) rural incomes have brought about stronger linkages with metropolitan centres. Our observations do not provide strong evidence of the development of decentralised production in this context. The decentralised industry which has grown, the silk industry, is not closely linked with agriculture through its inputs or outputs. Do our observations suggest then, that 'urban bias' − at least as a description − more accurately defines rural-urban relations in this case than the alternative view of the town as a growth centre? Our preliminary discussion showed that the 'urban bias' thesis asserts that financial mechanisms channel money from the country to the town without there being a reverse flow of investment.

The first obvious means whereby financial resources may flow from agriculture into non-agricultural sectors in the town is through interest payments on loans from financial institutions, as Kautsky suggests. Here we examine the recent history of pawnbroking, not in the belief that pawnbroking is necessarily typical of Arni's financial institutions, for pawnbrokers are relatively small-sized lending institutions, but because of the lack of comparability of information on other types of specialist money-lending agencies. We also comment on the new development of 'finance corporations'.[7]

Financial markets were and are segmented. The clientele of pawnbrokers consists of those ineligible for loans from nationalised or co-operative banks, not for lack of security, but because of the small size of the loan needed. It consists of those ineligible for loans from private trade for lack of paddy with which to repay. The pawnbrokers' clientele have inadequate security to enable them to borrow from private finance corporations with a promissory note.

In 1973 this clientele was predominantly agricultural. Eighty-two per cent of money loaned went to small farmers, to meet the cash requirements of crop production, or to agricultural labourers. The remainder went to weavers, coolies and clerks in Arni for gambling or for consumption. Pawnbrokers then registered a large recent increase in demand which they related to the arrival of high-yielding varieties of rice which necessitated increased cash inputs into the production process. Terms and conditions for loans on jewels were variable, particularistic and bore no relation to government regulations on pawning. The average interest rate, 18 per cent, would have guaranteed a net flow of at least Rs 2.6 lakhs into Arni, overwhelmingly from agriculture. Such flows were the main linkage between agriculture and these small financiers, for only 7.5 per cent of pawnbrokers' starting capital came from agriculture and no pawnbrokers had invested profits back into agriculture. Most starting capital was borrowed from relatives who were either pawnbrokers and jewellers, merchants or public sector employees. Investment portfolios were slender, limited to pawnbroking and urban property.

The expansion path encountered in 1973 has continued to the present. While in 1973 there were 44 pawnbrokers, mainly North Indians, there are now 70 firms, most belonging to members of South Indian castes. Total loans have expanded by a factor of five in current prices and have more than doubled in real terms. These financial institutions have greatly increased their trans- actions with the agricultural sector in absolute terms. There is a statistically insignificant decline, however, in the proportion of total loans to the rural sector (from 82 to 78 per cent). The rural clientele and the purposes for which money is borrowed have not changed their character, except that pawnbrokers can identify new borrowers from within Arni: office workers and government employees whose borrowing is for consumption and is related to the timing of their salary payments. Terms and conditions remain very variable. They are more adverse to borrowers than a decade previously. While loan ceilings have increased from Rs 1000 in 1973 to Rs 3-5,000, the percentage of the value of gold or jewels loaned has declined from 60-90 per cent (on average 75 per cent) in 1973 to 40-75 per cent (on average 65 per cent) in 1983, and interest rates have risen from 12-18 per cent per annum in 1973 to 24-36 per cent on gold jewels and to 60-120 per cent on watches and brass vessels. Interest payments from the agricultural sector could be in the region of at least Rs 1.6 million per annum. This flow has increased spectacularly over the decade. Other flows from agriculture remain much as before. The profits of agriculture supplied 15 per cent of pawnbrokers' starting capital. In the main, starting capital was derived from profits from goldsmithing in Arni itself. The increased returns from pawnbroking were invested in commercial and residential property in Arni and vehicles, ploughed back into pawnbroking, invested in shares in finance corporations, and saved for education and dowries rather than returned to agriculture. A quarter of our sample of pawnbrokers were hereditarily landed, all land being rented out.

Thus the evolution of this particular financial institution has provided a mechanism whereby agricultural resources flow to the urban economy and are invested in a further expansion of moneylending institutions and urban property.

A further development which seems to bear out Kautsky's prognosis concerning the relatively increased circulation of money in the town economy is the emergence of 24 'finance corporations' in the last four years. The first of these, and still the largest, was set up in 1979 by nine partners who included the seven largest silk manufacturers of Arni. Each partner put up a capital of Rs 10,000, it being important for taxation reasons to keep the total business capital below Rs 100,000. The minimum size of loans extended by this corporation is currently Rs 10,500 and the maximum Rs 100,000. Loans are short term, rarely for more than three months, and the standard rate of interest payable is 3.6 per cent per month. All the borrowers are urban people such as other silk manufacturers and silk brokers, and also professional moneylenders. The smaller corporations usually have between six and ten partners, who commonly include government staff, teachers, traders and a few larger farmers. The partners will each have put up capital of Rs 5,000 or more and the corporations extend short-term loans on which rates of interest of the order of 3.5 per cent per week are payable. Their clients are mostly (reportedly 90 per cent) small business people and other government servants. Very few agriculturalists make use even of these small corporations, so this new financial institution seems to recirculate money at great velocity but within the town itself.

Financial resources may flow between country and town at slower velocity via the mobilisation of capital for the starting of firms on the one hand and the investment of accumulated profit on the other. Agricultural profits and sales of agricultural land appear always to have been quite important sources of the starting capital for business investment, as Table 7 shows, though never of dominant importance. Neither does our evidence indicate the existence of any particular trend in levels of investment of agricultural profits into business in the recent past. On the other hand the interests of business people in agriculture and agricultural investment have remained constant, and of relatively modest importance. The proportions of business people owning agricultural land in the 1973 and the 1983 samples were not significantly different (44 per cent and 46 per cent of the total, respectively), though the average holding size in 1983 was 7.5 acres when in 1973 it was only 5.4 acres. Roughly 20 per cent of business people in each sample had invested in agriculture, and in only very few cases in either year was agriculture a major avenue for investment. Fewer of the 1983 than of the 1973 sample had purchased agricultural lands from business profits (9 per cent as opposed to 17 per cent), and more had *sold* agricultural land (25 per cent as opposed to 16 per cent). It is just possible that interest in agricultural investment has declined therefore, which may not be surprising in view of the relatively low rates of profit in agriculture as compared with other investments in 1973 [*B. Harriss, 1981: 76-90*].

TABLE 7

ORIGINS OF CAPITAL – ARNI, 1982 ('000 Rs)

Period	No. of firms	Profits from ag.		Profits from trade		Sale of inherited property		Savings from wages		Jewels		Loan		Sale of ag. land		Profits from money-lending		Total raised locally	Total raised outside	Total from ag.	Total
		a	b	a	b	a	b	a	b	a	b	a	b	a	b	a	b				
Pre 1940s	10	5.1	25	37	–	–	2.5	15.1	–	2	–	–	–	–	–	–	–	57.2	27.5	30.1	86.7
1940s	6	36	–	20	–	25	–	–	–	–	–	6	2	–	–	–	–	87	2	36	89
1950s	9	15	–	74	–	–	–	10.3	–	0.6	–	–	30	5	–	–	–	104.9	30	20	134.9
1960s	31	104	–	94.8	5	40	–	28	5.3	–	6	14.5	–	33	–	–	3	314.3	14.3	137	328.6
1970–4	21	55.7	–	148	–	0.5	2	10	10	25	2	10.2	15	10	–	–	–	259.4	34	65.7	293.4
1975–9	23	38	25	151	–	–	–	38.0	7	3	–	38.1	20	3	–	30	–	301.1	52	66	353.1
1980–2	13	20	–	–	–	–	–	4	–	3	54	61	53	–	60	–	75	88	242	80	330.0
TOTAL		323.8		529.8		70		127.7		95.6		249.8		111		108					

a = raised in Arni or immediate hinterland
b = raised outside hinterland

Note: Some of these data clearly rely on respondents' recall over a long period. It is not felt that this affects their reliability as much as agricultural production data, for example, are affected by recall. There may have been under-estimation of the extent of investment using profits from moneylending.

Study of the investment patterns of Arni's businessmen is complicated by the fact that our two snapshots, in 1973 and 1983, catch businesses at different stages in their development. We have attempted to compensate for this by examining the frequency of occurrence of different types of investment in firms of different ages in the 1983 sample. Given the difficulty involved in obtaining accurate and internally comparable data on investment our analysis at this stage is only in terms of frequency and not of financial value. Investment in urban property has generally been the most important single focus (64 per cent of businesses have made this kind of investment). Much of this has been in houses, although 19 per cent have invested in shops. Almost as high a proportion (55 per cent) have invested business profits in one or other form of moneylending, and only trading in consumer goods has attracted a comparable number of businessmen (41 per cent) – though especially amongst the younger firms and for reasons suggested earlier.

In short, there is not a great deal of evidence here that 'those in the urban centre' put much surplus value back into circulation in the rural hinterland, or do so in such a way that Arni functions as a 'growth pole'. Rather the evidence (i) shows some drawing of financial resources from agricultural for urban business investment; (ii) suggests a relatively weak and possibly declining interest in agricultural investment by urban business people; and (iii) indicates patterns of investment which are urban (property), or which – according to our analysis of pawnbroking – may tend to draw further funds from agriculture (moneylending), or which connect the town more closely with metropolitan centres (trade in consumer goods). Of course it is true that the silk industry in particular, and urban business in general, have been paying wages to absolutely and relatively increasing numbers of rural dwellers. But we saw that real wages have generally remained more or less constant, while profits – to judge from the trend of gross value added on turnover – have increased. Still, we estimate that the total sum paid in wages to rural dwellers employed by Arni businesses would have been around Rs 50 million in 1983, which must have compensated for some, at least, of the transfers of money from country to town in the form of interest payments. This figure of Rs 50 million works out, on a per capita basis, to be the equivalent of 10 per cent of the average per capita expenditure by rural dwellers in Arni that we reported above. The town *does* have generative functions in relation to its hinterland, but – *pace* Mellor's proposition – these have not developed primarily as a result of the expansion of agricultural production in the region.

CONCLUSIONS

The 'real world' of Arni and its hinterland, as we have observed it and allowing for the acute difficulties of measurement, appears much more complicated than do hinterland-small town relations in the theoretical schemes which we sketched out at the beginning. The fact that average rural effective demand has probably increased by about twice as much as urban effective demand indicates a relative shift in favour of the 'rural' sector, as geographically defined, in a period of agricultural expansion. While this finding might appear to go against the prognosis of the full 'urban bias' argument we do not yet know how widely distributed this increase in spending power has been within the rural population.[8] If, as seems possible, the increased demand has come disproportionately from the larger farmers, then it would be possible for a supporter of Lipton's thesis to argue that the finding is *not* inconsistent with the 'urban bias' argument. (It would be taken as evidence that the dominant rural group has been compensated for its part in the 'urban class alliance'.) Other important findings of our study clearly support the view that the urban centre of Arni is 'parasitic' rather than 'generative' in relation to its rural hinterland. It is true that there has been considerable growth in one decentralised industry – the silk handloom industry. But neither through inputs nor through outputs is this industry strongly linked with the agricultural economy of the region, and its growth is not directly or indirectly due to the expansion of the local agricultural economy, for this has contributed insignificantly to the demand for silk saris. The industry is responsible for increasing employment for rural people, and by this means for transferring some money in the form of wages to the hinterland. But the value of wages in relation to turnover is small in comparison with the profits which accrue to the urban silk manufacturers, and which are not invested in the rural economy or very much in other productive activities. In general it appears that agricultural expansion has *not* encouraged that decentralised labour-intensive production which would help to make Arni a 'generative growth centre', but has rather brought about much stronger metropolitan trading links. These mean that there is a relatively greater flow of money from Arni to the big city centres. In this respect, as well as through the transfer of money from the hinterland to Arni through financial institutions, and through the investment patterns of Arni businessmen, it seems to us that the town plays a role in relation to the hinterland which corresponds more closely with Lipton's model than with Mellor's. It is not surprising that Mellor's strategy should *not* be seen to be working out in practice when policies which he identified as being essential for it are not being pursued with vigour in Tamil Nadu. But there must be no illusions about the practical and political difficulties involved in implementing a policy of small-scale industrialisation for the production, mainly of consumer goods.

   To argue that there is an 'urban bias' in the relations of a small town with its hinterland (in the sense that it plays a 'parasitic' rather than a 'generative' role) does not necessarily imply an acceptance of Lipton's model as an explanatory framework. We have pointed out that his thesis postulates a political alliance of large farmers and of dominant urban groups, and that it is the power and the policy preferences of this coalition which determines the 'bias' that is observed in resource flows and allocations. The argument that the 'bias' which we have observed can be explained more adequately in these terms than by reference to a model like Kautsky's of the development of commodity production remains, to say the least, contentious.

NOTES

1.   For a discussion of the application of the 'growth centre' concept in Indian planning, see B. Harriss [*1976a*].

2. Washbrook's analysis of the political economy of the dryland districts of Tamil Nadu in the later nineteenth and early twentieth centuries includes an account of the increasing integration of rural and urban economic interests by a small class of dominant land controllers [*Washbrook, 1976*]. His account suggests that processes like those referred to by Kautsky had effect. But Washbrook too argues that these processes are to be explained principally by reference to the effects of the increased commercialisation of the period.

3. Our procedure, of drawing up a census by means of observation, is clearly susceptible to some errors. It is also time-consuming. But there is no other way of proceeding. Official lists, such as the Census of the Assistant Inspector of Labour, and the List of Dangerous and Offensive Trades (etc.), are all incomplete and also inconsistent with each other.

4. Constraints of space preclude the publication here of the results of our census of urban activities in 1973 and 1982–3.

5. As yet we have no contemporary data for milk, cattle and groundnuts.

6. The estimations in this paragraph imply that all the people in the hinterland of the town trade through Arni. This is a simplifying assumption for there are smaller commercial centres within the hinterland [*see B. Harriss, 1976b: 174*].

7. The major moneylending of Arni consists of advances in cash or kind by traders against repayment, post harvest, in cash or kind.

8. The results of the research conducted in North Arcot District in 1982–3, by a team from IFPRI and the Tamil Nadu Agricultural University, will provide information on this point.

REFERENCES

Farmer, B. H. (ed.), 1977, *Green Revolution? Technology and Change in Rice-growing Areas of Tamil Nadu and Sri Lanka*, London: Macmillan.

Harriss, B., 1976a, 'The Indian Ideology of Growth Centres', *Area*, 8, 2, pp. 263-9.

Harriss, B., 1976b, 'Rural-Urban Economic Transactions: a Case Study from India and Sri Lanka', in, S.W.R. de Samarasinghe (ed.), *Agriculture in the Peasant Sector of Sri Lanka*, Peradeniya: Ceylon Studies Seminar.

Harriss, B., 1981, *Transitional Trade and Rural Development*, New Delhi: Vikas.

Harriss, J., 1982, *Capitalism and Peasant Farming: Agrarian Structure and Ideology in Northern Tamil Nadu*, Bombay: Oxford University Press.

Harvey, D., 1973, *Social Justice and the City*, London: Edward Arnold.

International Food Policy Research Institute, 1980, *Proposal for Study of the Growth Linkages of the Green Revolution*, Washington D.C. (mimeo).

Lipton, M., 1977, *Why Poor People Stay Poor*, London: Temple Smith.

Mellor, J., 1976, *The New Economics of Growth: a Strategy for India and the Developing World*, Ithaca and London: Cornell University Press.

Washbrook, D. A., 1976, *The Emergence of Provincial Politics: the Madras Presidency, 1870–1920*, Cambridge: Cambridge University Press.

Categorising Space: Urban-Rural or Core-Periphery in Sri Lanka

By Mick Moore*

The notion of a clash between distinctive urban and rural interests does not provide a convincing explanation either of the pattern of public resource allocation in Sri Lanka or of the political conflicts which underlie these allocations. The concept of a core-periphery continuum, centred around a densely populated urban and rural region incorporating the capital city, does however furnish a useful framework for the analysis of the politics of agricultural policy. The applicability of this framework to Sri Lanka is in large part the result of contingent historical, topographical and agro-climatic factors, but analysis centred around this framework does illustrate the importance of certain factors of general significance to the analysis of rural-urban politics.

INTRODUCTION[1]

Is Sri Lanka urban-biased? Any reader who has delved thus far into this collection will know better than to anticipate a simple answer. It depends in the first place on what the question means. Does 'urban bias' refer to the constellation of political forces which determine public sector resource allocations, or to the pattern of resource allocation itself? On the first interpretation let us withhold comment for the moment. If the second interpretation is adopted then, for Sri Lanka in the period since the Second World War or independence (1948), the answer is ambiguous.

On the one hand the independent Sri Lankan policy has accomplished a massive transfer of material resources from agricultural producers to the state and to food consumers. Five main mechanisms have been employed:[2]

1. Heavy direct taxes on exports of tea, rubber and coconuts, the mainstays of the Sri Lankan economy and balance of payments.
2. An overvalued exchange rate, combined in the period 1967–77 with a dual exchange rate regime, which jointly and individually served to redirect a proportion of the world market value of these cash crop exports from the exporters and producers to the state and to domestic importers.
3. Retail price controls and, more importantly, periodic bans on the export of coconut products, which kept domestic consumer prices low at the expense of the earnings of those producers who marketed coconuts.

* Institute of Development Studies, University of Sussex. The author is grateful to Don Funnell, John Harriss, Michael Lipton and Gavin Williams for useful comments on an earlier draft, but wishes to make it explicit that none of them are responsible for the errors. At least one of them disagrees quite fundamentally with the method and the conclusions.

4. The import of wheat flour and rice at artifically low prices due to the over-valuation of the rupee. This helped depress the market price for the most important domestic smallholder crop, paddy.
5. Sales of imported foodgrains at a loss by the Food Commissioner, which further depressed the market price received by domestic paddy producers.

The export crops, especially tea and to a lesser extent rubber, are mainly, though decreasingly, produced on large estates, the bulk of which were nationalised in the early 1970s. That the estate sector has been the milch cow for government financing since independence[3] is widely recognised. It is equally widely believed that the smallholder sector, especially paddy producers, have been the beneficiaries of state largesse. The contrast is however over-drawn. It is true that the paddy sector taken as a whole has been a net beneficiary of government action, mainly via large expenditures on irrigation and land development in the extreme periphery (Map 1). The number of beneficiaries is however small in relation to the total number of paddy farmers. And taken as a whole the smallholder sector, including smallholder producers of tea, rubber and coconuts, has been a net victim of 'urban bias' through public intervention in the pricing of agricultural inputs and outputs. In the early 1970s the net transfer of resources from smallholder producers of export cash crops via public action was three times as large as the net transfer to paddy producers [*Moore, 1981: 464*]. Using categories as aggregated as 'agriculture' and 'non-agriculture', agriculture as a whole (and the smallholder sub-sector) have been victims of 'urban bias' in the sphere of input and output pricing.

On the other hand, it is far less easy to plaster the label 'urban-biased' on Sri Lanka if one examines the pattern of public expenditure. The absence of any detailed analysis of the inter-sectoral distribution of spending is incon-venient but for present purposes unimportant, considering the excellence of Sri Lanka's record in providing a wide range of welfare services, notably free education, health care and subsidised food rations, to a large proportion of its total population, and thus necessarily to much of that proportion (78 per cent in 1981) defined as rural. When it became fashionable in the 1970s to construct physical quality of life indices covering such variables as infant mortality rates, life expectancy and literacy, Sri Lanka emerged as having achieved a physical quality of life for its citizens which − with the important exception of Indian Tamil estate labourers − was extraordinarily high in relation to its low income levels [*Isenman, 1980*]. It is a further indicator of the extent of the rural impact of public expenditure that, very unusually among developing countries, Sri Lanka has experienced very low rates of net rural-urban migration since independence, and virtually none between the censuses of 1963 and 1981.[4] Rural living remains relatively attractive.

That the appropriateness to Sri Lanka of the term 'urban bias' is so variously a function of the definitions adopted is certainly grounds for suspecting that the political process underlying public resource allocation revolves around axes considerably more complex than the conflict of rural and urban interests. This paper makes a less qualified claim. To understand conflicts of interest over the allocation of resources between agriculture and non-agriculture and between different categories of agriculturalists, the

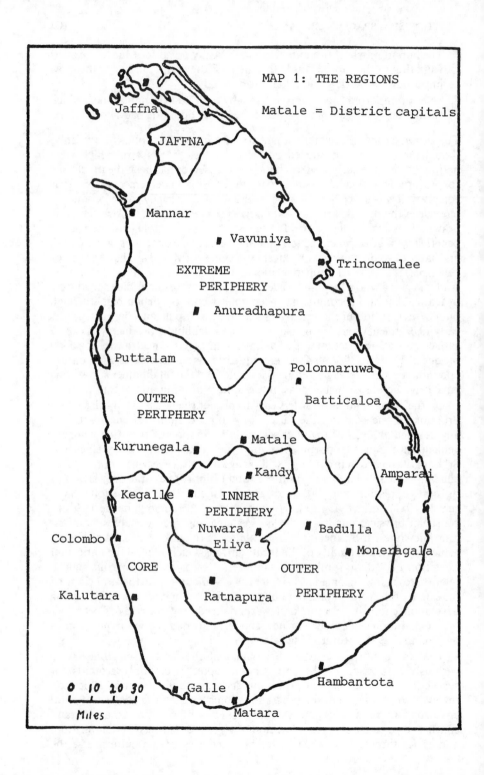

MAP 1: THE REGIONS

Matale = District capitals

Jaffna

JAFFNA

Mannar

Vavuniya

Trincomalee

EXTREME
PERIPHERY

Anuradhapura

Puttalam

Polonnaruwa

Batticaloa

OUTER
PERIPHERY

Kurunegala

Matale

Kandy

Amparai

Kegalle

INNER
PERIPHERY

Colombo

Nuwara
Eliya

Badulla

Moneragala

CORE

OUTER
PERIPHERY

Kalutara

Ratnapura

0 10 20 30

Miles

Galle

Hambantota

Matara

rural-urban dichotomy is of very limited use. Yet interest group and class analysis is also inadequate without a genuine spatial — as opposed to a sectoral — dimension. For Sri Lanka, one can locate interest group and class analysis by using the concept of a core-periphery continuum. The capital, Colombo, lies at the very heart of the core. But the adjacent rural areas have both different interests from and more power than the more distant rural areas, and are most usefully categorised as part of the core. The population of the core exercises disproportionate influence in various senses and for various reasons. The long-established political and bureaucratic elite is concentrated in the core, both residentially and in the sense that its sources of income and of patronage and thus local-level political support are drawn from core areas. This interacts with spatial proximity to give the core population generally privileged access to politicians and the public bureaucracy. The core is the historical locus of the Sri Lankan political system. The pattern of party and interest group conflict reflects the socio-economic structure of the core. The economic policy issues of greatest objective concern to the periphery, especially agricultural product pricing, are crowded off the national political agenda.

It is important to establish from the outset the modesty of the claims made here for the utility of the core-periphery concept. It is used here as a framework for organising data rather than as any kind of rigorous model.[5] It helps to draw attention to and to analyse the consequences of the greater political power of a large segment of the population. But it does *not* imply the absolute dominance of core over periphery in all spheres. Nor does it imply any notion of spatial hierarchies *à la* Gunder Frank [*1969*], in which surplus value is consistently extracted from the periphery and concentrated in the core.

The core-periphery concept does not provide a complete framework for understanding Sri Lankan politics, for which an appreciation of interest conflicts of a broadly 'class' nature, including conflicts between core-located groups, is essential. One of the advantages which this concept has over the 'urban bias' analysis of Michael Lipton [*1977*] is that it allows one to separate 'class' analysis from sectoral/spatial analysis, while accepting that the two are related. Indeed the core-periphery continuum is so useful because distance from the core is closely associated with differences in rural economic activity patterns, and thus differences in political interests; it is a concept which encapsulates, initially in a purely descriptive sense, spatial-cum-economic variation.

The core-periphery concept does not imply any generalisable model of the functioning of national polities or economies. The high degree of appropriateness to the Sri Lankan case results in part from certain contingent historical, climatic and agro-climatic factors. The sole element which is generalisable is the recognition of the importance of distance — as opposed to simply rural/urban sectoral location — as a political variable. Urbanites dwelling near the seat of government are indeed well-placed to have their voices heard [*Smith, 1776: 222-33; Lipton, 1977: 13*]. But those rural dwellers living near the capital are also better placed than those from distant areas to influence politics, both in the more formal sense of the term (the making of governments and policy decisions) and the day-to-day routines of administrative actions.

ORGANISATION

Immediately below it is argued that the discrete rural and urban categories cannot easily be applied in Sri Lanka without considerable ambiguity and imprecision. It is a short step from this to a regional core-periphery categorisation which demarcates consistent patterns of intra-rural differentiation in economic activities, coinciding with a degree of access to the capital. The historical, topographical and agro-climatic correlates and causes of this core-periphery pattern are then summarised. Finally, it is demonstrated that this pattern provides a useful framework for beginning to understand how conflicts over material resources – especially agricultural resources – have arisen and been pursued.

Although a continuous gradation between core and periphery is intrinsic to the core-periphery concept, one must make some discrete divisions between territorial spaces in order to bring quantitative data to bear. The categorisation, based on aggregating groups of administrative districts, is summarised in Map 1. Based originally on agro-climatic criteria, this categorisation is also useful for present purposes as it also encapsulates roughly coincident areal differences in: effective access to Colombo; degree of historical contact and involvement with Western culture, mercantile capitalism and large-scale formal organisation, especially public bureaucracy; and population density.[6]

Sri Lanka has been divided into five regions. Apart from the core, the inner periphery, the outer periphery and the extreme periphery, Jaffna, for reasons explained below, stands alone as a kind of sub-core for the Sri Lanka Tamil population, and one which can usefully be seen as being in conflict with the Colombo core.

URBAN AND RURAL IN SRI LANKA

Of the range of meanings which are variously implicit in the juxtaposition of the terms 'urban' and 'rural' [*Moore, this volume*], three – the ecological, the functional and the occupational – can usefully be examined here. The available data do not permit any fruitful comment on the rather doubtful sociological perspective on this question: that urbanness and rurality are each associated with different and generic patterns of social interaction [ibid.]. One might however mention in passing that, although many data series on Sri Lanka use a tripartite sectoral population division – urban, rural and estate – in this paper the term 'rural' subsumes the latter two. The question of the degree of sociological distinctiveness of the estate sector is not germane to this paper.[7]

At the most elementary level the difference between urban and rural is one of ecology or landscape. Rural implies the predominance of natural-occurring environmental features – vegetation, watercourses, animals, etc. – while urban suggests the predominance of structures made of artificial materials, notably buildings, roads and vehicles. It is an extension of this perspective to identify urbanness with densely-clustered human populations.

This minimal definition of the rural-urban divide is more difficult to operationalise for Sri Lanka than for many other countries. Settlement is traditionally dispersed rather than nucleated, each household standing alone in the midst of a cultivated homestead.[8] Wherever possible, this practice is also followed in towns. Most of the rural nucleation which does exist is related to the high degree of commercialisation of rural life and to very high rates of use of road transport. One consequence is a high preference for roadside homesites, and another the prevalence of small bazaars, invariably clustered around road junctions and bus-stops, which constitute the major foci of economic and social activities. 'Villages' are not clearly separated one from another, and there is an unbroken continuum from the very small local bazaar to the commercial centre large enough to be classified as a town. Add to this the very high rural population densities of much of the core and inner periphery regions (Table 1, row c) and one can understand why, for example, the traveller on the main road along the crowded south-western coastal strip often has very little visual basis for deciding whether he is in an 'urban' or a 'rural' area. Official categorisations of rural and urban areas correspondingly often appear rather arbitrary.

Some comment on the usefulness and feasibility of a functional classification of rural and urban areas is implicit in the preceding paragraph. The essence of this approach is to classify settlements according to the nature and extent of the commercial, administrative, etc. services which they provide to surrounding populations. The key concept is the economic geographers' term 'central places'. One can in principle demarcate as 'urban' those centres providing more than a minimum level of service functions, as well as rank towns by function. However, in Sri Lanka the prevalence of small 'central places' at local level and the existence of an apparently unbroken continuum by scale makes it difficult to draw any useful and non-arbitrary dividing line between 'urban' and 'village' centres. Sri Lankans commonly use the English word 'town' to describe local centres which to the outsider appear in some indefinable sense to be evidently rural.

The third approach to the urban-rural dichotomy is to look at occupations, specifically for an association of rural with agriculture and urban with non-agriculture. National level statistics initially indicate this to be a satisfactory procedure. In 1971, less than 7 per cent of the urban population was employed in agriculture, compared to 59 per cent of the rural population, even if this still left the great majority (62 per cent) of those employed in non-agriculture living in rural areas. The inter-regional differences are however considerable (Table 1, row j). In 1971 only 39 per cent of the rural population of the core region were employed in agriculture, while in the extreme periphery the figure was 71 per cent. The absolute difference between the two figures was the same as the difference between the rural core and all urban areas.

CORE AND PERIPHERY

The relative clarity and consistency of inter-regional socio-economic differences, as illustrated by the statistics in Table 1, is the direct obverse and consequence of the absence of a clear urban-rural dividing line, especially within the core region. The figures reveal that the rural areas of the core are in many respects similar to urban areas: populations are dense, levels of school

TABLE 1

SELECTED INDICATORS OF REGIONAL SOCIO-ECONOMIC DIFFERENTIATION, EARLY 1970s[1]

Region	Core	Inner peri-phery	Outer peri-phery	Extreme peri-phery	Jaffna	Sri Lanka
(a) Rural population (thousand persons)	2,867	2,072	2,946	1,490	468	9,482
(b) % of regional population defined as rural.	52%	90%	92%	84%	45%	78%
(c) Persons per square kilometre	718	436	139	65	281	196
(d) % of population aged 5-24 { urban	49%	52%	49%	44%	57%	49%
(e) years attending school { rural	50%	44%	43%	39%	53%	45%
(f) $\frac{d}{e}$	0.97	1.18	1.16	1.14	1.08	1.09
(g) % of employed population { urban	9%	11%	10%	11%	10%	11%
(h) in professional(2) jobs { rural	5%	3%	3%	3%	7%	4%
(i) $\frac{g}{h}$	1.63	3.61	3.12	4.31	1.48	2.37
(j) % of employed rural population { Agriculture(3)	39%	70%	63%	71%	42%	61%
(k) working primarily in { Paddy production	15%	16%	37%	53%	16%	27%
(l) % of farm operators spending 50%+ of their time in agricultural work.	59%	69%	75%	77%	55%	68%
(m) Estimated % of paddy farming household not producing enough paddy to meet household food needs. (4)	82%	67%	66%	19%	74%	61%

(1) The data in rows (a)-(k) relate to 1971, those in row (j) to 1973, and those in row (k) to 1976.

(2) 'Professional employment' refers to occupational code 0/1 ('Professional, technical and related workers'), constituting 5% of the total workforce in 1971. 60% of those included within it were schoolteachers, and the other major employments, in order of magnitude, were: indigenous ('ayurvedic') physicians; mechanical and civil engineering technicians; medical doctors; professional midwives; creative artists; pharmacists; religious func-tionaries; accountants; engineers; and lawyers. It does not include clerical workers.

(3) Relates to the agriculture, forestry, fishing and hunting industrial category; the numbers in the latter three categories are negligible.

(4) These estimates do not take into consideration the availability of public rice rations, and constitute slight over-estimates because no data were available to permit adjustment for the fact that households with larger land areas probably contain above-average numbers of people. The inter-regional differences are not affected.

Sources: (a) and (b) - 1971 Census of Population, Volume 2, Part 1: Table 4; (c) - 1971 Census of Population, General Report: Table 3.1; (d) and (e) - 1971 Census of Population, Volume 1, Parts 1-22: Table 12; (g) and (h) - Ibid.: Table 16; (j) and (k) - Ibid.: Table 17; (l) - 1973 Census of Agriculture, General Report: Table 3; (m) - Moore, 1980.

attendance high, and the proportions of the work force engaged in agriculture and in professional occupations low and high respectively. As is evident from the first four figures in rows (f) and (i) or Table 1, the differences between urban and rural areas in respect of access to education and professional employment are much sharper within the core than in the periphery. It is in the periphery that the urban-rural divide appears most clear cut.

There is little doubt that the main single variable underlying this pattern is population density. It is the dense clustering of people in the rural core which explains why its population is so well-provided with public services and infrastructure like schools, roads, medical care and communication facilities, why they can command *in situ* the services of relatively highly paid and educated professionals, why relatively small proportions of people can find employment in agriculture, and why so many of those who do succeed are obliged to combine this with non-agricultural employment (Table 1, row l). It is population numbers, and thus aggregate need and demand for services per square kilometre, which matter rather than per capita income levels. Once allowance is made for the concentration of high income earners in Colombo, available statistics do not indicate that the rural population of the core are especially non-poor in the Sri Lankan context. Indeed, the acute scarcity of land can mean extreme hardship for families without land or access to stable non-agricultural employment.

The diehard advocates of sectoral analysis might be tempted to suggest a redefinition of terms. Since the rural core is not really agricultural, perhaps one should redraw the urban-rural line to distinguish the densely-populated areas, whether formally rural or urban, from the (agricultural) remainder? Apart from injecting so much elasticity into conventional terminology as to make dialogue and analysis almost impossible, this would lead one to ignore a crucial feature of the core-periphery pattern in Sri Lanka: the *juxtaposition* of the densely-populated rural areas to the capital city. While such a juxtaposition is by no means unusual, it is not inevitable, and in the Sri Lankan case is contingent upon a number of historical, topographical and agro-climatic factors to which we now turn.

THE EVOLUTION OF REGIONAL PATTERNS

When in the fifteenth century European traders began to encroach upon its trade, Sri Lanka was an important source of such valuable commodities as cinnamon, gems, arecanut and elephants and an importer of Indian rice. Control over trade was the material base for the Sri Lankan kingdoms based in the south-western quadrant of the island – both the central Kandyan hills (approximately our 'inner periphery') and the Low Country (approximately our 'core' region) – where most of the population was concentrated. Trade was channelled through a string of ports along the south-western coast. Muslim traders had a foothold in these ports and also, as they do today, a considerable trading and farming presence along the east coast around Batticaloa. A long-standing Sri Lanka Tamil polity based on Jaffna was closely connected to Tamil Nadu in India across the narrow, shallow Palk Strait, but separated from the Sinhalese areas in the south-west by the wide no-man's-land of sparsely populated Dry Zone jungle, which more or less corresponds to our extreme periphery region.

The establishment of European (Portuguese) control over the Low Country began in the early sixteenth century and was completed by the early seventeenth century. The loci of this control were the south-western ports. Urban life however did not develop on a large scale, partly because of continual warfare. Apart from European rivalries, each successive conqueror – Portuguese, Dutch and British – had to face the opposition of the Kandyan kingdom, ensconced in the central hills and protected from superior European firepower by difficult terrain. When Kandy finally came under British control in 1815, the Sinhalese of the Low Country had been under European rule for two centuries and subject to major European influences for three. These contrasting experiences helped to crystallise a divergence between Kandyan and Low Country Sinhalese which continues to have considerable political significance. Coastal location, foreign contact, trade and continual immigration from India had probably already engendered in the Low Country a society which was relatively loosely-structured, innovative and entrepreneurial, while Kandy remained feudal, hierarchic, conservative and subject to the rule of those who controlled the land. The adaptation of the Low Country Sinhalese to Christianity, commerce, formal education and European culture only exacerbated this difference, which emerged also at the levels of ideology and consciousness. Having resisted Europeans for two centuries and maintained a Buddhist kingdom, Kandyans saw themselves as the repository of pure Sinhalese and Buddhist traditions and culture. The Low Country people by contrast saw in the Kandyans conservatism, lack of education and commercial naivety.

These conflicting perceptions became more pointed after the Kandyan hills were 'opened up' for plantation development, first for coffee production in the 1840s, and then, from the 1870s, for tea. The commercial opportunities which emerged in such spheres as wholesale and retail trade, estate supply, land clearance and development under contract, and transport services were to a large extent seized by Low Country Sinhalese. The Low Country already had a substantial nucleus of mercantile capitalists, especially from the population groups located on the coastal fringe. The general expansion of the plantation economy provided them with many new opportunities [*Roberts, 1982*].

A further consequence of plantation development in the Kandyan areas was the emergence of Colombo as the premier port and city in the Island. It had previously been no more than *primus inter pares*, and closely rivalled by the southern port of Galle. However the development of the Kandy-Colombo road (and later, railway) as the main supply and export route into the plantation areas, and the decline of sailing ships, for which Galle offered technical advantages, in favour of coal power, led to the rapid development of Colombo and the relative demise of Galle and the other ports, none of which offered deep-water anchorages. Today, Colombo 'stands like a Triton among the minnows' [*Farmer, 1972: 812*], and has a population fifteen times larger than the second-ranking urban area, Jaffna.

This process of concentration of urban activities in Colombo did not however impair the position of the Low Country Sinhalese as a whole, including those from the southern districts of Galle and Matara, as the leaders of commercial, educational and political development among the Sinhalese. Taking advantage of their established position and easy transport along the coast, the Low Country people took a large proportion of educational and public sector posts, sharing them with other minorities, notably Burghers (Eurasians) and Sri Lanka Tamils to the near-exclusion of the Kandyan Sinhalese (and the total exclusion of the Indian Tamil estate population). When in the early twentieth century Sri Lankan capitalists began to invest in plantations on a large scale, it was the Low Country Sinhalese (along with Sri Lanka Tamils and members of a few other small minority groups of recent Indian origin – Chetties, Borahs, etc.) who were most prominent. Most Sri Lankan-owned estates were either in or on the fringes of the Low Country – tea estates in the upland areas of Galle and Matara, rubber estates in the interior of all the Low Country districts and, above all, coconut estates in the north of Colombo district and in the adjacent Kurunegala and Kegalle districts.

REGION AND STATE

In comparative perspective one of the distinguishing features of Sri Lanka's experience of integration into the global economy under colonial rule was the extent of development of a Sri Lankan capitalist class. Further, mercantile capitalism, plantation ownership and incipient industrial capitalism provided the material base from which this class expanded into advanced Western education, the professions and local political leadership, thus developing the characteristics of an all-round elite – a distinctive group of people, socialised around similar Western culture and educational experience, which provided leadership in economic, social and political spheres. This elite and the much more numerous 'middle class' which underpinned it were able to stake a successful early claim to succeed the British. In 1931 Sri Lanka was granted almost complete domestic political autonomy under a government elected by universal adult franchise. Before independence the 'localisation' of the public service was almost complete.

While in some degree representative of almost all ethnic and social groups, regions and spheres of economic activity, both the elite and the middle-class were in composition strongly concentrated in particular regions. The elite, especially that section which took over political leadership under universal franchise, was comprised largely of Low Country Sinhalese, almost all resident in Colombo itself, but generally having strong local political bases in the Low Country where their estates were located. There has also been a Kandyan element among the Sinhalese elite, while the outer and extreme peripheries are hardly represented at all. The 'middle class' (or 'middle classes'), formed mainly around trading and education and jobs in the public sector and in related white-collar occupations – education, journalism, law, etc. – represented above all the Low Country and Jaffna. Indeed, there are close parallels to be drawn between Jaffna, the heartland of Sri Lanka Tamil culture, and the Low Country, especially the southern districts of Galle and Matara. Both areas are relatively distant from the capital, ill-favoured by nature, lacking local industry, dependent locally on relatively unproductive small-scale agriculture, and historically outward-looking. Both developed a major stake in island-wide trading and in white-collar occupations, especially in the public sector. Both experienced a continual population movement to and from Colombo, and saw public sector employment, underpinned by excellent local educational facilities, as one of their primary 'industries'. If the state is to be viewed in terms of the origins of the people who drew a (generally good) material sustenance from occupying positions within its apparatuses, then the Sri Lankan state, especially in the late colonial and early post-independence period, was to a large degree a Low Country Sinhalese – and secondarily a Sri Lanka Tamil – state.

Cultural nationalism and mass politicisation have almost inevitably entailed a reaction against the colonial state. In Sri Lanka the dominant aspect of this process has been the substantive and symbolic 'Sinhalisation' of the state since 1956. Apart from the small Westernised Burgher population, many of whom have emigrated, the main victims have been the Tamils: the Indian Tamil estate population, most of whom were disenfranchised in 1948 and whose numbers have remained more or less constant in absolute terms, thus declining in proportionate terms because of 'repatriation' to India; and above all the Sri Lanka Tamils, whose shares in advanced education and public sector employment have been methodically cut back to something nearer their (13 per cent, in 1971) proportion of the population. At the same time, and in a far quieter fashion, the traditionally-disadvantaged Kandyan Sinhalese have successfully asserted a claim to a larger share of public resources and a greater role in the state apparatus. Their main vehicle has been the Sri Lanka Freedom Party (SLFP) governments of 1960–5 and 1970–7 led by the Kandyan Mrs Sirimavo Bandaranaike and a coterie of Kandyans, most of them from prestigious land-owning families.[9]

However, the strength of the 'Kandyan reaction' has not been such as to nullify the overall Low Country domination of the Sri Lankan polity. It is to an analysis of this domination that we now turn.

REGIONS AND POLITICAL POWER

In justifying the assertion that the core region (Low Country) has been dominant in the post-independence Sri Lankan polity one cannot avoid some initial discussion of the concept of political power itself. The central problem of concern to us was originally elaborated in what has become known as the 'community decision-making debate' [*Lukes, 1974*]. And the relevant conclusion is that one cannot adequately measure and evaluate the relative power of different actors simply by studying the outcome of conflicts which have become political 'issues', i.e. which have entered into the conscious agenda of politics. For one of the most effective methods of exercising power by the forces of the *status quo* is to prevent threatening potential questions from ever becoming political 'issues' at all. The classic example quoted is the success of industrial interests in preventing factory pollution from ever becoming a matter of concern in local politics [*Lukes, 1974: 42-5*]. Power resides firstly in the ability to set the political agenda, and only secondarily in the ability to influence the outcome of issues on the agenda. It follows that any adequate evaluation of relative power must be based on a diagnosis of what are the 'objective' interests of the parties potentially involved, and thus on a determination of the *potential* political issues. Conservative scholars argue, not without some justification, that this method is potentially dangerous. Given the absence of any single criterion for assessing 'interests' once 'demands' are rejected as inadequate, there is nothing to prevent the analyst from attributing whatever 'objective interests' he cares to light upon to any given population. In particular, the conservatives are worried about the common Marxian method of assuming that class polarisation, the weakening of capitalism and proletarian revolution are the dominant 'objective interests' of working classes. While respecting this concern, the present author believes that their own method makes a great deal of the most interesting and important political analysis impossible. The question of the differences between the actual and the potential political agenda is central to this paper.

Trying to make the best of limited data, the argument for the usefulness of the core-periphery concept for the analysis of the Sri Lankan polity proceeds as follows. It is first demonstrated that this polity is dominated by personnnel from the core region. Then it is argued that the main thrust of agricultural policy, which has been to provide generous input subsidies and services to smallholders but to depress farm output prices, has been to the relative advantage of the core both because of differences between core and periphery in farm structure and economy and because of the greater *de facto* ability of the core population to get control of scarce subsidised inputs. The conclusion is that the political agenda as a whole has been dominated by established conflicts within the core, and between the core and Jaffna, thus allowing no scope for the peripheral agricultural populations to assert their interests in high producer prices and more *efficient* (rather than simply more) publicly-provided services.

REGION AND POLITICAL LEADERSHIP

To demonstrate that people from a given area predominate in the high-level positions in any polity is not in itself conclusive evidence that the interests of that region are pre-eminent. It is however good presumptive evidence, especially when it conforms to other parts of a total picture.

The prevalence of Low Country Sinhalese in public employment has been discussed in general terms above. The background factor of privileged access to higher education has been documented in detail by Uswatte-Aratchi [*1974*]. It is a relatively simple matter to demonstrate the pre-eminent role of personnel from the core region in high elective political positions, a pre-eminence that tends to increase the higher up the scale one goes.

Since independence Sri Lanka has had seven elected heads of government, all of them prime ministers until the introduction of the post of Executive President in 1978. One represented a Colombo city electorate (J. R. Jayawardene); three sat for rural Colombo district electorates (Dudley Senanayake, S.W.R.D. Bandaranaike and Mrs S. Bandaranaike), and W. Dahanayake represented Galle town in the core region. The remaining two,

D. S. Senanayake and J. L. Kotelawala, represented electorates in the areas where their families owned large coconut estates and which, while outside the core region as defined here, are in fact only just over the boundary, in Kegalle and Kurunegala districts respectively. The dominance of the core region as a whole, not just Colombo city, is evident. The same pattern is found in the location of the electorates of successive finance ministers, who have probably on average been the most powerful ministers after the elected heads of government. In the 36 years between 1947 and 1983 the finance portfolio has been held by representatives of core electorates for all but six and a half years.[10]

Table 2 indicates a similar although less marked pattern in respect of all cabinet ministers. Although the peripheries have been deliberately over-represented in the allocation of parliamentary seats [11] (Table 2, row d), both

TABLE 2

REGIONAL LOCATION OF ELECTORATES OF ELECTED CABINET MINISTERS, 1947–77[1]

	Region	Core	Inner peri-phery	Outer peri-phery	Extreme peri-phery	Jaffna	Total
(a)	Location of electorates of elected Cabinet Ministers − number	51	24	12	18[4]	1	106
(b)	Location of electorates of elected Cabinet Ministers − %	48%	23%	11%	17%	1%	100%
(c)	% distribution of all Parliamentary electorates (2)	33%	18%	25%	17%	7%	100%
(d)	Average number of persons per Parliamentary electorate, 1963 (thousands) (3)	78	75	69	56	56	70

(1) The figures relate to the first cabinet formed after each of the eight general elections between 1947 and 1977, and exclude 13 cabinet posts held by non-elected Senators between 1947 and 1965.

(2) Parliamentary electorates were distributed under three different delimitations − 1946, 1959 and 1976. The inter-regional distribution of electorates however hardly varied at all. The figure given here is the average.

(3) These figures are calculated from the 1963 census population data and the 1959 demarcation of Parliamentary electorates.

(4) Nine of these eighteen were Tamils or Muslims.

Source: De Silva, G.P.S.H., A Statistical Survey of Elections to the Legislatures of Sri Lanka, 1911–1977, Colombo, Marga Institute, 1979; and Census of Population 1971, Volume 2, Part 1: Table 4.

the core and the inner periphery regions have provided larger proportions of cabinet ministers than MPs.[12] The apparent lack of under-representation of the extreme periphery is an indirect consequence of the fact that almost every cabinet has included representatives of the main minority communities − Muslims in all cabinets but one, and Sri Lanka Tamils in half the cabinets. Apart from the Colombo Central electorate, which regularly returns a Muslim

MP and, rather irregularly, a few Kandyan electorates, the choice of Muslim cabinet ministers is made from among a number of Muslim electorates on the East Coast, i.e. the outer periphery. There have been no Tamil MPs elected from outside the main Tamil areas in the North and East. Jaffna, the heartland of Sri Lanka Tamil society, has been the home of Tamil separatist sentiment, has become increasingly estranged from Colombo, and has become dominated by separate − and increasingly separatist − Tamil parties. It has provided no cabinet minister since G. G. Ponnambalam in 1952−3. The choice of Sri Lanka Tamil ministers has therefore been limited to a few Tamil electorates in the extreme periphery which are willing to return members of the main national political parties, the United National Party and the SLFP. Of the eighteen elected cabinet ministers based in the outer periphery, nine were Muslims or Sri Lanka Tamils. They accounted for three-fifths of all elected cabinet ministers from these two communities. In so far as there is a conflict − and there is (see below) − these minority ministers have been expected to serve as representatives of their communities on a national basis rather than as representatives of their region.

The fact that leading elective positions continue to accrue disproportionately to politicians from the core (and the inner periphery) is causally related to the continuity of elite political leadership. Any major replacement of the elite by politicians from lower social strata could be expected to broaden the geographical base of the leadership. Continued elite leadership does not however mean that policy has always favoured its material interests. Indeed, part of the price and explanation for this continuity has been the willingness of the elite to respond to and channel grassroots political demands which are inimical to its interests. The clearest case is the willingness of the elite to sacrifice most of its plantation income, and the local patronage networks associated with plantation ownership, by accepting heavy taxation of plantation exports (see above) and the nationalisation of most of their plantation assets in the early 1970s [*Moore, 1981: 139-59*].

In a similar way, the continued dominance of people from the core in positions of political and administrative leadership does not mean that all major policies are advantageous to the core. The heavy taxation of export crops, while mainly disadvantaging the plantation-dependent populations of the inner periphery, also adversely affects substantial populations in the core and the outer periphery regions. Only the extreme periphery and Jaffna, which grow scarcely any tea or rubber and few coconuts, can be said to be clear winners in regional terms. The conflicts of interests here are not regional but 'class' in the loosest sense of the term: essentially − and despite the existence of Sinhalese smallholder export-crop producers and a Sinhalese minority among estate labourers − conflicts between, on the one hand, Sri Lankan and foreign capitalist estate owners and Indian Tamil estate labourers and, on the other hand, the state,[13] the (mainly Sinhalese) beneficiaries of state expenditure and the mass of food purchasers.[14] Class conflict in a broad sense is in fact a central feature of politics and party alignments in the core region (see below). Regional conflicts are much more evident in relation to policy towards the smallholder sector, especially to its main component: paddy production.

AGRICULTURAL POLICY

The dominant characteristics of agricultural policy in independent Sri Lanka have been the combination of measures depressing farm output prices with the generous public provision and subsidisation of agricultural inputs, especially fertiliser, credit, tractors, land development and surface irrigation [*Moore, 1981: Chapter 5*]. It is rather unlikely that any of those responsible for this strategy realised or intended that it should benefit the smallholders of the core rather than those of the peripheries, but this is in fact the result. There is one clear exception: almost all public land and irrigation development has been in the Dry Zone — the extreme periphery. Such a policy was almost inevitable given Sri Lanka's big food deficit and the availability of large sparsely-populated spaces. And given that Dry Zone agricultural development has involved a great deal of Sinhalese migration from the core and inner periphery regions, the distribution of benefits cannot be posed as a simple region versus region issue. The regional *origins* of Dry Zone farmers must be taken into account.

What is clear is that the strategy of subsidising agricultural inputs but depressing agricultural output prices is of greatest relative benefit to those rural populations whose rate of use of purchased inputs is high relative to the proportion of their produce which they market. In Sri Lanka this means the smallholders of the core and, secondly, the inner periphery regions. The farmers of the core, having small holdings and relatively very low paddy yields, produce paddy mainly for auto-consumption (Table 1, row m). The present author has elsewhere used sample farm management data to illustrate the relative effects on paddy farmers of the core, the inner periphery and the extreme periphery of four different hypothetical measures to channel more public financial support to paddy farmers: reductions in the sale price of fertiliser and agro-chemicals, subsidies on tractor hire charges and increases in the market price of paddy. Regardless of the amount by which these prices are changed, the relative advantage to the extreme periphery always lies in increasing the market price of paddy, and to the core in increasing subsidies on inputs. The inner periphery stands between the two [*Moore, 1981: 306*]. Most households in the extreme periphery are sellers of paddy; in the core the majority, even of the relatively smaller proportions who are cultivators, are actually net purchasers of paddy. Thus low paddy prices are of net benefit to a majority of even the paddy farmers of the core, and the policy of 'helping' farmers by subsidising inputs while depressing paddy prices benefits them doubly.

The same study examines a related issue: the relative success of the paddy farmers of different districts in actually obtaining scarce, subsidised and publicly-provided fertiliser in the early 1970s. The degree of success is very closely related to physical proximity and ease of physical access to both Colombo and the sub-core of Jaffna [*Moore, 1981: 308*]. There is no direct evidence on the reasons for this pattern. One can however reasonably guess, on the basis of general knowledge on the functioning of public sector institutions in Sri Lanka, the likely range of factors involved: better physical transport, storage and distribution facilities near the core, partly perhaps because of denser populations;[15] the greater ease with which politicians in or near core areas can put pressure on public institutions; and the lesser effectiveness of public agencies in the peripheral areas because so many of their staff have their homes and family in the core areas and are frequently absent from their workplaces.

None of this suggests any intention to benefit the core in agricultural policy. But it does suggest a number of other things. One is that, unless the above case is very atypical, the general strategy of providing subsidised inputs through public agencies – even if not motivated by any clear perception of relative regional impact – is most likely to be approved and least likely to generate opposition in the core region. The core is better able than the peripheries to tolerate the undoubted inefficiencies of many public distribution systems. Distance, or distance tempered by some measure of ease of travel and communication, appears to be a significant variable underlying effective access to public resources and, perhaps less directly, to the shaping of public policy.

This case also suggests the inapplicability to Sri Lanka of the view that the practice of subsidising scarce fertilisers is a device for ensuring, whether consciously or not, that politically-powerful large farmers actually obtain the bulk of this cheap input, which they use to produce a surplus to be sold cheaply to feed the towns, whereas small farmers would use fertiliser to produce more food for auto-consumption [*Lipton, 1977: 289*]. If the Sri Lankan polity were to practise such pure 'urban bias' it would have to direct fertiliser to the extreme periphery, where the surplus-producing paddy farmers are located and where the marginal returns to fertiliser use are almost certainly greater than in the core areas.[16]

THE AGRICULTURAL POLICY AGENDA

It is one thing to demonstrate that the general thrust of agricultural policy has tended to be of benefit to the core rather than the peripheries. It is quite another to explain the origins of the policy itself. In what sense if any does it stem from the greater power of the core populations? Because the 'strategy' is the cumulative result of a long series of measures, one cannot hope to find any easy explanation by examining one or a small number of policy 'decisions', even if the relevant information were available. The issue has apparently never been publicly elaborated or debated in the way in which it is framed above. It is this silence which is in fact our point of departure. One can examine the issue by looking at what has not been said or demanded: by studying the absences from the public agricultural policy agenda.

What is it that has not been said? Let us begin to answer that by looking at the objective interests of the rural population of the extreme periphery. The extreme periphery is characterised by a very high dependence on agriculture, especially paddy production; a clear objective interest in high market prices for paddy (and other food crops); and a high degree of reliance on publicly-provided agricultural services, especially for fertiliser, credit and irrigation water. Its population has been very clearly disadvantaged in post-independence agricultural policy in two major respects: the state has depressed the producer price of paddy (see above), and the efficiency with which agricultural services have been provided by public institutions has been low. Fertiliser has already been discussed above. Because of the non-enforcement of repayment of agricultural credit, resulting in an arbitrarily distributed net subsidy to some farmers (and non-farmers) in all parts of the island, the volume of credit has to be curtailed, and at the local level credit is only intermittently available. This is to the clear disadvantage of the peripheral farming areas, where the very marked seasonality of harvests and the dearth of part-time non-farm employment make farmers very dependent on extra-household credit of some kind. Dry Zone farmers are also heavily dependent on irrigation water from large, publicly-managed gravity irrigation systems, but the standards of water management have been very low, and the consequent losses of crops and income high [*Moore, 1981: 189-97*].

It is *not* being suggested that Dry Zone farmers are in any very evident sense exploited or disadvantaged in the distribution of public expenditure. Even while keeping domestic paddy producer prices below world market levels, the state has subsidised the difference it has paid farmers for (some of) their paddy surplus and the price at which it sells publicly-procured rice to consumers. Dry Zone farmers share in the large subsidy element in agricultural credit and pay nothing for the irrigation water which is made available to them at such high cost by the state.

The point is that Dry Zone farmers have not raised their voices or attempted to use their electoral power to challenge those aspects of agricultural policy which are clearly disadvantageous to them: maintenance of low paddy prices through state action; the preference for supporting agriculture through input subsidies which are relatively much more beneficial to the core areas; and the emphasis on the quantitative provision of state services rather than qualitative efficiency, where inefficiencies bear hardest on them. That the rural peripheries have not challenged these policies is evident when one examines the political agenda, as revealed in the content of parliamentary debates, party election programmes and politicians' speeches. Demands for higher agricultural prices have been rare and easily squashed. Advocacy of more overall efficiency in public distribution systems – as opposed to the voicing of individual grievances – has been only marginally less rare. By contrast, the public agenda has been packed with questions about the level of public subsidy and support to the rural population – the extent of Crown land to be alienated or developed for irrigation; the level of subsidy on fertilisers, the appropriateness of attempts to enforce repayment of credit; the price of tractors and the level of hire charges; and outraged reactions to hints that farmers might be asked to contribute to the cost of land development and irrigation water [*Moore, 1981: Chapter 5*].

The language, metaphor and ideology suffusing these policy discussions is characteristic of that of Sri Lankan politics as a whole, and conforms closely to actual policy. It is based on a widely-accepted premise that the role of the state is to redistribute material resources as widely as possible, with a special emphasis on protection and support for 'the masses', 'the poor' or 'the working classes'. Since 'the masses' are implicitly the Sinhalese, calls for the state to intervene on their behalf is also often a way of pursuing ethnic conflicts in a coded language which is understandable without being offensively explicit [*Moore, 1981, Chapter 5*].

At its broadest level the agenda of Sri Lankan politics has been about conflicts between different groups – including classes in the broad sense and ethnic groups – over access to the very large volume of material and symbolic resources distributed by the state. Our argument about the political domination of the core over the periphery can be reduced to four main points. The first is that agricultural policy conforms to this agenda and the second that policy has been to the relative disadvantage of the periphery over the core. The third point is that the peripheral populations have implicitly accepted this agenda, participated fully in an electoral and party system organised around it, and 'failed' even to struggle for a different agenda which would provide an opportunity for them to push for their interests in high producer prices and efficient service delivery. The fourth point is that the 'domination' of the core lies in the fact that the agenda and the pattern of party and electoral conflict supporting it arose in the core and reflects the interests, including the conflicts of interest, within the core.

Even to sketch out a justification for these claims three further points need to be explained. The first is that the core region has been the most politically creative and dynamic region in Sri Lanka in that it has been the locus of virtually every major new political movement or conflict which has emerged in Sri Lanka over the past century: the Buddhist revival, the temperance movement and nationalism in the late nineteenth and early twentieth centuries; the organised labour movement in the 1920s to 1940s; much of the cultural nationalism and indigenism which underlay the creation and meteoric rise to power of the SLFP in the 1950s; and the radical JVP movement which came close to overthrowing the state by force in 1971 [*Moore, 1981: Chapter 9*].

The second point follows closely: the contemporary party system, which all the time it remains stable places limits on the content of the political agenda, arose in the core and reflects conflicts of interest in the core. It dates from the creation of the Lanka Sama Samaj (Socialist) party in the 1930s on the basis of the conflict of capital and labour in the core. There emerged a relatively clear conflict between a Marxist Left and a conservative Right, drawing their main support from lower and upper social strata respectively. When the SLFP emerged as a major party and became the main opposition to the UNP, it too found the core of its support in lower social strata. What did not emerge was any kind of rural or peasant party distinctively associated with the smallholder sector. The SLFP has mainly been rural, but is not a peasant party. The Dry Zone would have been the natural base for such a rural party, but a part at least of the reason why none has emerged is that by the time post-war migration of Sinhalese to the Dry Zone and the improvement of communications provided the potential for the Dry Zone to become a major electoral force, the core-based party system was already firmly in place. Lacking any indigenous elite, and under the political leadership of traders and public servants, many originating in the Low Country, the Sinhalese Dry Zone was fitted into the existing political system as an area of UNP-SLFP electoral competition [*Moore, 1981: Chapters 8 and 9*].

There is however a further reason why the Dry Zone has not nurtured any 'peasant' or 'farmer' party or political programme. This constitutes our third point. The Dry Zone farmers whose interests lie in high paddy prices and a more production-orientated pattern of public service delivery are divided along ethnic lines between Sinhalese, Sri Lanka Tamils and Muslims. In fact, the producers of large marketed paddy surpluses are especially likely to be Tamils or Muslims [*Moore, 1981: 329-36*]. That they are members of different socio-cultural groups is of course not in itself an explanation for the failure of Dry Zone farmers to co-operate politically; the explanation lies in the salience of ethnic conflict, especially between Sinhalese and Sri Lanka Tamils, in the Sri Lankan polity as a whole. What are the sources of this conflict? One source certainly lies within the Dry Zone itself: public land and irrigation development has resulted in areas of the Dry Zone traditionally considered Tamil becoming populated by Sinhalese. The significance of this as a source of conflict at the *local* level can easily be exaggerated, because these are areas previously virtually unpopulated. It is not that the migration of Sinhalese to the Dry Zone has actually resulted in significant numbers of Sri Lanka Tamils being displaced. There has long been a net migration flow from Jaffna to the Dry Zone which is exactly analogous to the Sinhalese migration from the core and inner periphery [*Moore, 1981: 476*]. Much of the hostility generated among Tamils at public (Sinhalese) land colonisation programmes lies in the realm of the symbolic: at the Sinhalisation of areas traditionally considered Tamil and, more concretely, in the physical diminution in the area which can credibly be claimed as the natural territory of a separate Tamil state.

The failure of Dry Zone farmers to co-operate politically on inter-ethnic lines is in part a result of the core-periphery pattern and of the conflict between the Sinhalese core and the Sri Lanka Tamil sub-core of Jaffna.[17] While undoubtedly having an important symbolic dimension, the main cause of this conflict is competition between Tamil and Sinhalese traders and aspirants for higher education and public sector posts. It is a conflict of little intrinsic relevance to the Dry Zone farmers. Yet history has led them to line up with their own ethnic groups, and in the process to jeopardise considerably the chances that their own distinctive material interests will be pushed on to the national political agenda [*Moore, 1981: Chapter 8*].

CONCLUSION

The concept of a clash of distinctive urban and rural interests is difficult to apply to Sri Lanka because of the permeability of the urban-rural divide and the diversity of farming interests consequent upon the coexistence of export and food crop production and estate and smallholder farming. Intra-rural variations in population density, occupation, access to services, cropping patterns and farm structure form a spatial pattern which can relatively easily be fitted into a core-periphery framework; their political consequences can be analysed in tandem with purely spatial considerations. The 'fit' of this core-periphery framework is in large degree the consequence of factors peculiar to Sri Lanka. However, the use of the framework to analyse the politics of agricultural policy does illustrate the importance of certain principles of political analysis which tend to have been ignored in, for example, Michael Lipton's [*1977*] quasi-vulgar Marxian treatment of the political dimension of rural-urban relations. Like other prominent theorists of the rural-urban relationship [*Moore, this volume*], Lipton has tended to derive an assumed pattern of political conflict from the nature of the economic relationships between different class/sectoral categories; reduce the concept of political interest group to the concept of economic sectoral/class group; and predict the outcome of these interest conflicts on the basis of assumptions about the mainly material resources available to the different groups. This paper suggests that this analytic procedure is inadequate for at least three reasons.

1. Access (the ability to make a case to and put direct pressure on) to politicians and public servants is a significant variable affecting policy outcomes, and distance, in addition to simple class affiliation or sectoral location, is an important determinant of this access.

2. The connection between interest and political resources on the one hand and policy outcomes on the other is less direct and more complex than the arguments of Lipton and others imply. The connection is mediated in particular by the process through which an actual pattern of interest articulation and an actual political agenda emerge from the very wide range of potential interest groups and potential agenda items. Patterns of economic relationships do not provide a manageably small political agenda without the assistance of political variables. It is widely accepted that this narrowing-down process is strongly influenced by dominant social groups [*Lukes, 1974*]. The Sri Lanka case suggests that pre-existing patterns of political and party competition can also seriously constrain the terms under which new potential interest groups (i.e. Dry Zone surplus farmers) enter into the political system.[18]

3. The state cannot be treated simply as an arena within which interest conflicts arising within civil society are pursued. The ways in which 'the state' or aspects of it might have and pursue distinctive interests are varied [*Nolan and White, this volume; Nordlinger, 1981*]. This paper has dealt only with the regional bias in the origins of the state personnel and the ways in which their resultant perceptions or interests might influence policy.

NOTES

1. This paper is a distillation of an argument presented at length in the author's D.Phil. thesis [*Moore, 1981*], especially Chapter 6, and also parts of Chapters 7 and 9. Supporting references and footnotes are provided here only if deemed essential, thus saving considerable space.
2. See ibid, Chapter 5 for details.
3. This has been much less true since the late 1970s, as low world tea and rubber prices have forced reductions in export taxes.
4. *Census of Population, 1971, General Report*: 40; and *Census of Population and Housing, 1981, Preliminary Release No. 2*: Table 9.
5. 'Consequently it seems that centre-periphery theory will remain an analytical idiom rather than a rigorous theory' [*Newby, 1980: 91*].
6. The same data are presented for individual districts in *Moore, 1981: passim*.
7. For discussion of that issue see ibid: 141-50.
8. The main exceptions are to be found in old-settled villages in the Dry Zone which are often nucleated around small irrigation tanks.
9. The SLFP was not an especially Kandyan-based organisation when it emerged in the early 1950s, and indeed much of the élan behind its surprise election victory in 1956 derived from the vigorous support of Low Country Buddhist priests and Low Country Buddhist revivalist sentiment generally. It was only after the emergence of Mrs Bandaranaike as leader that the party came under the control of Kandyan 'notables'.

10. The information is obtained from de Silva [*1979: 302-28*].
11. There are two mechanisms involved. The weightage for area as well as population, originally introduced to devalue the Marxist vote which was concentrated in the Low Country, benefits the outer periphery, extreme periphery and Jaffna regions. The inner periphery benefits from the fact that, although not Sri Lanka citizens and disenfranchised since 1948, the Indian Tamils are still counted as part of the population for the purposes of electoral delimitation. Because the figures in Table 2, row (d) include non-citizens, the superior electoral power of the average inner periphery voter compared to the average core region voter is not fully evident. For details of electoral delimitation, see Jupp [*1978: 190*].
12. The figures in row (a) of Table 2 somewhat under-represent the importance of the core because they exclude non-elected cabinet ministers sitting in the Senate (abolished in 1972). The majority were apparently core-based. On the other hand, a reverse bias operates due to the increasing number of cabinet ministers over time and the fact that there is a tendency, which this author cannot explain, for the over-representation of the core to increase over time, independently of the identity of the ruling parties.
13. This was far less true after the bulk of the estate sector was nationalised in the early 1970s.
14. Food consumers have benefited, at least in the short term, from policies depressing the market price of coconuts (see above in the text). Coconuts are a major item in the Sri Lankan diet.
15. The physical infrastructure for the distribution of fertiliser in Sri Lanka has been poor.
16. The periphery is relatively well provided with production inputs complementary to fertiliser, especially sunshine and irrigation water. Average levels of fertiliser application per unit of land are also lower than in the core areas.
17. One might also add that the Dry Zone Muslim farmers appear to accept that Muslim interests are essentially those of urban-trading Muslims of Batticaloa, Trincomalee, Colombo, Kandy, etc.
18. 'All forms of political organisation have a bias in favour of the exploitation of some kinds of conflict and the suppression of others, because organisation is the mobilisation of bias' [*Schattschneider, quoted in Lukes, 1974: 16*].

REFERENCES

De Silva, G. P. S. H., 1979, *A Statistical Survey of Elections to the Legislatures of Sri Lanka, 1911–1977*, Colombo: The Marga Institute.
Farmer, B. H., 1972, 'Ceylon', in Spate, O. H. K. *et al.*, *India, Pakistan and Ceylon. The Regions*, London: Methuen.
Frank, A. G., 1969, *Capitalism and Underdevelopment in Latin America*, New York and London: Monthly Review Press.
Isenman, P., 1980, 'Basic Needs: The Case of Sri Lanka', *World Development*, Vol. 8, No. 3.
Jupp, J., 1978, *Sri Lanka – Third World Democracy*, London: Frank Cass.
Lipton, M., 1977, *Why Poor People Stay Poor. Urban Bias in World Development*, London: Temple Smith.
Lukes, S., 1974, *Power. A Radical View*, London: Macmillan.
Moore, M. P., 1981, *The State and the Peasantry in Sri Lanka*, D.Phil. thesis, University of Sussex.
Newby, H., 1980, 'Rural Sociology', *Current Sociology*, Vol. 28, No. 1.
Nordlinger, E., 1981, *On the Autonomy of the Democratic State*, Cambridge, Massachusetts: Harvard University Press.
Roberts, M., 1982, *Caste Conflict and Elite Formation. The Rise of a Karava Elite in Sri Lanka, 1500–1931*, Cambridge: Cambridge University Press.
Smith, Adam, 1776, *The Wealth of Nations* (reprinted in 1977 by Harmondsworth: Penguin).
Uswatte-Aratchi, G., 1974, 'University Admissions in Ceylon: Their Economic and Social Background and Employment Expectations', *Modern Asian Studies*, Vol. 8, No. 3.

'Urban Bias' and Rural Poverty: A Latin American Perspective

by M. R. Redclift*

Despite evidence that the urban sector benefits disproportionately from the public allocation of resources, there has been little discussion of theories of 'urban bias' in Latin America. This is attributed to Latin America's economic dependency, in which the dominance of urban interests is seen as an outcome, rather than a cause, of underdevelopment in both rural and urban sectors. After examining the origins of urban dominance in the region, and the 'theory of sectoral clashes' proposed by Mamalakis, the paper focuses on recent food and energy policy in Mexico and Brazil. Although these policies provide evidence of the influence of large-scale capital in urban and rural areas, the greater differentiation of the rural sector in Latin America and the constraints imposed by the international economy weaken the case for 'urban bias' as formulated by Lipton.

INTRODUCTION

The Latin American development literature contains few references to the 'urban bias' debate initiated by Lipton [*1977*]. Yet this literature is concerned to explain the persistence of rural poverty, which Lipton saw as the outcome of 'urban bias'. Rural poverty, together with the concentration of political and economic resources in urban areas, are viewed in the Latin American perspective as the outcome of exogenous development processes. The debate about the political direction given to development policy in Latin America is less concerned with sectoral conflicts than with the degree of national 'autonomy' which international dependence affords Latin American economies. This concentration on the national/international level has effectively precluded any examination of 'urban bias'.

A close reading of Lipton's work, and the debate to which he contributed, suggests some basic confusions as to what constitutes 'urban bias'. Part of the time 'urban bias' is taken as a description of policy outcomes: the pattern of resource allocation induced by the use of public power. There is considerable evidence in the Latin American literature that urban areas receive preferential treatment at the expense of rural areas.[1] At other times 'urban bias' is used by Lipton and his critics in a weightier, explanatory way, to refer to collusion between 'urban and elite rural classes' in order to direct the development process towards their own ends.[2] The Latin American material does provide some illustrations of this kind of political process based on sectoral interests. In the work of Mamalakis, considered below, the 'clashes' between sectoral

* Department of Environment Studies and Countryside Planning, Wye College, Ashford, Kent, and Institute of Latin American Studies, University of London.

interests are not confined to the urban and rural sectors, but include other economic sectors which have expected to benefit from government policies.

The descriptive use of 'urban bias' raises interesting issues, especially in the evaluation of development policy, but will not be considered further in this paper.[3] The analytical question – how far 'urban bias' is an accurate, or heuristically useful, approach to understanding the politics behind Latin American development policies – constitutes the main axis around which the paper is written. Can rural poverty be attributed principally to the mobilisation of urban sectoral interests, or to the wider effects of uneven development in Latin America? The question is addressed by examining both the Latin American experience and some common interpretations of that experience: the historical role of cities in Latin America, the debate about 'sectoral clashes' and Import Substituting Industrialisation and the various interpretations offered of dependency theory. The final section of the paper considers two recent development policy initiatives, the Mexican Food System (SAM) and Brazil's ethanol programme, which illustrate the need for a revision of the 'urban bias' thesis.

RURAL-URBAN RELATIONS IN HISTORICAL PERSPECTIVE

Latin America has a long tradition of highly-developed urbanism, with the dominance of the urban sector over rural areas taking a variety of forms depending on the role of Latin American economies within global systems of accumulation. The Spanish and Portuguese established their colonial empires by adapting urban forms typical of southern Europe to the geographical and political exigencies of the new territories. Their cities were often built on the ruins of pre-Columbian civilisations, such as those of the Mayas and the Incas, which themselves exhibited highly developed urban forms [*Hardoy, 1975*]. Latin American urbanisation provided an historical link between land use and labour arrangements that were inherited from the pre-Conquest period, and shifts in metropolitan-satellite economic relations which were a feature of Latin America's position within the global economic system. The dominance of urban interests thus needs to be considered in temporal as well as in spatial terms, as the development process involved both 'backward' and 'forward' linkages in time and space. Agrarian institutions, such as the *hacienda* system, were fashioned to meet the needs not only of a burgeoning urban population but, at one remove, the markets created for primary products in Western Europe and North America.

The Spanish and Portuguese were important colonial powers before the Industrial Revolution had transformed Europe. This fact alone suggests that different historical baselines need to be drawn for Latin America as compared to Asia and Africa. When, towards the end of the nineteenth century, European colonisers were rushing to secure large tracts of tropical Africa, most Latin American states had been politically independent for almost half a century. Urban-rural relations in these states had been transformed, however, not only by independence but by the continent's three centuries of integration within the global economy.

The role of Latin America in the world economy during the sixteenth, seventeenth and eighteenth centuries was essentially that of providing commodities, especially precious metals, needed by the commerce of the metropolitan countries of Europe. Later, in the nineteenth century, the production of surplus foodstuffs and tropical crops assumed greater importance and the mercantilist policies engendered by dependence on a limited supply of gold and silver lost favour. In time the self-sufficient empires, which had been created around the supply of precious metals to the mother country, made way for new colonial economies in which trade was freer and foodcrops were cultivated for the internal market alongside plantation crops for the metropolitan states. Looting, plunder and piracy gave way to more subtle forms of surplus appropriation. On the eve of the Industrial Revolution in Britain the South American colonies were among those that had proved 'incapable of permanent expansion' and needed to be transformed if they were to recover their declining profitability [*Hobsbawm, 1967: 55-6*].

Latin American urban forms were intimately linked to the shifts in metropolitan-satellite relations. Most early towns were either extractive or trade centres (entrepôts). Agricultural production made use of indigenous labour to produce food for the mines and, gradually, the demands of the urban domestic market assumed critical importance. There were plantation economies like those in Asia and Africa, but in Latin America the permanent settlement of European people at an early date was combined with the widespread destruction or restructuring of indigenous agriculture. Population was sparsely distributed and the principal agricultural production institution, the *hacienda*, was more labour-extensive than any comparable institution in Asia or Africa. The *hacienda* basically existed to serve the city, as well as the population settled on it. Indigenous agricultural systems continued to exist, of course, but they were made increasingly dependent on the *hacienda* and, ultimately, the urban settlements which had given rise to it.[4]

During the nineteenth century there were growing signs of conflict between the landholding interests associated with the *hacienda* (or *fazenda* in Brazil) and the commercial bourgeoisie [*Roberts, 1978: 37*]. Urban development was hindered by checks on the expansion of the internal market and by the tight social control exercised over the rural labour force. The latter was however seen by the dominant rural and urban classes as a necessary prerequisite to social stability. The alliance between rural landholding and urban entrepreneurial classes was achieved at the cost of maintaining a sub-optimal agriculture, which was incapable of combining greater agricultural productivity with improved welfare for the rural poor. Land was conceived as a means of extracting rent, and capital was systematically diverted into urban centres, rather than reinvested in agriculture. The rural-urban bourgeois alliance thus offered gains and losses to both sides, and was not completely stable.

The hold of Latin American towns on their rural hinterland has been described by Morse as 'centrifugal', in contrast with the 'centripetal' force that obtained in most of Europe during the eighteenth and nineteenth centuries [*Morse, 1962*]. Towns exercised dominion over the rural hinterland rather than, as in the European model, serving as trading points for the rural areas. From the mid-sixteenth century onwards towns in Latin America served to control and administer resources based in the countryside, but unlike the situation in parts of India, for example, they were never just centres of control and administration. Towns developed 'as parts of more comprehensive plans for regional development, that included the mining and farming areas' [*Roberts, 1978: 38*]. Some writers have even suggested that these towns 'owned their hinterlands', in terms both of economic proprietorship and administrative control [*Portes and Walton, 1976: 9*]. In the Portuguese colony that became Brazil, this process was less marked than in the Spanish colonies, and political decision-making was less centralised. In general, Latin American cities were not large, at least until the mid-nineteenth century, but their role was decisive in linking colonial agriculture and mineral extracting activities to the metropolitan centre. Cities were 'bridgeheads to settlement' in which the elite were left free to consume that part of the surplus which was not exported [*Roberts, 1978: 42*].

Urban-rural relations were highly localised until the mid-nineteenth century. As Roberts puts it:

> In effect the situation that developed in Latin America towards the end of the colonial period was almost that of a city-state system; poor inter-regional communication and a weakly developed or non-existent inter-regional division of labour meant that the commercial and landed interests ... depended on the political and administrative power of their local city. [*Roberts, 1978: 43*]

This urban configuration was transformed by closer economic ties with the European, and later North American, metropoli, which developed from the third quarter of the nineteenth century onwards. In place of unilateral political dependence and deference to commercial monopoly, Latin American states developed multilateral commercial dependence. The development of manufacturing industry, in search of new markets and raw materials, combined with the lowering of transport costs to open up Latin America to much more intensive commercial pressure. In some respects the early nineteenth century had witnessed a partial reversal of the urbanisation process, as new opportunities for commercial agriculture diversified the rural hinterland and extended the frontier. The closer integration with European economies may also have served to undermine local manufacturing, as it did in other parts of the world [*de Silva, 1982: 43*]. Certainly, increased competition in the internal market of most Latin American countries was the outcome of closer links between the interests controlling the sale of foodstuffs and raw materials, and those controlling imported manufactured goods.

The late nineteenth and early twentieth centuries saw an intensification of these processes, leading to large-scale European capital being invested in parts of Latin America. Central government came to exert more control over provincial centres and urban primacy reached its zenith in the growth of large capital cities like Mexico City, Buenos Aires and Lima. By 1920 most Latin American countries had primate urban systems, with power and economic growth being concentrated in one large urban centre [*Roberts, 1978: 47*]. The nature of urban dominance had thus changed markedly.

It was from this basis in urban primacy and centralised control that import substituting industrialisation was to be attempted in succeeding decades.

Already, between 1870 and 1914, some countries (Argentina, Uruguay, Brazil and Cuba) had absorbed millions of immigrants from Europe. Immigration was renewed after 1919 and continued until the world crisis in 1930. Many of these migrants expected to become rural property owners, but few succeeded: 'the actual destination of the majority of the immigrants ... was the city' [*Hardoy, 1975: 49*]. When the opportunity arose – as it did during the Depression and the Second World War – for countries like Argentina, Chile and Brazil (and later, Mexico) to concentrate their attention on their own development needs, the benefits were captured largely by urban groups. The cities came to resemble magnets, increasing their holds on the rural hinterland, and incorporating a new generation of immigrants in the process of urban expansion.

IMPORT SUBSTITUTING INDUSTRIALISATION AND THE THEORY OF
SECTORAL CLASHES

The process through which some Latin American countries achieved a measure of industrialisation, particularly after the Great Depression (1929–31) has received considerable attention and need not detain us.[5] Accelerated industrialisation proved more difficult to accomplish than some of its advocates had anticipated, giving rise to criticism of 'export-led' industrialization and the search for alternative ways of achieving development.

The economists associated with the alternative model of import substituting industrialisation (ISI) had their base in the United Nations' Economic Commission for Latin America (ECLA). From about 1950 onwards they argued, with increasing vigour, that only the development of an internal market for consumer durable goods, and restrictions on the import of such goods from the developed countries, could secure a solid industrial sector. It is clear, in retrospect, that the ECLA 'structuralists' seriously underestimated the difficulties of applying such a policy, especially given the economic recovery of Western Europe in the postwar period. The heavy dependence on imported capital goods, and some raw materials, contributed to the economic fragility of those populist governments which had sought greater economic autonomy for Brazil, Argentina and Mexico. In turn a right-of-centre, non-structuralist position developed, which argued that ISI had resulted in the excessive 'taxing' of the agricultural and export sectors to support inefficient home industries, over-expanded bureaucracies and a fledgling 'welfare state'.

One of the indirect effects of the criticism to which the ECLA school was subjected was Mamalakis' 'theory of sectoral clashes' which, when it was first formulated in the pages of *Latin American Research Review*, attracted considerable attention from scholars throughout Latin America.[6] Mamalakis' work is interesting because, like Lipton, he developed a theory of politics based on an analysis of inter-sectoral economic relations (see Moore's introductory paper). His work also raises an issue central to the reassessment of the 'urban bias' framework of analysis. How have efforts to reduce Latin America's economic dependency been initiated by social forces opposed to urban-led development in the region? This is discussed briefly in the section on Mexican Food Policy (the SAM) below.

In Mamalakis' model, the government regulates the competition between different economic sectors. In return, 'sectoral teams' try to enlist the support of the government in an effort to maximise their share of gross national product. Mamalakis places great emphasis on the relative autonomy of the state which, in his view, acts to ensure that capitalist growth is not 'retarded' by the operation of free-market forces. The view that Latin American governments should put a brake on the working of the market appears slightly quaint in the light of recent attempts to apply the monetarist theories of the Chicago School to the Southern Cone. However, one should recall that in the 1960s industrialisation was seen in Latin America as the only means of bringing stability to economies that were firmly based on exports. Modernisation and government-sponsored industrialisation went hand-in-hand.

Mamalakis distinguished between what he described as 'suppressed sectors' and those which were economically stagnant. Agriculture, for example, could be both expanding and strategically important, and yet still be suppressed, disfavoured by government [*Mamalakis, 1969: 14*]. Government could favour 'dominant' sectors while discriminating against other, rapidly expanding, sectors. The principal mechanism was the allocation of public investment. Agriculture had been a suppressed sector 'in Argentina, Chile and Colombia' partly for non-economic reasons, including 'resentment against the conservative oligarchy ... (and) anti-imperialist feelings' [*1969: 15*]. Mamalakis also notes that agriculture is sometimes suppressed because 'it is associated with backwardness, stagnation and the undesirable segment in a dualistic economy' [*1969: 15*]. The fate of the agricultural sector is dependent not only on the existing sectoral relations with the urban industrial sector − terms of trade, fiscal policies, migration, etc. − but on the tendencies of governments to penalise rural groups because of the general backwardness of their economy.

Echoing Lipton's approach, Mamalakis sees the stagnation of agriculture and bottlenecks in food supplies, as the result of policies designed to accelerate the flow of funds from agriculture to industry. The principal mechanism is price control of agricultural commodities. Mamalakis notes that this has the paradoxical effect of stimulating other countries' agricultural sectors. As we shall see, such an interpretation looks less convincing today than it did in the 1960s and early 1970s, before industrial and financial capital became heavily committed to agricultural production and food processing in Latin America. Price controls discriminate not only − or mainly − between sectors but within them, by penalising the petty commodity producer and subsidising agribusiness.

LATIN AMERICAN DEPENDENCY AND URBAN BIAS

Mamalakis' work possesses originality within the Latin American context because although he differs from the ECLA structuralist school in identifying sectoral rather than class interests at work in Latin American development, he avoids direct recourse to a rural-urban dichotomy. It is important to recognise, however, that 'the theory of sectoral clashes' lies outside the mainstream of writing on Latin American development. That tradition sees 'urban bias', in the descriptive sense, as the outcome of international, rather than domestic intersectoral, economic relations. Urban dominance is expressed *in terms of* international political economy rather than, as in Asia, an alternative to it. As we shall see, such a perspective cannot easily be reconciled with the 'urban bias' model in the stronger, more analytical sense referred to at the beginning of this paper.

The disparities within Latin American countries have usually been interpreted by the neo-Marxist school as evidence of metropolitan-satellite relations [*Frank, 1967, and 1969*] or internal colonialism [*Stavenhagen, 1975; Walton, 1977*]. Debate has revolved around several aspects of these relationships, notably the room for manoeuvre which is implied by the concept of dependence [*O'Brien, 1975; Dos Santos, 1973*] and the extent to which economic dependency implies underdevelopment [*Cardoso, 1972; Sunkel and Paz, 1970*]. At the inter-sectoral level discussion has centred on the extent to which the modes of production in rural areas are 'capitalist' [*Laclau, 1971*] and, more recently, the characterisation of the migrant labour force in Latin American cities and its utility or disutility for the development of capitalism [*Quijano, 1974; Scott, 1979; Lopes, 1978; Oliveira, 1972*]. Until recently much of this discussion was conducted solely at a theoretical level, partly as a reaction to the atheoretical approaches of the preceding 'modernisation' school. However, during the last few years attention has shifted from purely analytical considerations to their empirical referents. Important work includes that by Roberts and Long on the regional economy in Peru [*Roberts and Long, 1978*], the exploration of urban labour markets [*Sinclair, 1978; Bromley, 1979*], and the organisation of urban settlements [*Moser, 1978; Ward, 1978; Eckstein, 1977*]. By contrast, relatively few attempts have been made to analyse current development policy from the perspectives of 'urban bias'. Below, we examine the limitations of 'urban bias' as a tool for a better understanding of these policy initiatives.

THE LIMITATIONS OF A SECTORAL APPROACH

During the 1970s it was assumed that inequalities within the rural sector of Latin American countries were a major hindrance to industrialisation. For the industrial sector to grow it was necessary to enlarge the internal market, and this required agrarian reform. The highly unequal distribution of land, meticulously chronicled in the studies undertaken by the Inter-American Committee for Agricultural Development (CIDA), was also thought to constitute an invitation to rural revolution on the Cuban model [*Barraclough, 1973*].

The last twenty years have served to throw doubt on several aspects of this analysis. First, a series of agrarian reforms in a number of Latin American countries (Chile, Peru, Ecuador, Panama, among them) have done little to improve rural living standards and enlarge the internal market. Second, the land tenure system which was considered an obstacle to capitalist development in the 1960s has proved to be nothing of the sort. Indeed, land reform has usually succeeded in being 'a means of speeding the transformation from a feudal to a capitalistic ... society' [*Barraclough, 1973: 38*] without radically affecting the *distribution* of land.

Perhaps the most notable effect of agrarian reform has been the way it has facilitated capital penetration into the rural sector. This, in turn, has brought increased social differentiation, not merely between rural wageworkers and petty commodity producers, but also between the latter and large-scale agro-industry. The process of rural proletarianisation has certainly been marked in Latin America, as in India. In the Latin American case, however, rapid rural proletarianisation in some areas has been combined with the reproduction of petty commodity production in others. The petty commodity producer in the late 1980s is generally linked either to large-scale private capital or, more commonly, to the state. Increasingly, it is the state which provides inputs, credit and technical assistance to that strata of small commodity producers where surplus is also controlled by the public sector [*Burbach and Flynn, 1980; Goodman and Redclift, 1981; de Janvry, 1981*]. The landholding system of Latin America did not constitute a brake on the development of capitalism in agriculture. Nor did it prevent countries like Brazil and Mexico experiencing high rates of overall economic growth in the 1960s and 1970s. Clearly, one reason for this is the restructuring that has occurred in the last two decades within the rural sector, as well as between urban and rural sectors. This has enabled industrialisation to proceed on the basis of a restricted internal market, and much of the rural sector to experience 'development' without a radical transformation of land tenure arrangements. In this interpretation, rural poverty is not the outcome of collusion between urban social classes, but of increased penetration of some parts of the rural sector by some urban interests. Rural poverty is an outcome of the differential effect of capital on the rural sector.

Further limitations of a sectoral approach to Latin American development are illustrated by two recent departures from conventional development policy: 'Mexico's Food System' (SAM) and Brazil's programme to convert sugar into alcohol (ethanol). After considering these cases in some detail we return to the question posed at the beginning of this paper: Can rural poverty be attributed principally to the mobilisation of urban sectoral interests or to the wider effects of uneven development in Latin America?

Mexican Food Policy: the SAM

Many of the basic food crop producers in Latin America have been ignored by agricultural development policy. The clearest example is that of maize and bean producers in Mexico and Central America, although we might also include potato producers in the Andean countries and cassava producers in Brazil. The prices which governments and intermediaries have offered for these crops have consistently lagged behind those for cash crops, whether exported or destined for the domestic market. One effect of this neglect of foodcrop production has been to reduce the self-sufficiency of some Latin American countries in staple items of the national diet. In Mexico the crisis reached such proportions that an attempt was made to reverse these processes of food dependence. The Mexican Food System (known by its Spanish acronym, SAM) is an interesting case of public policy seeking to redress rural poverty and meet increased urban consumption within the existing economic and social framework of dependent capitalism, both aspects of Lipton's programme to overcome urban bias.

Despite considerable success in improving wheat production through the dissemination of new 'Green Revolution' varieties, Mexico's production of maize and beans declined throughout the 1970s. At the same time crops such as sorghum and alfalfa were increasingly grown for animal feed, while fruit and vegetables were exported to the United States on a seasonal basis. The benefit they provided the balance of payments, like other export crops such as coffee and tobacco, was not passed on to the rural poor.

The Mexican Food System was introduced in 1980 because of an awareness of the deepening crisis over food production, and the increasing evidence that other forms of state intervention in rural Mexico had not helped the poorest rural groups. The SAM was basically a package of related policies drawn up after initial research by some twenty government committees. The proposals were intended to achieve three objectives: to increase domestic production of strategically important food crops (maize, beans, rice and sugar); to streamline food delivery systems serving the urban and rural poor; and to improve the nutrition of vulnerable target groups in both areas. Specific measures included raising the price of maize by 31 per cent and beans by 25 per cent. Improved seeds would be made available to poor farmers, and they were promised the free delivery of 600,000 tons of fertilisers at prices 20 per cent below commercial rates [*Meissner, 1981*]. Resources for combating plant diseases were to be increased and the cost of crop insurance reduced for the peasant farmer. Perhaps most important of all, agricultural credit policy was redesigned with the interests of the maize-producing farmer in mind, freeing him from exploitative intermediaries.

Efforts were also made to improve food delivery systems. Sections of the food industry that collaborated with the SAM were given a financial boost by the injection of state funds. Specifically, the SAM strove 'to encourage vertically integrated agricultural undertakings which would combine labour intensive agricultural production with capital intensive transformation processes' [*Meissner, 1981: 223*]. More agribusiness was placed under government control.

In addition to the agricultural production aspects of the SAM there were important nutritional elements in the package. It was calculated that about 35 million Mexicans, more than half the population, failed to reach *per capita* daily food intakes of 2,750 calories and 80 grams of protein. Of this number over half − 13 million in rural areas and 6 million in cities − were estimated to have fallen well below these 'minimum' nutritional levels. The most vulnerable were rural women and children, whose nutritional levels would be improved through subsidising a Recommended Basic Food Basket, reducing its cost to poor consumers to about 13 Mexican *pesos* per day per head. (This was about 26 British pence in January 1980.)

The SAM recognised that to reach the target population it was necessary to increase the number and efficiency of the retail outlets used by poor people, especially those of the government's food distribution organisation, CONASUPO. In the cities poor people tended to use small grocery stores or public markets, many of which were mobile (*mercados sobre ruedas:* 'markets on wheels'). Different prices were established for specific marketing channels, enabling the state's subsidy to be relatively selective.

This ambitious programme was only possible because Mexico was in the fortunate, and rather unusual, position of having enormous petroleum reserves. By 1980 it was the world's fifth largest oil producer, and the country's potential reserves were ranked second only to Saudi Arabia's. In 1938, under President Cardenas, the Mexican government had nationalised the petroleum industry and PEMEX, the government's oil monopoly, was linked with the nationalist aspirations of both Left and Right. In 1980 the subsidies received by the SAM amounted to almost four billion United States dollars. The Mexicans, following on the heels of the Venezuelans in the early 1970s, were 'sowing their petroleum' [*Meissner, 1981*]. The implementation of the SAM proved difficult for a number of reasons summarised in the conclusion below [*Redclift: 1980, 1981, and 1984*].

Brazilian Energy Policy: the Ethanol Programme

Brazil's dependence on imported sources of energy is a direct result of the development path it has followed for the last three decades. In 1940, 80 per cent of Brazil's energy consumption was derived from biomass, principally firewood. Only 15 per cent came from hydroelectricity. In 1980 electricity represented over a quarter of the total and the biomass had been replaced by petroleum [*Cardoso, 1980: 114*]. The modernisation of Brazil's energy sector, made necessary by rapid industrialisation and urbanisation, exacerbated the country's external dependence. Domestically, the development model placed emphasis on the rapid diffusion of consumer durables and the exacerbation of income and regional inequality, all of which were made possible by oil imports.

TABLE 1

BRAZIL: PRIMARY ENERGY SOURCES (IN PERCENTAGES)

	Petroleum	*Coal*	*Hydroelectric*	*Biomass***
1970	38	4	19	39
1975	44	3	24	29
1977	42	4	26	27
1978	43	4	26	27
1979	41	4	28	26
1980*	41	5	28	26

*   estimated.
** In 1980, of the 26 per cent of energy derived from biomass, 7 per cent was attributable to the alcohol programmes, 16 per cent to fuelwood and 2 per cent to charcoal.

Source: Van der Pluijin [*1982: 87*].

Brazil's dependence on the internal combustion engine cost it 11 billion US dollars in 1980 [*Saint, 1982: 223*]. The principal factor in Brazil's energy dependence is its heavy reliance on motor transport for private and commercial purposes. It has been calculated that in 1978 96 per cent of passengers and 70 per cent of freight were transported by road [*Cardoso, 1980: 115*]. Although

Brazil has an important hydroelectricity programme, liquid hydrocarbons, derived from petroleum and coal, are only partially replaceable by electricity, and only for industrial consumption. Transport, rather than manufacturing industry, accounts for the lion's share of energy consumption.

In view of the country's commitment to its present development model, with the implied increase in dependence on imported energy sources, the military government has been forced to introduce new policies since 1979. These policies were designed to restrict the consumption of petroleum and replace it with alcohol derived from biomass. Brazil's National Alcohol Programme had been initiated four years earlier, but worsening trade conditions accelerated its promotion. It has rapidly become one of the most disputed programmes to emerge from the biotechnology revolution. The alcohol programme, with a budget of over 5 billion US dollars, is designed to stimulate ethyl alcohol (ethanol) production based largely on the use of sugar cane and cassava as feedstocks. The plan envisages a major substitution of alcohol for gasoline, accounting for three-quarters of all liquid combustible fuel by the year 2000 [*Saint, 1982: 223*]. Liquid fuel production from energy crops promises to be increasingly important for other countries with similar resource advantages for energy farming, severely limited fossil fuel supplies and a balance of payments situation distorted by petroleum imports. The environmental implications of Brazil's alcohol programme are serious enough to warrant close attention. Among the most important effects of the alochol programme the following can be identified: the progressive neglect of staple foodcrops and domestic food supply, the increased concentration of land and worsening regional inequality.

The decision to stimulate sugarcane production in Brazil is of immediate benefit to the 250 plantation-owning families who control two-thirds of sugar production and the entire processing industry [*Saint, 1982: 224*]. Based on the experience of existing irrigated plantations, plans have been drawn up to develop 750,000 hectares of irrigated cane for alcohol production within the watershed of the Sao Francisco River valley where yields are high and production costs particularly low. Such projects rely heavily on seasonal wage labour and serve to increase the importance of Sao Paulo at the expense of states in the poor North-East, where sugar production is less cost efficient [*van der Pluijin, 1982*].

The decision to concentrate on increasing sugar production was made after considering the possibilities offered by cassava production for alcohol. Brazil is the world's largest producer of cassava which, unlike sugar cane, grows well under a variety of agroclimatic conditions. It is grown largely by resource-poor farmers on small plots of land, throughout the year. As is so often the case with crops grown by peasant farmers, cassava has received little research funding and has been systematically neglected in credit and extension programmes [*Saint, 1982: 226*]. If existing technology to increase cassava yields were employed, it would become roughly competitive with sugar cane in terms of alcohol production.

The development of ethanol from sugar cane rather than cassava is likely to contribute further to land concentration. The available evidence suggests that between 1974 and 1979 the 362,000 new hectares of land devoted to cane were cultivated largely at the expense of food crops. The cultivated area of corn and rice declined by 35 per cent in these years. At the same time, the price of food staples rose dramatically in the cities. As Saint argues:

> In a country where an advantaged 20 per cent of the population owns almost 90 per cent of the automobiles and a disadvantaged 50 per cent spends at least half their income on food, the policy decision ... comes perilously close to choosing between allocating calories to cars or to people. [*Saint, 1982: 230*]

Even commentators whose sympathy lies with the sugar ethanol programme admit that the intended increase in acreage devoted to sugar is likely to have a negative impact on the production and availability of food, as well as on income distribution [*van der Pluijin, 1982: 92*].

The specifically environmental consequences of the ethanol programme are more disputed. Cardoso notes that the production of sugar cane alcohol generates an extremely polluting by-product which is currently responsible for considerable river pollution [*Cardoso, 1980: 119*]. On the other hand, alcohol contributes less to air pollution than petroleum fumes, largely because its vapours do not contain carbon monoxide or lead. Interestingly, industrial waste from alcohol production can be used as a fertiliser, and this becomes cost-effective if small distilleries are substituted for large ones. However, this option has not been given the attention it deserves by the Brazilian government [*Saint, 1982: 233*].

The issues raised by Brazil's ethanol programme should not be restricted to the economic efficiency of the programme as a means of saving foreign exchange [*Barzelay and Pearson, 1982: 144*]. As Cardoso remarks, the basic choices must not be limited to the analysis of technological substitutes, important as these may be, for the underlying issues concern '*who* consumes energy and *for what purpose*' [*Cardoso, 1980: 119*]. The decision to commit Brazil to grow more sugar as a form of import substitution, to meet domestic fuel needs, is important from a number of standpoints. It provides an illustration of a development policy which is not in the interests of most rural producers, who derive no benefit from government-financed investment. Like the SAM in Mexico, however, the ethanol programme was conceived partly as a means of reducing Brazil's economic dependence, in this case on imported fuels. Although in technological terms the ethanol programme is innovative, it implies continued commitment to Brazil's highly-concentrated industrialisation model. At first sight, those who stand to benefit from a reduction in transport costs, especially of food, are urban consumers. But subsidies for transporting food are no alternative to a cheap food policy, while foodcrop producers may derive little benefit from transport pricing. In many urban areas, where food shortages have precipitated riots during 1983, poor people are well aware of the class biases in Brazil's current development model. The ethanol programme illustrates how the consequences of new technological policy, tied to old economic policy, fall unevenly on the poor and the rich in both urban and rural sectors.

CONCLUSION

This paper began by commenting that although Latin American countries exhibited 'urban bias' in the descriptive sense and development policy favoured urban areas in the allocation of resources, the discussion of urban bias had received little attention in the region's development literature. An examination of the history of urban dominance since the colonial period helps account for this omission. Latin American countries were relatively urbanised at an early date, and their elite groups were located in urban centres. Most explanations of underdevelopment in the rural sector perceived 'urban bias' as outcome rather than cause of the basic features of the economic environment: not only were urban forms dependent on changing economic relations between 'centre' and 'peripheral' countries, but endogenous development within Latin America was conditioned by external economic relations.

If the outcome of development policy has favoured urban areas and urban classes, does this enable us to use Lipton's concept of 'urban bias' in the stronger, explanatory sense? Would such a use be compatible with the broadly 'dependency' position advocated by most Latin American scholars? The answers to these questions are more difficult to resolve. Clearly, development processes within the rural sector have ensured that urban and rural capital-owning classes have been able to join forces in the political arena. Agribusiness has reached relatively sophisticated levels of operation in many parts of Latin America, incorporating petty commodity producers in the labour process and making effective use of capital provided by the state. The rural sector is more internally differentiated as a result of these trans-sectoral processes.

At the same time, public policy throughout Latin America continues to wrestle with the contradictions imposed by transnational as well as trans-sectoral development. The SAM in Mexico was an attempt to reverse that country's food dependence and provide incentives for small-scale agricultural production. The inspiration for this approach was partly found in the 'Food First' school at the Institute for Food and Development Policy in California [*Luiselli, 1979; Lappé and Collins, 1977*] and partly in an older neo-populist tradition of Mexican agrarianism [*Redclift, 1980*]. The implementation of the SAM proved to be difficult for a variety of reasons. Mexican state agencies were so discredited in many rural areas that they failed to cement the 'alliance with the peasantry' that had been sought. Pressure from foreign-owned banks, spiralling debts and the displeasure of the International Monetary Fund easily persuaded an incoming president to discontinue the SAM in 1982. The financial crisis of that summer had finally put paid to a policy whose benefici-aries had little political voice in Mexico City, let alone Washington and New York. And yet the fact remains that a reformist, redistributive policy of a Liptonian kind was partially implemented in Mexico during the 1980s. Clearly, an awareness of the external dependency with which urban bias is associated had led Mexicans to attempt to reduce both.

Brazil's *ethanol* programme raises other issues of importance to the debate about 'urban bias'. The need for such a programme arose because of Brazil's increased dependence on imported fuel, which threatens the very basis of the country's industrialisation. The allocation of state resources to the programme indicates that countries experiencing 'dependent development' can take measures to defend their precarious position. However, the principal beneficiaries of the programme are those urban groups who have a considerable stake in the current development path, and the costs are likely to be borne by those who have received least benefit from the 'Brazilian miracle' in both urban and rural areas. If the ethanol programme illustrates a development bias, it is that of large-scale Brazilian capital and its primarily urban dependencies. It is an illustration of *scale* bias as much as urban bias.

The examples drawn from Brazil and Mexico should make us reflect on the linkages between inter-sectoral bias and international development. Changes in the international economy, notably the recycling of petrodollars, have served to increase the indebtedness of those Latin American countries with relatively high rates of industrial activity. This has helped to create tensions between domestic groups seeking to pursue more nationalist economic policies, including a complete moratorium on foreign debts, and those groups which have seized the opportunity of indebtedness to discredit redistributive policies. These tensions are not unlike those of the postwar years when populism was married to a structuralist analysis, and the opposition to structuralism sought to reopen Latin American economies to foreign capital. Provided that 'urban bias' is identified with these cross-cutting alliances, cutting across class divisions as well as sectoral ones, it has utility in the 'strong' analytical sense. But it was Lipton's intention to place the burden of proof on those who rejected 'urban bias' and could formulate a more plausible model. If we revise 'urban bias' to take account of Latin American experience we are witnessing the end of the concept as it was originally used. As so often in the social sciences, theoretical refinement ultimately leaves a vacuum that cannot immediately be filled.

NOTES

1. Gilbert is one of the few to discuss 'urban bias' in Latin America, arguing that it 'is most likely to be relevant to those countries in which urbanization has been rapid, as in Africa or in Latin America' [*Gilbert and Gugler, 1981: 165*]. It is not altogether clear why urban bias should *necessarily* be linked to rapid urban growth, which has been less marked in India (Lipton's case *par excellence*) than many other countries.
2. This distinction owes much to the comments on an earlier draft of this paper by David Booth, Mick Moore and John Harriss.
3. An example is Mexico's integrated rural development programme (PIDER), which was conceived in an attempt to reverse the bias in resource allocation towards large urban centres. (See *World Bank, 1979 and 1983*.)
4. It should be noted that the large estate in Brazil (*fazenda*) had greater autonomy than its Spanish American equivalent. In general, Brazilian history suggests less urban dominance and centralisation than in Spanish America.
5. Among the most useful summaries of the ECLA view and its critics are Baer [*1972*] and Hirschman [*1968*].
6. The debate was taken up by political scientists rather than economists, Mamalakis, like Lipton, being an economist-turned-social theorist. The countries to which a 'sectoral clash' analysis was applied include Argentina, Bolivia, Chile, Cuba, Peru and Mexico. (See *Mamalakis, 1971: 121, footnote 3*.)

REFERENCES

Arias, P. and Bazan, L., 1979, *Demandas y Conflicto: el poder político en un pueblo de Morelos*, Mexico City: Ed. Nueva Imagen.

Baer, W., 1972, 'Import Substitution in Latin America: experience and interpretations', *Latin American Research Review*, Vol. 7, No. 1.

Barraclough, S., 1973, *Agrarian Structure in Latin America*, Cambridge, Mass.: D. C. Heath.

Booth, D., 1975, 'André Gunder Frank: an introduction and appreciation', in Oxaal, I., Barnett, T. and Booth, D. (eds.), *Beyond the Sociology of Development*, London: Routledge & Kegan Paul.

Bromley, R., 1979, 'Introduction' in Bromley, R. and Gerry, C., *Casual Work and Poverty in Third World Cities*, Chichester: John Wiley.

Burbach, R. and Flynn, P., 1980, *Agribusiness in the Americas*, New York: Monthly Review Press.

Byres, T. J., 1979, 'Of neo-populist pipe-dreams: Daedalus in the Third World and the myth of urban bias', *Journal of Peasant Studies*, Vol. 6, No. 2.

Cardoso, F. H., 1972, 'Dependent Capitalist Development in Latin America', *New Left Review*, No. 74.

Cardoso, F. H., 1980, 'Development and Environment: The Brazilian Case', *CEPAL Review*, 12.

Cardoso, F. H. and Faletto, E., 1969, *Dependencia y Desarrollo en América Latina*, Mexico: Siglo XXI.

Dos Santos, T., 1973, 'The Crisis of Development Theory and the Problem of Dependence in Latin America', in Bernstein, H. (ed.), *Underdevelopment and Development*, Harmondsworth: Penguin.

Eckstein, Susan, 1977, *The Poverty of Revolution, The State and the Urban Poor in Mexico*, Princeton: Princeton University Press.

Frank, A. G., 1967, *Capitalism and Underdevelopment in Latin America*, New York: Monthly Review Press.

Frank, A. G., 1969, *Latin America: Underdevelopment or Revolution*, New York: Monthly Review Press.

Germani, G., 1970, 'Mass Society, Social Class and the Emergence of Fascism' in Horowitz, I. L. (ed.) *Masses in Latin America*, Oxford: Oxford University Press.

Gilbert, A. and Gugler, J., 1981, *Cities, Poverty and Development*, Oxford: Oxford University Press.

Griffin, K., 1969, *Underdevelopment in Spanish America: an interpretation*, London: Allen and Unwin.

Goodman, D. and Redclift, M., 1981, *From Peasant to Proletarian: Capitalist Development and Agrarian Transitions*, Oxford: Basil Blackwell.

Hardoy, J. (ed.), 1975, *Urbanization in Latin America: approaches and issues*, Garden City, New York: Anchor.

Hirschman, A. O., 1968, 'The Political Economy of Import Substituting Industrialisation in Latin America', *Quarterly Journal of Economics*, No. 82.

Hobsbawm, E. J., 1967, 'The Crisis of the Seventeenth Century', in Aston, T. (ed.), *Crisis in Europe 1560–1660*, New York: Doubleday.

de Janvry, Alain, 1981, *The Agrarian Question and Reformism in Latin America*, Baltimore: Johns Hopkins University Press.

Kitching, G., 1982, *Development and Underdevelopment in Historical Perspective*, London: Methuen.

Laclau, E., 1971, 'Feudalism and Capitalism in Latin America', *New Left Review*, No. 67.

Lappé, F. M. and Collins, J., 1977, *Food First: Beyond the Myth of Scarcity*, New York: Houghton Mifflin.

Lehmann, D., 1982, 'Agrarian Structure, Migration and the State', in Peek, P. and Standing, G. (eds.), *State Policies and Migration*, London: Croom Helm.

Lipset, S. M. and Solari, A., 1967, *Elites in Latin America*, Oxford: Oxford University Press.

Lipton, M., 1977, *Why Poor People Stay Poor: a Study of Urban Bias in World Development*, London: Temple Smith.

Lopes, B. J. R., 1978, 'Capitalist Development and Agrarian Structure in Brazil', *International Journal of Urban and Regional Research*, Vol. 2, No. 1.

Luiselli, C., 1979, 'Agricultura y alimentación en México: premisas para una nueva estrategia', Estudios Rurales Latinoamericanos, Vol. 2, No. 3.

Mamalakis, M. J., 1969, 'The Theory of Sectoral Clashes', *Latin American Research Review*, Vol. IV, No. 3.

Mamalakis, M. J., 1971, 'The Theory of Sectoral Clashes and Coalitions Revisited', *Latin American Research Review*, Vol. VI, No. 3.

Meissner, F., 1981, 'The Mexican Food System (SAM): cultivating the oil revenue', *Food Policy*, Vol. 6, No. 4.

Morse, R., 1962, 'Latin American Cities: aspects of function and structure', *Comparative Studies in Society and History*, Vol. 4, No. 4.

Moser, C., 1978, 'Informal sector or petty commodity production: dualism or dependence in urban development?' *World Development*, Vol. 8, No. 9/10.

O'Brien, P., 1975, 'A Critique of Latin American Theories of Dependency', in Oxaal, I., Barnett, T. and Booth, D. (eds), *Beyond the Sociology of Development*, London: Routledge and Kegan Paul.

Oliveira, F. de, 1972, 'A Economia Brasileira: crítica á razão dualista', *Estudos CEBRAP*, 2 (October), 5-82.

Portes, A. and Walton, J., 1976, *Urban Latin America: The Political Conditions from Above and Below*, Austin and London: University of Texas Press.

Quijano, A., 1974, 'The Marginal Role of the Economy and the Marginalised Labour Force', *Economy and Society*, Vol. 3, No. 4.

Redclift, M. R., 1980, 'Agrarian Populism in Mexico – the "via campesina"', *Journal of Peasant Studies*, Vol. 7, No. 4.

Redclift, M. R., 1981, *Development Policymaking in Mexico: the Sistema Alimentario Mexicano*, Working Paper in U.S.-Mexican Studies, No. 24, University of California, San Diego.

Redclift, M. R., 1984, *Development and the Environmental Crisis: Green and Red Alternatives*, London: Methuen.

Restrepo, I. (ed.), 1980, *Conflicto entre cuidad y campo en América Latina*, Mexico City: Nueva Imagen.

Roberts, B., 1978, *Cities of Peasants*, London: Edward Arnold.

Roberts, B. and Long, N. (eds), 1978, *Peasant Cooperation and Capitalist Expansion in Central Peru*, Austin: University of Texas Press.

Saint, W., 1982, 'Farming for Energy: Social Options under Brazil's National Alcohol Programme', *World Development*, Vol. 10, No. 3.

Scott, A. M., 1979, 'Who are the self-employed?' in Bromley, R. and Gerry, C. (eds.), *Casual Work and Poverty in Third World Cities*, Chichester: John Wiley.

de Silva, S. B. D., 1982, *The Political Economy of Underdevelopment*, London: Routledge and Kegan Paul.

Sinclair, S., 1978, *Urbanisation and Labour Markets in Developing Countries*, London: Croom Helm.

Stavenhagen, R., 1975, *Social Classes in Agrarian Societies*, New York: Anchor Doubleday.

Sunkel, O. and Paz, P., 1970, *El Subdesarrollo Latinoamericano y la Teoría del Desarrollo*, Mexico: Siglo XXI.

Van der Pluijin, T., 1982, 'Energy versus Food? Implications of Macroeconomic Adjustments on Land-use Patterns: The Ethanol Programme in Brazil', *Boletin de Estudios Latinamericanos*, 33.

Veliz, C. (ed.), 1965, *Obstacles to change in Latin America*, Oxford: Oxford University Press.

Veliz, C. (ed.), 1967, *The Politics of Conformity in Latin America*, Oxford: Oxford University Press.

Walton, J., 1977, *Elites and Economic Development: Comparative studies on the political economy of Latin American cities*, Austin: University of Texas Press.

Ward, P., 1978, 'Self-help in Mexico City: social and economic determinants of success', *Town Planning Review*, No. 49.

World Bank, 1979, *Measuring Project Impact: Monitoring and Evaluation in the PIDER Rural Development Project Mexico*, Washington D.C.: Staff Working Paper No. 332.

World Bank, 1983, *A Social Methodology for Community Participation in Local Investments: the experience of Mexico's PIDER program*, Washington D.C.: Staff Working Paper No. 598.

Urban Bias Revisited

by Michael Lipton*

In his book 'Why Poor People Stay Poor' the author has argued that urban bias is the moving force behind needlessly slow and inequitable growth in contemporary developing countries. This claim is defended against three main criticisms: that the methods chosen to test it are not appropriate; that the evidence tendered is not relevant or sufficient; and that the rural-urban polarity is not clear-cut or does not represent the prime conflict within contemporary developing countries.

INTRODUCTION

The urban bias (UB) hypotheses are summarised in Lipton [*1981: 3-7*].[1] UB does not apply to all less developed countries (LDCs), for example, to some very open economies such as Fiji [*Ellis, this volume*]. Where UB does apply, not all institutions always demonstrate it: Maharashtra's Employment Guarantee Scheme mainly benefits rural people at mainly urban expense [*Herring and Edwards, 1983*].[2] Nor, of course, is it implied, because 'the disadvantaged are rural and the gainers urban', that UB 'explains ... regional ... racial ... sexual and inter-generational inequality' [*Byres, 1979: 215*]: only that UB (as the 'moving force behind maldistribution-with-growth') 'ensures that the rural sector both retains disproportionate shares of' women, children, blacks in South Africa, or Bengalis in pre-1971 Pakistan, 'and gives them less chance to advance' than the towns [*Lipton, 1977a: 74, and 1977a: 28; cf. Seers, 1977: 6-7; Griffin, 1977: 108*]. While it is important, in these three ways, not to claim too much for UB, it is indeed advanced as the main explanation of 'why poor people stay poor' in post-colonial LDCs.

This claim raises four main groups of issues. First, what *methods* are appropriate to test it? Second, are the *facts* adduced to support it relevant and sufficient? Third, does the *urban-rural polarity* – especially if interpreted as a class conflict – usefully survive the existence of poor townsmen, rich villagers, spatial continuities and alternative polarizations; or does such survival compel one, untenably, 'to define a class as an interest group' or, implausibly, to allocate rural elites sometimes into and sometimes out of the 'urban class' [*Corbridge, 1982, p. 101*]?[3] Fourth, do plausible *remedies* exist, if state structures are indeed dominated by classes bent on urban advance at the cost of efficiency and equity?

The first three questions are treated sequentially below. Space constraints made it impossible to deal with the fourth here.

---

* Institute of Development Studies, University of Sussex.

METHODS

UB is tested in Lipton [*1977a*] by two main methods. Chapters 5-8 comprise multi-country generalisations, comparing rural-urban income disparities, and seeking to associate them with disparate (and generally inefficient) capital endowments relative to output. Are such tests useful? Chapters 9-13 comprise discussions of particular issues (e.g. pricing, migration) with numerous examples, but with no assurance that the evidence is complete or typical of the realities. Is such exemplification over-dependent on countries with more data (and authorial experience), notably India, at the expense of (say) China, where UB may be negative, small, or just irrelevant? And is any form of multi-country comparison (as opposed to case-studies) too ahistorical to be acceptable?

Income and Capital Disparities

The urban-rural disparity is estimated − perhaps slightly over-estimated[4] − by r, the ratio of Non-agriculture (N) to Agriculture (A) in respect of output (or income) per person. This ratio is available for 63 LDCs around 1970, and for nine now-developed countries (NDCs) 10-30 years after modern growth acceleration. For the NDCs, r was: below 1.8 in six; 2.7 in two; and 3.4 in one (Norway 1865). Yet, around 1970, in all 63 LDCs except Dahomey (r = 1.6), r was above 1.8. In 52, including 40 of the 44 LDCs in Africa and Asia, r was above 2.7; and in 36 r was 4 or more [*Lipton, 1977a: 435-7*]. This unprecedented and widespread (and non-diminishing) disparity[5] is associated with the distribution of capital; LDCs vary greatly, but typically some 70 per cent of workforce is engaged mainly in A, producing some 40 per cent of GNP with some 20-25 per cent of 'capital stock' [*Lipton, 1977a: ch. 7*]. Such allocations, however inequitable, cannot be associated with 'bias' unless they are also inefficient: unless (a) investment-per-person is also much greater in N [*Lipton, 1977a: 444*], yet (b) the rate of return on investment is significantly greater in A. My evidence for (b) mostly uses the k-criterion: that the incremental capital/output ratio should be (but is not) about as high in A as it is in N.

This use of the k-criterion, which underpins my main multi-country systematic (as against topic-specific) evidence for UB, has been much criticised.[6] First, on 'prescriptive use of capital-output ratios ... the controversy has ranged long and hard, and it is surprising ... to find someone still willing to use them so unreservedly' [*Byres, 1979: 220-1*]; but most of the controversy surrounds the use of a projected, aggregate ratio to infer needed national investment for desired GNP growth − not (as in my argument) the use of past, sectoral ratios to infer relative capital efficiencies.

Second, some 'object strongly' even to this inference [*Rosen, 1978: 612*]; but the valid grounds of objection in fact suggest that even the high ratios of k_N to k_A in most LDCs tend to underestimate shortfalls of urban behind rural capital efficiencies [*Lipton, 1977a: 198-209*]. In particular, the abundance of rural labour (and its capacity to form 'labouresque' capital [*Sen, 1968: 82-7*] at slack-season opportunity-cost well below the wage rate) tends to strengthen the case for raising A's share of investment, not to weaken it as implied by Kitching [*1982: 88*].[7]

Third, there exists a set of arguments, associated with Marx and Dobb, for investing in capital-goods production – in order to lay the basis for long-term growth – although the short-run yield from such investment may be low (and, presumably, *because*, not 'although', such yield tends to go into reinvestible profits rather than into consumable, poorer people's, wage incomes). I indeed say little about such arguments [*Byres, 1979: 221-2*] because they are confined to large, closed economies, with (as Dobb advocates for planners) zero time-preference. Even there, as I stress too elliptically [*Lipton, 1977a: 20*], deadweight efficiency and equity costs are great; reasons for not (on analogous arguments) restricting investment to 'machines to make machines to ...' *ad infinitum* are obscure; and hence – even for an industrialisation-maximiser – arguments for preferring Dobbian policies to the larger GNP (and potential surplus) from conventionally efficient allocation are dubious.[8]

The Search for General Theory

The k-criterion – in conjunction with the r-comparisons – seems to me a correct, indeed essential, method in establishing necessary conditions for allocative UB. It can be used in many countries, and the r-comparisons (and other indicators of growth and poverty) can be regressed upon indicators of explanations alternative to UB, as outlined in *Why Poor People Stay Poor*, Chapter 3. I do believe in such searches for generality, not just in detailed case-studies as advocated by many critics [*B. Harriss, 1980: 17; Byres, 1979: 217*]. Unfortunately, on particular topics, there are too few reliable data to permit even suggestive statistical analysis. One is driven into *a priori* theorising, to which many also object [*Byres, 1979: 216*] but which seems acceptable if the assumptions are credible or testable;[9] or into taking 'examples from many countries, one per point, at various points in time', which may conceal 'contradictions which would develop if only one country were used' [*B. Harriss, 1983: 15*]. The latter danger is real, but can be reduced if (as I try to do) one searches the literature,[10] and never knowingly conceals counter-evidence.[11]

Many more case-studies are certainly needed, however, if even the most honest of 'lists of examples' is to be really convincing. My major disappointment is the relative scarcity of attempts to test UB, using it not as dogma but as research agenda. Striking exceptions are Urwick [*1983*], demonstrating much qualitative but little quantitative UB in secondary education in Sokoto; and Bates [*1981*], validating many of the political sequences of the UB hypothesis in specific African contexts by linking it to analyses of economic rent and social choice.[12] Fortunately, however, there are some issues relevant to UB – doctor allocation, primary schooling, urbanization – where there are sufficient broadly comparable data sets to generate considerable faith in the 'lists' approach.

Indian Bias?

It is, in particular, claimed that my UB evidence leans too heavily on India [*Seers, 1977; Baker, 1979: 171; Byres, 1979: 217*]. India contains as many people as Africa and Latin America combined, yet far less than one-third of my evidence is Indian. Almost all the comparative work (much of it cited in Lipton [*1977a: Tables*] indicates that UB is much more acute in most African LDCs than in India, where − at least in respect of credit, and of public investment − it probably diminished somewhat in the 1970s.

In the introductory paper to this volume Moore rightly points out that, though my *evidence* for UB may not be unduly Indian, the *model* sometimes appears to be so. The particular version of UB often discussed there: (a) has urban elites extracting mostly food surpluses, not surpluses of exportables, so that some price twists do not obviously harm some rural people (net food buyers); (b) has some rural inputs subsidized (at least nominally) − rather than implicitly taxed − for surplus farmers and regions. However, to relax these Indian-style special-case assumptions tends to make UB harsher, and simpler for the urban class to operate. The nature of the urban-class-based state may well be different in the 'African ideal type', with surplus extraction much more dependent on export crops than in India; or in the 'Latin American ideal type', with massively more intra-rural inequality (and an urban, absentee rural elite) than in India; but UB extraction is common to the three types of state, and analytical methods that combine evidence from all three are not obviously unacceptable.

Are There Exceptions?

A more serious methodological criticism of UB is that, due to the severe problems of genuine research access, too little attention was paid to socialist LDCs. I was too ready to accept claims that such countries featured relatively little UB. Thus Tanzania (arguably 'populist' rather than Socialist in its stated aims) is shown by much recent analysis to have suffered severely from UB; extreme price twists are revealed by Ellis in this volume. The problem is authoritatively, but perhaps doubtfully,[13] attributed to lack of rural political participation [*Nyerere, 1979: 8*]. As for China, rural people appear to remain (since 1953) virtually 'barred from bettering themselves in the cities'. Such movement control is in itself a massive imposition on villagers. Also, the state's need for such controls is testimony to villagers' relative deprivation in other aspects, well summarized by Nolan and White in this volume: urban income-per-person standing at about double rural levels in 1936, 1956 and today; a static agricultural share (about 12 per cent) in 'basic construction investment' during most of 1958−78; and since 1978 − despite some fall in the urban/rural wage ratio, and some further [compare *Khan, 1978: 834*] increase, though to well below world levels, in farm-nonfarm terms of trade − a 'more explicitly urban-centred' strategy, alongside a moderation of former rural emphases in health and education. The massive, rural and largely unreported famine deaths of 1959−61 [*Sen, 1983*] show how an urban-centred state, however pro-rural in its rhetoric, can (with a controlled press and no democracy) neglect silent, remote suffering. UB in India has no match for this tragedy.

Hence Chinese and Tanzanian experience strengthens the evidence (though not necessarily my explanation) for allocative UB. Also, notwithstanding Currie [*1979*], Latin American and other middle-income LDCs − which include such contrasts as Brasilia and the Brazilian North-East – are pervaded by inefficient (and inequitable) underallocation to, and extraction from, rural activity.[14] Peru has apparently exemplified extreme urban bias for three decades at least [*Alberts, 1981*].

The Relevance of History

But are the 'lists of examples' and 'generalized testing' methods, or my uses of them, hopelessly unhistorical? Some readers of Lipton [*1977a*] complain – with much justice – that 'countries flash on and off ... with unsettling speed ... chosen because they happen to illustrate the point [with] no sense of a detailed knowledge of ... their history, social structure or contemporary evolution' [*Byres, 1979: 217*]. In contrast to Marx's 'central question of the historical origin of institutions', the analysis often 'fails to pose the question in terms of historical development: where, when, how and why the modern urban-rural split arose' [*Lambert, 1979: 41*]. Some of these weaknesses, however, are implicit in any attempt to construct a general theory (e.g. that the persistence of poverty is in the great majority of LDCs due mainly to UB) that is *testable*, in respect of both assumptions and conclusions. The two methods used do imply a serious lack of historical denseness, especially for countries that an author knows only through a couple of books or papers. That is why case-studies [e.g. *Urwick, 1983*] matter so much. However, the methods at least render UB testable and modifiable as a multi-country theory to predict and explain phenomena currently observable. The sacrifice of such testability – in a much broader sense than Popper's – is the weakness implicit in the Marxian strength: in the methodology of building up general theories of history from nationally specific accounts of class-struggle as a development process.

Nevertheless, one can provide a broad-brush check-list of 'how it has come about' – not 'as a kind of Third World perversion of nature' – that in LDCs generally today (but not in the NDC past) 'the state ... acts to resolve the divergence of interests ... decisively in favour of the urban class' [*Byres, 1979: 234*].

> Small, interlocking elites of ... businessmen, professionals, bureaucrats [etc.] ... can in a modern state substantially control the distribution of resources. In the great majority of [LDCs], such urban elites spearheaded the fight against the colonizing power [,] formed, and have since dominated, the institutions of independence .... Urban power – by comparison with [NDC history[15] – has in LDCs] been out of all proportion to the urban share in either population or production. Rural people ... are much more dispersed, poor, articulate and unorganised. On the whole, rural groups fight each other locally; nationally, they seek to join or to use urban power and income, but not [to oppose them in the interests of] the rural sector. [*Lipton, 1981: 3*]

This *is* an account of an historical process – albeit one inevitably compressed into over-generality. It badly needs substantiation. For some countries and activities, this underpins the 'anti-colonial' history of UB's origins (on Indian heavy-industry policy, see Esho, [*1980: 4*] and Hanson [*1966*]; on the Sri Lankan successor elite, see Moore, [*this volume*]). In other cases [*H. Rao, 1978: 1699*], the origins lie mainly in urban colonial enclaves, and UB can perhaps be undermined by democratic rural institutions. In much of Francophone Africa, both colonialism and anti-colonialism were overwhelmingly urban-led and rurally-extractive [cf. Fanon, as cited in *Lipton, 1977a: 110, 139-40*]; probably independent India, too, both *inherited* non-farm salary structures and 'a norm that would justify ... only years of low farm prices as normal' and *initiated* 'industrialisation policies which ... demanded that farm prices remained in check' [*Tyagi, 1979: A-121*]. The social scientist must seek, and test, general explanations of the shared UB outcomes of these three distinct processes. He must, therefore, risk some unhistorical comparisons of current situations, to the neglect of specific historical sequences and class conflicts. What do India and China, colonizing and decolonizing origins, etc., *share*, to generate and maintain UB now? Surely, the common features are: (a) *state technologies* – political, military, communications – that now permit, more effectively than when Marx wrote, 'uniform actions from a supreme [state] centre upon all parts' of the peasantry [cited in *Lipton, 1977a: 120*]; and (b) *production and consumption technologies* that, much more than a hundred years ago, raised urban capital-intensity (and capital 'requirements' – though not efficiencies!) relative to those of near-subsistence rural activities. Such technologies, in turn, arise because of the 'history' of social confrontation, not just of natural science; but, once extant, they predispose LDCs, of *whatever history and capital-labour structures*, towards UB outcomes.

FACTS

So much for methods: what of facts? Most critics of the UB hypothesis accept the claimed facts – extreme rural underallocation, its relative recency, its inefficiency and inequity – but reject some of the explanations [*Griffin, 1977: 108; Southall, 1978: 2; Chase-Dunn, 1978: 83;* and implicitly on Latin America, *Redclift, this volume*; on Tanzania, *Ellis, this volume*; and on selectively urban electrification in Bihar, *Rothermund, 1980*]. Indeed, the rare exception – in repeatedly claiming 'rural bias' in India – can ground his remark only as 'deliberate mocking' [*Byres, 1979: 241*]. In India (or almost any LDC) a comparison of, say, urban with rural death-rates, productivities, investments or teacher-provisions rather suggests 'unconscious self-mocking'. The facts *are* disputed, however, in two possible areas for state action to transfer rural incomes townwards, viz. prices and taxes; in one area of possible rural self-compensation, namely, urbanisation with subsequent remittances; in one area affecting relative rural entitlements (and taxable capacities), namely, the claim that urban income inequality generally exceeds rural; and in respect of some aspects of NDC history.

Terms of Trade

My main emphasis, in discussing farm-nonfarm[16] terms of trade, is on their *levels*. How much of their current bundle of purchases could farmers buy with their current bundle of sales, if non-market interventions[17] affected prices neutrally? If over 100 per cent, those interventions are biased against farmers; if under 100 per cent, the bias is pro-farmer.

One critic expatiates sardonically upon his quite inaccurate claim that 'no specific countries are cited' [*Byres, 1979: 228*] to illustrate anti-farmer terms-of-trade bias; its very large effect was in fact documented in Pakistan and Kenya and (for particular interventions only) in Argentina and India [*Lipton, 1977: 306*]. The total impact is now confirmed by 1976 data for Pakistan and Argentina (as well as Egypt, Thailand and Yugoslavia), all showing large price twists against agricultural producers − costing them \$1.8-2.1 billion in Egypt alone [*Bale and Lutz, 1979: 12, 19*]. Apart from such total indicators, agricultural output price twists alone give a fairly good indication of public-sector-cum-cartel impacts on farmers' terms of trade (at least in countries where modern inputs comprise below 10 per cent or so of farm output value): in all 13 African countries sampled by the World Bank [*1981*] substantial negative nominal protection was found for almost all crops; a current study of 16 commodities and 29 countries from the developing regions shows average producer prices over 30 per cent below border prices, of which gap perhaps a quarter to a third might comprise marketing costs [*FAO, 1984: ch. 4, pts. B-C*]. In most cases, however, one has to look at the impact of particular measures − input and output taxes and subsidies, food-aid disposals, exchange-rate decisions, etc. − on the level of the farm-nonfarm terms of trade.

While this *relative level*, compared with the border-price ratio (or some other indicator of the level with neutral interventions), is an indicator of static price-related UB, I reject the use of *absolute changes* in the farm-nonfarm terms of trade to indicate changes in − or, even worse, levels of − UB. This is because such absolute changes are due to exogenous changes in (a) demand (in conjunction with supply elasticities) and (b) supply (in conjunction with demand elasticities), and not merely in (c) the extent of urban, or rural, bias that is exogenously pushing supply and demand conditions around. To equate terms-of-trade changes to (c) alone is no less arbitrary if they 'are calculated over a suitably long period ... say, 1950−75', as suggested by Byres [*1979: 229*]; this may iron out fluctuations, but does nothing to allow for (a) and (b).[18]

The above argument for measuring 'levels, not trends' is rejected by B. Harriss [*1980: 16*] and Baker [*1979: 171*]. The latter claims that 'After much criticism of the use of the terms of trade as an analytical tool, he uses this on p. 295 in the same partial way which he criticises so heavily earlier and in so doing he selects the two years (1967/8) which show the reverse of Thamarajakshi's study of the period 1950−69.' The latter study is of *movements* in the terms of trade − due to changes in supply, in demand, and in UB. My 1967−8 data (citing Dandekar) show that 'about a quarter of Indian cereal marketings were publicly procured, at prices about 25 per cent lower than were obtainable in the market' for free sales: part of public-sector action to reduce the static *level* of producer prices, below what would prevail if such action were neutral.

Although trends in farm-nonfarm terms-of-trade suggest absolutely nothing about levels, or even changes, in urban bias, two comments on such trends are in order. First, if such absolute trends consistently and significantly moved relative prices to favour (or to reduce disfavour for) agriculturalists, that would be an interesting *limitation on the impact* of price UB. Byres suggests this happened in India. Yet, from 1951/2 to 1965/6, 'sectoral improvement [of agriculture's] net barter terms of trade is marginal' [*Thamarajakshi, 1969: A-99*], even using price series later shown to substantially exaggerate such improvements [*Tyagi: 1979*]; on more appropriate series (and contrary to Mitra [*1977: ch. 8*]), more recent trends have been clearly unfavourable to farmers [*Kahlon and Tyagi: 1980*]: all this in three decades of rising income-based demand for food per person yet with a near-static supply (per-person rises in food output being closely matched by falls in imports plus rises in stocks). Second, especially for export crops, it is sometimes possible to set farmers' price trends against world price trends, thus inferring increased [*Ellis, this volume, Table 2*] or decreased resource-extraction in respect of major farm outputs.

Ellis's ingenious statistical work demonstrates deepening UB in Tanzanian pricing policy. He doubts this, because he believes such UB exists only if (a) *food* underpricing is used, to enable urban employers to pay lower money-wages and increase investible profits; and (b) such surpluses finance 'a sustainable contribution to non-farm growth'. However, (a) export marketing boards are a classic medium of UB surplus extraction via pricing [*Lipton, 1977a: 295*] − a surer route to higher re-investable surpluses than is artificially cheap food, which need not always mean commensurately higher re-investible urban profits [*Ellis, this volume: fn. 5*]; and (b) urban-biased policies, alas, carry no guarantees of even non-farm success.

A more difficult question − a prime candidate for the UB 'research agenda' − concerns the impact of price twists. Major rural *employment effects* cast further doubt on 'the conventional lay wisdom that if farm product prices' were less repressed by State action in LDCs then 'poor people would be hurt' [*Bale and Lutz, 1979: 9-10; Table 2*]. In India, moreover, *wage-price relationships* suggest that 'in the long run high prices are in the interests of agricultural labourers and low prices against them', though the reverse may apply in the very short run [*Tyagi, 1979: A-118-9*].[19] Evidence of substantial market dependence by small farmers (and of course labourers) in respect of their *gross* purchases of *grain* [*Mitra, 1977: 120*] − relating as it does, to a systematically incomplete (gross) indicator, of consumption only (not wages or employment) and with no implication for non-food prices − seems insufficient to overturn the above indications that less-repressed farm prices would usually help the rural poor. They would gain absolutely, but probably less so than the rural rich, even if the higher prices induced faster rural growth [*Van Arkadie, 1977: 413*].

But would it? Some authors [*H. Rao, 1978: 1701; Mitra, 1977: 121; B. Harriss, 1980: 18*] claim low Indian aggregate agricultural supply elasticities, but underestimate these because they overestimate the favourable trend in farm prices [*Tyagi, 1979*]. Long-run effects, at least where new technology is for many farmers near the margin of attractiveness, certainly raise total price-elasticities of farm supply well above the 0.1-0.2 levels normally accepted in partial-equilibrium analyses [*Peterson, 1979*]. And the responsiveness of marketed surplus – at least – to price is sufficiently clear and large [*Sah and Stiglitz, 1983: 8*] as to render quite incoherent any policy that *both* turns terms-of-trade heavily against farmers (to urbanise savings) *and* seeks, by kinder methods than Stalin's, to urbanise food or exportables. This inconvenient fact will not go away just because it is termed a 'cheap gibe' or 'utter nonsense' and confused with arguments about the optimal roundaboutness of investment [*Byres, 1979: 223*]. However, I concur fully with those who doubt that much can be done for agriculture, especially in Africa, by improved price-incentives alone.

Taxes

On taxes, my position [*Lipton, 1977a: ch. 12*] is simple. In most LDCs, persons in 'agriculture and the rural sector ... are ... undertaxed' absolutely – tax rates and yields, at least for the better-off, should be raised. But rural persons are overtaxed by comparison with: (a) urban persons of similar capacity-to-pay; and (b) the share of state benefits going to rural areas – especially since rural taxes are costlier to collect, less stable and less income-elastic than urban taxes, and are likelier to be diverted from essential forms of consumption or high-return forms of investment. So urban tax take should rise relative to rural. The *sign* of urban tax bias is usually positive, but its *size*, positive or negative, is seldom large.

These facts have not been disputed, but my position has been – no doubt unintentionally – misrepresented. Thus I am referred [*Byres, 1979: 224-6*] to a series of reports showing that *direct* taxation in India is a smaller share of farm than of non-farm *income*; this is indisputable, and perfectly consistent with my evidence that *total* taxation, in each available year (1950–1 to 1961–2), was a slightly larger share of rural than of urban *taxable capacity* [*Lipton, 1977a: 282*].[20] Moreover, rural or agricultural taxes appear to exceed corresponding outlays in Tanzania and Pakistan as well as India [*Lipton, 1977a: 284*]. Byres further states that for me, higher overall taxation in LDCs 'must not be rural taxation: urban workers and the urban rich can be taxed, but not farmers of any kind' (earlier in the chapter he has defended kulaks against taxation – pp. 279-80) [*Byres, 1979: 227*]. Contrast [*Lipton, 1977: 279-80*]: 'If taxes are imposed on better-off farmers, the efficiency and equity case for taxation is much stronger [reasons are given] but some caveats are in order .... None of this is meant as a general case against taxing big farmers [but] the emphasis on mopping up, for urban development, the often modest "gains" of the "green revolution" may be misplaced'. Readers of Byres [*1979*] need to recall the warning *caveant emptores*.

Urban Remittances

A major objection to UB is that losers could 'vote with their feet' by moving townwards, and then remit incomes to their families. Townward migration, however, at least in most of Asia and Africa, is far less than official data suggest, and has very limited power to reduce the *proportions* living in rural areas, because of demographic and economic mechanisms linking it to slowed urban natural increase. Urbanisation also provides very limited remittance (or other) benefits to the poorest rural people, but concentrates [despite *Breese, 1978: 773;* see *Connell et al., 1976: 59-63*] on the educated, constituting a 'rural skill drain' [*Lipton, 1977a: chs. 9, 11*]. Again, these facts have scarcely been disputed. They limit the uses of urbanisation as an effective 'safety valve for the rural sector' [*H. Rao, 1978: 1700;* cf. *White, 1979: 298* and *Lipton, 1982*]. Some commentators rightly stress that townward migration usually benefits migrants, is part of healthy economic development, is accordingly significant in middle-income countries (especially Latin America), and should not be artificially impeded [*Currie, 1979*]. All this is true; but the rising marginal *social* costs of townward migrancy,[21] however advantageous privately, militate strongly against encouraging it artificially by means of UB.

As for urban-rural remittances, the evidence is that − while gross figures can be very large for particular, mostly wealthy, families, and for exceptional villages (often surveyed precisely because of the high incidence of townward movements) − inflows net of rural-to-urban remittances are very small proportions of rural incomes in typical villages in most LDCs. Such remittances could, perhaps, sometimes 'counteract much of the damage done to the village by urbanization' (not by 'urban bias', as attributed to me by Byres [*1979: 230*]). Byres cites − from [*Connell et al., 1976*], which (as he states) I co-authored − several instances of Indian families, even a few villages, with high ratios of gross remittances to income; but he does not cite the village data relevant to this issue. These are the data for *net* remittances as a proportion of income of villages (not selected explicitly for their remittance-intensity). These proportions are available for 17 villages (in Tamil Nadu, Gujarat and Rajasthan) in the 1960s. For just one village, net remittances were indeed 33.1 per cent of total incomes; for the other 16, they averaged just 1.8 per cent. The few non-Indian data sets on out-remittances also suggest that net inflows are small indeed [*Connell et al., 1976: 101-2, 107-8*] − seldom, perhaps, offering a very high return on the educational and other costs that the migrant's family has invested *within* the village. Possibly Byres's remark that 'a little probing will transform agnosticism into first surprise and then into other emotions' might better be applied, not to my assertions on remittances, but to his methodology of 'citation'?

Intra-sectoral Income Distribution

If, and only if, rural equality exceeds urban equality, several strong conclusions follow. First, even if average rural and urban income is identical, rural taxable capacity is lower than urban. Second − provided that power in a community is distributed roughly according to (if perhaps more unequally than) income and assets − a given amount of *extra* income will probably be distributed more equally (and will thus generate more welfare) in rural than in urban areas.[22] Third, therefore, the 'overlap of efficiency and equity', associated with urban-to-rural transfers of investible incomes, is strengthened by intra-sectoral income distributions.

I chose a measure of intra-sectoral inequality that also helps assess the concentration of intra-sectoral power: sectoral income share of the richest 20 per cent. This was significantly[23] higher in rural areas in only one of the ten countries cited from Ahluwalia; but in urban areas, in five, plus one (Malaysia) cited at the same point [in *Lipton, 1977a: 388, fn. 13*; see also *Abdullah, 1979: 90*] but not listed in Byres [*1979: Table 1*]. This was not 'three out of ten ... selective use of evidence' [*Byres, 1979: 219*] for the hypothesis of greater intra-rural equality, but six out of seven, plus four draws. Later evidence changes the score to eleven out of thirteen (plus five draws): rural areas are clearly more unequal in Argentina, but towns in Puerto Rico [*Weiskoff, 1976: 43-50*], almost certainly (since regional and national Gini coefficients are so much higher in metropolitan than in rural areas [*Thomas, 1982: 86*]) Brazil, and certainly Sri Lanka, South Korea and Bangladesh, with the Philippines 'drawn' [*Asian Development Bank, 1977: 64*]. African data are absent, but almost all would surely show intra-rural inequality far below intra-urban.

True enough, even where rural distribution is not very unequal 'it cannot be concluded that future distribution will follow this pattern'. For instance, rural income gains from the 'green revolution' disproportionately favoured the rural rich [*Byres, 1979: 219*]. I contend only that: (a) the richest *urban* 20 per cent generally have a greater inter-sectoral 'head start' than the richest rural 20 per cent, so that (b) urban elites are even better placed to appropriate gains from extra intra-sectoral investment than are rural elites. This is indeed *ceteris paribus*, but not necessarily 'static'. It is a testable hypothesis, for the research agenda, not a grand theory; I hope that is true of all the component hypotheses of the UB approach.

NDC History

A final, occasionally challenged, factual claim is that almost all NDCs featured far less UB than do today's LDCs. First, NDCs then − like LDCs now − 'relied upon industrialisation rather than agricultural development for their economic growth [, which] inevitably also meant urbanisation as the dominant style of economic development'; can we not read NDC history as 'a triumph of UB in engineering economic development without the continuing adverse effects on rural development'? This criticism would apply − and UB would fail as a theory, because it would seek 'to explain the history of development, by attributing ... to special circumstances' [*V. Rao, 1980: 83*] the above triumph (by contrast to the persistence of rural underdevelopment today) − if, and only if, UB were equated with industrialisation and urbanisation. In fact, UB is defined as *resource allocations* that are both inefficiently and inequitably over-urban, plus *dispositions* to advocate and induce them. In almost all NDCs − by contrast to LDCs now − the structures of thinking, of power, and (above all?) of technology for state action (and for economic activity) did not significantly induce UB. That is shown by the low A-N disparities [*Lipton, 1977a: 437*].[24]

New Evidence

Finally, four new areas of factual support for the UB hypothesis have emerged recently. First, nutritional behaviour indicates that far larger proportions of people in rural than in urban areas reveal urgent food needs − by maintaining, in spite of increases in income, the three ratios food/outlay, cereal/food, and coarse/fine grains [*Lipton, 1983: 40-9*]. Second, in India, this is probably related to a clear excess of rural over urban death-rates, in each age-group and for both sexes [*Mitra, 1978: 223; Grawe, 1980: 130; Ruzicka, 1982: 20, 39*].

Third, peri-urban land expansion – while often a natural consequence of development, and of townward migration – becomes symptomatic of UB if: (a) such migration is artificially encouraged by direct resource allocation (or price policies) disfavouring the rural sector, or by increasing its surplus/ output ratio by rendering it more unequal (for the inequality-migration link, see Connell *et al.* [*1976*]); or (b) new rural farmland or residential land – by means of compulsory purchase, restriction of existing urban densities, price policy or otherwise – is rendered especially vulnerable to urban expansion. Some trenchant critics of these trends [*Eckholm, 1976*] perhaps distinguish too little between justified and excessive de-ruralisations of LDC land, but the latter are substantial and closely related to UB [*Brown, 1978; Coleman, 1976; Habitat Asia, 1979*].

Fourth, the important role of corrupt payments in diverting rural benefits has recently been documented [*Herring and Edwards, 1983: 581; Wade, 1982*]. Initially this diversion may well be intra-rural, from labourers seeking public-works jobs to supervisors, or from farmers to irrigation allocators; but there is an almost inevitable process by which the implied quasi-rent, earned from occupying ever-higher posts (supervisor, assigner of supervisors), sucks the corrupt payments towards ever higher, more centralised places, whether in the contracting firm, political party or civil service. This is a largely unmeasured but probably major component of rural-to-urban flows of payments.[25]

THEORISING URBAN BIAS

> The larger landowners ... become honorary members of the urban class as the towns succeed in buying off 'the powerful country interests' .... Conversely, the urban poor, the unemployed, the self-employed in the informal sector and other migrants ... appear to be assigned to the rural class .... We thus have a bizarre situation in which the people who control over half the land in rural areas are counted as beneficiaries of UB while the people who account for over half the labour force in urban areas are assigned to the rural classes and suffer from UB.

The class theory of UB, if thus correctly summarised by Griffin [*1977: 109*], indeed looks like what Popper called a conventionalist strategem: 'semantic short-circuiting of empirical attack ... by simply relabelling ... sectors and classes on the back of a series of alliances'. Moreover, even where Griffin's objection failed because 'formulation of ... policies, and the resultant distri-bution of the spoils, ... correspond to the rural-urban divide' [*Corbridge, 1982: 98*], would not UB – in rightly rejecting Griffin's implicitly essentialist definition of 'economic classes [as] located always and only by definite relationships to the means of production' [*Corbridge, 1982: 100*] – unaccept-ably (a) 'define a class as an interest group', and (b) reduce 'policies and plans' to the expression of the interests of the urban 'class' thus (mis)defined [*Corbridge, 1982: 101*]?

Such criticisms of UB theorising are intellectually much more serious than some other commentators' denials of the realities: viz., of the prevalence, historical novelty, inequity, or inefficiency of systematic anti-rural outcomes in the vast majority of LDCs. These four realities (see Schickele [*1968*] and Mamalakis [*1970*] – neither known to me in 1977 – and Todaro and Stilkind [*1981*] for more evidence), however, surely require *some* theory. I hope the critics of UB theory will either modify it, or suggest alternative theoretical explanations of the realities.

Below, the theoretical issues are 'layered' as follows. Can a UB-type account encompass (a) urban people with little affluence, power or status, (b) rural people with much, yet in an 'urban alliance'? If so, are 'urban' and 'rural' still (c) usefully definable, (d) dichotomous? If so, (e) is 'urban-rural' better than other (or no) dichotomies? Only after this bush-clearing can we see the big game: (f) class theory and urban bias.

The Urban Poor

There are many petty capitalists in the poorest, least powerful, and lowest-status (say) quintiles, in Italy or France [*Berger and Piore, 1980*]; yet it is acceptable to theorise that such countries' socio-economic systems feature bias towards a dominant capitalist class. 'Competition among capitals', in which the successful capitalists increase their gains-per-person by exclusion (and inheritance) per person is recognised. What, then, is the force of claims that in LDCs the numerous poor, powerless, or low-status people in urban areas disprove the existence of bias towards an urban group?

The claim could mean that the *incidence* of urban poverty and powerlessness is so high that UB becomes implausible. To this, there are three rejoinders. Firstly, the incidence is far lower than in rural areas, due to the much higher average urban income (and despite the usually greater urban inequality). Secondly, many families containing urban informal self-employed and other migrants (and many educated unemployed) *are* in the higher deciles of affluence and power, and thus can be 'assigned to the urban class' [*Griffin, 1977: 109*] without problems. Thirdly, many other families, while poor and resident in cities, can legitimately be described as poor rural victims of UB: most of the 8-10 per cent of Indian (and other LDC?) urban persons dependent mainly on agriculture [*UN, 1980*]; poor migrants, who would return to the village but for urban-biased prospects and income-distribution there.

The claim may be that there is no group commonality of benefit between the urban rich and the permanently urban poor (who *are* in the urban class); and, conversely, no clear conflict between the apparently urban poor who are 'really rural' and other townspeople. As for commonality, is 'the more ready availability of urban services very meaningful to the bottom quarter of the urban income structure' [*van Arkadie, 1977: 412*], in making their lives preferable to those of rural people with similar income-per-person? Yes, surely, if they have access even to urban standpipes and emergency medical services. Conversely, as for conflict, the essentially rural and temporary presence of many of the 'urban' poor – often seen by established townspeople (especially workers) as a quasi-ethnic challenge, from Southern tribals in Khartoum or from Tamils in Bombay – provides a distinct form of labour-power: dismissible by bosses, or seasonally withdrawable by workers at agricultural peaks; competing on different terms with urban employees (casual as against permanent wage-labour); and thus preventing urban labour solidarity precisely because a rural class provides the labour-reserve, and an urban class the labour elite. A brilliant exemplification is Rothermund [*1980*].

Particularly in Latin American cities, however, 'the marginal sector is not of such marginal and transient importance' as I may have suggested; there, a significant part of the 'immense grey economy of working poor' [*Seers, 1977: 8*] cannot be decomposed into those who share urban-class benefits (or soon will) and those who are 'really' rural. Would an assault on UB help this part of the 'vast pool of desperately poor people in or around the major cities and large towns' [*Singh, 1977: 51*]? Certainly, more labour-intensive urban growth, and not *only* a reallocation of capital towards (anyway more labour-intensive) rural activities, is required to bid up employment, wage-rates and hence the share in GNP of the rural and urban poor. But urban labour intensification, without rural resource reallocation, will mean more townward migration. Anyway, will it happen, while the UB coalition – of rurally extractive employers, big farmers and urban labour elites – remains dominant?

The Rural Rich

Despite the reality of urban poverty in LDCs, few deny the much greater incidence, severity, instability and 'inescapability' of rural poverty and powerlessness. On the other hand, the wealth and power of 'big' farmers, 'kulak lobbies', rural leaders, etc. are sometimes claimed to be comparable or superior to – or the same thing as! – those of the apparently 'urban' rich or powerful. The 'rural strong', therefore, are a greater challenge to UB than the 'urban weak'.

The role of rural elites, in any plausible model of group relations, is complex. They share with the rural poor an interest in more rural investment, schooling, research, etc., and in furthering this interest they would be in direct competition for outlays against the urban sector.[26] Yet they share with the urban elite an interest in (a) concentrating rural resources – and incentives – on those groups that use them to create and 'urbanise' surpluses of food, exportables, savings and human capital; (b) avoiding major *intra-sectoral* redistributions of power or wealth. The UB hypothesis claims, first, that – because of the urban-centred power and technology of most LDC states, and the role of rural surpluses – these conflicts of interest normally result in a political outcome in which the rural elites receive concessions (e.g. selective subsidies on inputs or credit) but accept urban bias in output prices and in allocations of human and physical capital; and, second, that this alignment of rural elites with decision-taking townspeople produces anti-rural, inefficient and inequitable outcomes.

Such ideal-typical simplifications of the complex realities of 100 or more LDCs are dangerous enough, albeit essential to form testable generalisations. But further simplification – that the UB hypothesis 'simply defines the rural privileged as "rural urbanists"' [*Kitching, 1982: 88*]; or involves 'conscription of the rural rich into the urban class' [*Ellis, this volume*]; or even, less crudely, requires that rural elites 'belong to the urban class [, are] bought off [by it,] or, more correctly, absorbed into [it] by virtue of its coincident interests' [*Corbridge, 1982: 97*] – risks caricature.

Certainly, 'the urban rich as well as bureaucracy are increasingly recruited from the class of rural rich through the process of education[and migration' [*H. Rao, 1978: 1700*] (although, especially in Africa, such 'rural rich' are usually much less rich, and weaker, than the urban rich whom they seek to join). A dominant group or class (though it will try to pass on many benefits of dominance to its offspring) will, if wise, strengthen itself and weaken rivals by admitting their wealthier, more powerful and intelligent members, thus pre-empting effectively-led counter-actions and keeping some hope alive for those who, without hope, might rebel.

The acid test of the role of rural elites in UB is not whether LDCs' dominant groups include many rural-born politicians [*Griffin, 1977: 109*] or businessmen – of course they do – but how such people use their rural incomes and urban power.[27] Generally their priorities are: (a) to transfer residence, ambience, investible surplus, offspring, and group interests to the town, while keeping rural assets, vote banks, and clients; (b) to arrange state policy for rural areas in ways that, while not diverting many urban resources, mainly help better-off rural groups (including absentees), especially in the process of townward surplus transfer. For example, in parts of India agricultural policy renders it profitable to use agricultural surpluses to finance, not farm re-investment, but urban food transfers by private merchants [*B. Harriss, 1981*] – and, by food zoning down to District level and below, not only parallels this process by easing the states' compulsory food levies but also creates corrupt incomes (from those seeking to evade zoning) which, as described earlier, are inevitably sucked upwards to urban and central levels. It is incorrect to ascribe these processes to 'the dominant position of the larger farmers and rural capitalists, and their conflicts with less powerful rural groups, rather than urban pressures' [*Rosen, 1978: 612*]. Rather, urban groups – formal labour, business, political – with a shared interest in surplus make it more attractive for urbanising rural elites to subserve urban interests than to advance those of rural people as a whole.

Especially in democracies, the mass of poor rural voters can secure major concessions [*Rosen, 1978: 1700*], including substantial independent parts of non-monolithic state systems directed exclusively to helping it. Although even here benefits tend to trickle up, such processes are perhaps the best short-term hope for undermining UB. But long-established elites are skilful at safe-guarding their position – not least by obtaining recurrent 'reorganisations' of institutions that look like helping the rural poor at their expense. This, like much else, suggests the apparently 'reactionary' conclusion that the rural poor, except in revolutionary situations, need to ally themselves with (at least some of) the rural (moderately) rich: to detach them from the urban alliance.

Far from being 'absurd ... unrealistic ... utterly ignor[ing] the deep and fundamental class divisions of rural society' [*Byres, 1979: 240*], such a strategy builds on the reality that the power of the urban class to extract rural sur-plus depends on these divisions, in two senses. It depends on the political urbanisation of the rural leadership – in South Asia and Latin America on raising the rural share of, in much of Africa on virtually creating *de novo*, kulaks and merchants able to save (thanks partly to cheap labour) and willing to transfer townwards their surpluses both of outputs (food and exportables) and of savings (supporting physical capital and human skills). Rural deprivation will seldom be ameliorable without a realignment of substantial parts of the rural middle-income groups, including their urbanising members, in politics and business, to fight, not (as co-opted parts of the urban alliance) for their own, urban share in rural-to-urban extractions, but (in a rural class) for rural resources – through either reduced extractions or, as in the Japanese case (and in Harvey's italicised remarks that commence B. and J. Harriss's article in this volume), extractions reinvested rurally. The urbanisation of rural surplus and control of the state, not 'coincident interests' as claimed by Corbridge [*1982: 97*], are the aims that unite the 'urban alliance', and what makes it an urban class rather than an interest group.

Four final points about the role of the rural better-off or more-powerful in the urban alliance need stressing. First – contrary to Byres [*1979: 239*], Baker [*1979: 171-2*] and Herring and Edwards [*1983: 588*] – my repeated denials that UB is a conspiracy theory were serious! Urban businessmen and politicians, plus rural 'big men' with urban contacts, indeed find it easier than dispersed villagers to meet in small groups to achieve their goals, because they are spatially more concentrated and closer to power. However, such groups seldom meet each other, would often disagree if they did, and anyway frequently produce urban-biased outcomes without such inter-group meetings (and often without secrecy, or explicitly anti-rural interest) merely by separate action, given their joint power. Second, UB can persist, even if the power-groups (urban rich plus rural-based 'joiners') use its benefits, not to industrialise, but to build bigger bureaucracies [*Ellis, this volume*] or even palaces. Third, better-off 'non-agricultural landless' [*B. Harriss, 1980: 23*] in rural areas – merchants, lenders, the rare big artisan – face incentives to urbanise their surpluses (and hence class allegiances) rather as big farmers do, though usually[28] in respect of savings rather than of outputs. Fourth, of course there are conflicts of interest (a) within the urban alliance, (b) among its rural victims, who include richer peasants who do *not* significantly urbanise surpluses, but who do oppose the rural poor on some issues. 'Undifferentiated groups of peasants' [*B. Harris, 1980*] are rare; indeed, the thrust for urbanism to differentiate them (so as to extract the surplus) is bound to create some borderline cases of farmers half in and half out of the urban alliance.

The Rural-Urban Dichotomy

How strongly does a UB model require a clear urban-rural dichotomy [*Moore, this volume; di Giorgi, 1979: 47*]? It does not require dichotomous types of human activity, but it does require some dichotomy of settlement patterns. If each human's activities (including assets, residence, work, income sources, and output types) were either fully rural or fully urban, then the 'urban alliance' would require deals (probably implicit) between the town leadership and the rural surplus-generators. The possibility that better-off households can shift residence, savings, etc. between town and country, thereby on balance transferring surpluses and power townwards, provides a plausible and testable alternative pattern for the 'urban alliance'. Hence a not-too-discrete separation of urban from rural activity − as opposed to settlement patterns − actually enriches the UB model (although complete continuity, with everyone, rich or poor, half in and half out of rural life, would render the model implausible, perhaps unworkable).

Some dichotomy of settlement patterns, however, is needed for UB. It involves the use, by urban ruling groups, of economies of *political* agglomeration, organisation and scale in the exercise of power (in markets and in politics) *vis-à-vis* dispersed rural places. If everyone lived in settlements of the same size, or if space were settled at uniform densities with no clear urban-rural distinction, there could be no UB. There might be some − but it could only be mild − if very large proportions of people, especially powerful people, concentrated their activities (residence, assets, work, etc.) in 'rurban' places − as appears clearly not to be the case in most LDCs. More data are now available than could be cited in Lipton [*1977a: 368, fn. 24*].

UB also requires some overlap between (a) human activity, (b) settlement patterns and (c) the density of both. If (a) and (b) did not overlap substantially − in particular if towns were as agriculture-dependent as villages − the wish to extract regional (rural) surpluses for special forms of non-agricultural development in other (urban) regions would be inoperative. If (b) and (c) did not overlap − if towns were no denser in population than villages or groups of homesteads − townspeople would lose a major advantage in extracting a surplus from country people: greater ease of intra-urban than of intra-rural communication, organisation and control. If (a) did not overlap with (c) − if (chiefly urban) industry required no more persons or capital per acre, at optimal levels of activity, than (chiefly rural) agriculture − the economic basis for the overlap of (a) with (b), of steel-mills with urban life and of farms with rural life, would disappear, as would the economic basis for higher urban densities.

'Rural-urban' is not a categorisation of space alone. To see it like that is to underpin an incorrect absolute distinction between geographical (residence, density), occupational, sectoral and class categorisations of households. The overlap 'rural, agricultural,[29] labour-using, dispersed' *vis-à-vis* the overlap 'urban, non-farm, capital-using, concentrated', while imperfect (and complex in operation), does define a central class conflict.

Alternative Categorisations

The empirical validation of overlaps between rurality and lower density, smallness and dispersion of settlements, agriculture-dependence, low capital-intensity, low income-per-person, and political and economic underdog or 'extractee' status − and even of fairly substantial differences between the probabilities that persons in rural places will be (say) mainly agricultural, poorer or the victims of price-twists − does not suffice to justify the central place accorded in Lipton [*1977a*] to the rural-urban dichotomy. Other dichotomies than rural-urban might, in some or all LDCs, better separate groups of persons, households or places into (say) rich or poor, strong or weak; or might better indicate where to seek causes and/or cures.

The proposal to replace 'urban vs. rural [by] rich vs. poor' [*H. Rao, 1978: 1699*] is unhelpful, because we seek to know *why* poor people stay poor. The proposal does, however, warn against any view 'that the rural rich should be provided unfettered opportunities for development through state aid'. However, this error is not implicit in my claim that productive manna from heaven (or the state) and its yields will be less unequally, more poverty-reductively, distributed in rural areas than in the city. The city normally: (a) provides fewer extra working hours and units of GNP per unit of extra 'manna' (be it investment, schooling or health care); (b) distributes them less equally (to the extent that extra income distribution depends on initial inequality);[30] (c) uses a much smaller proportion of them (and of the 'manna') to make, and hence to cut the price of, poor people's consumables – some 60-85 per cent of which comprise foods, mostly cereals and roots.

If townward migration is severely and effectively restrained, and if rural elites are repressed also, then one would expect core-periphery models to categorise space, as in China, where 'increments to rural incomes have been distributed along a continuum defined by ... proximity to cities, especially large ones' [*Nolan and White, this volume*]. However, in other circumstances I am unconvinced by attempts to replace UB by core-periphery models where the capital city is 'a Triton among the minnows' [*Moore, this volume*, citing B. Farmer]. Dense rural populations near such a capital city – often part-time farmer-commuters with land values pulled up by it – can indeed show many urban interests and features. However, I see this as consistent with a model of an encapsulated, urbanising rural elite, and find the alternative core-periphery model unconvincing. First, why does similar capital-city primacy do so little to ameliorate UB around, say, Dacca? Second, even in Sri Lanka, why is it so unclear what should be part of the periphery? (There is a sense in which the historic centres of Sinhalese Buddhist tradition, Kandy and Anuradhapura, retain their significance in the interface of politics with Buddhism, yet they are in Moore's periphery. There are problems with a model where surplus farmers are mostly in the periphery and deficit farmers in the core. Within the periphery, as Moore *et al.* [*1983*] have shown, control over headwaters of canal irrigation systems concentrates in towns – sometimes small or even new towns – and is associated there with many other character-istically urban media for rural extraction, including the control of draft power.) Third, it is easier to account for Sri Lanka's distributional experiences in a UB context by allowing for the distinction between plantation crops – in 1948–74, largely controlled by one set of voteless foreigners and worked by another, and thus squeezed on both wages and profits[31] to support islanders' welfare – and food crops, especially rice. Here, research, investment (in irrigation) and growth have been very heavily concentrated on increasing the urbanised rice surplus from the 'peripheral' Dry Zone, to the neglect of the 'core' Wet Zone areas, but in conformity with the standard UB model. Do similar rural trifurcations – squeezed ethnic-minority export-crops, privileged food-surplus areas, deprived food-deficit areas – characterise the operation of UB in other post-colonial plantation economies?

Some commentators [*Heisey, 1978*; implicitly *Ellis, this volume*] find dif-ficulty with my use of urban-*rural* dichotomies, alongside stress on *agricultural* investment. The major roles of rural non-agriculture (increasingly researched [*Chuta and Liedholm, 1979; Lipton, 1983b*]) and of urban agriculture (persistently neglected, but employing 5-15 per cent of LDC urban labour) justifies this concern. The response is that, in LDCs, the scale of rural activity and the nature of rural spatial organisation are much more embracing than – yet heavily influenced by – the resources, technologies and institutions of agriculture; that these are massively effected by urban-rural power balances (rather than by farm-nonfarm ones); and that urban activity as a whole rests upon transfers, not necessarily extractive, of rural-produced foods and/or exportables.

The final dichotomies of exploitation, frequently held up as 'better' than rural-urban, are *labour-capital* and *domestic-foreign*. That capital exploits labour is – unlike UB – situated, we are told, in 'the historical origins of institutions, of the mechanisms of motion and sources of structure .... Marxism recognises ... (the) rural-urban difference but interprets it as ... a reflection of an underlying process that is rooted in the dominant mode of production' [*Lambert, 1979*]. Rural 'differentiation is proceeding apace, and with it polarisation along class lines and increasing immiserisation: with a class of kulaks growing immensely in power ... and rising numbers of landless labourers' [*Byres, 1979: 235*]. As Lehmann [*1977*] stresses, the UB hypotheses '[do not] deny the existence of ...[32] conflict within agriculture', but it is unhelpful to force such conflicts into the moulds of nineteenth-century Marxian theory, either definitionally as Lambert does, or by empirical near-caricature as Byres does. Lambert has to explain the persistence and severity of rural-urban distortion in non-capitalist societies (e.g. the barriers against townward migration in China, price twists in Tanzania). Byres has to explain the absence of the phenomena he mentions in capitalist societies whose rural inequality was initially small and/or was reduced by land reform, and where rural surpluses were either not extracted or ploughed back into research-based agricultural investment (Taiwan?). Moreover, in India, the trend of *land* distribution shows decreasing class polarisation [*Vyas, 1979*]; *input* distribution has indeed tended to raise the relative strength of kulaks, but this concentration of 'green revolution' benefits upon them is due mainly to Indian state priority for an urbanised food surplus.

As for the domestic-foreign polarity, it could seem odd that the UB argument attributes much rural poverty to rural-urban relations within LDCs, yet denies that much LDC poverty is attributable to LDC-DC relations. The reason for the latter is empirical: poverty and slow growth are statistically unrelated to involvement, or lack of it, in the world economy. This involvement is measured [*Lipton, 1977a: ch. 3*] by extremely crude indicators (trade/GNP ratios) as stated there and as stressed by several critics. However, strident calls for (unspecified) subtler measures, or for more display of information about detailed cases [*Byres, 1979: 218*], seem misplaced, if the association of persistent poverty (or urban-rural maldistribution) with the intensity of DC-LDC relations[33] falls at the first fence.

Seers [*1977: 11*] makes the better-founded point that foreign influences can provide channels for UB: by providing the technology of 'government-organised terror', the exemplars for luxurious life-styles and, as in the 'Singer model', the world research biases (because research enjoys economies of scale) towards production and consumption preferences in the main areas concerning multinationals, namely, towards urban and heavy-industrial production (see also *Esho, 1980: 7*) and towards urban and high-income consumption. But − short of armed intervention − the North thereby provides only the menu; LDC states, firms and consumers choose the courses.[34] For instance, Latin American import-substitution (reducing integration into the world economy) was no less urban-biased − and no less directed towards large-scale industrial production at the cost of equity and efficiency − than the later stages of export-promotion. Moreover, many recent options, initially Western-researched or at least -financed, are, like high-yielding cereals [*Lipton, 1978*], of their nature favourable to the poor; if most of Africa has neither adopted nor adapted them, and most of Asia has wrenched their benefits towards surplus farmers (and urban consumers), UB cannot be simply blamed on technological or cultural imperialism or paternalism.

Are Dichotomies Needed?

The case for 'urban-rural' as the central dichotomy underlying Third World poverty therefore seems to be unrefuted, though still in great need of testing and refinement. Before linking it to the problem of class, we should ask whether dichotomies are needed at all. Briefly, whether resource-allocation (or relative pricing) is seen as urban-rural, urban-rurban-rural, or continuous from largest and densest settlement to smallest and sparsest, the impact of UB on equity, efficiency and growth need not be fundamentally altered. To take 'town' and 'country' as ideal types may be convenient, both for measure-ment and prediction. Whether most people live in clearly urban or clearly rural places; if so, whether group membership can be clearly associated with advancing the interests of people firmly committed to living in such places; if so, whether arrangements between urban sectors and rural elites take the class form postulated in the UB hypotheses − these are empirical, not theoretical, issues, and the review of evidence in the section above entitled 'Facts' bears upon them.

Class and the State

So far, it has been argued that the urban-rural conflict 'leads' the polarisation of groups in most LDCs, though not that no other polarities matter, nor that everyone is always 100 per cent rural or urban. Further, the existence of urban poor-and-weak (many, but not all, rural in main allegiance) and of rural rich-and-strong (increasingly either urban in main allegiance, or accepting urban priorities in return for concessions) does not invalidate the model of most LDCs as dominated, at the cost of both efficiency and equity, by an urban group that under-allocates resources to, extracts surpluses from, and turns prices against a rural group. But all this, even if true, does not turn the groups into 'classes', nor validate the claim that urban bias is a *class* theory for LDCs, based on product *types* rather than on relationship to the *means* of production [*Lipton, 1977a: 13, 109*]. What does this claim mean?

Corbridge [*1982: 101*] rejects 'any attempt to define a class as an interest group' on the grounds that it would 'lead to a fruitless multiplication of classes' with each member's (multiple) class allegiances 'prone to rapid and recurring shifts'. Several critics believe I have adopted this definition [*Corbridge, 1982: 101; Moore, this volume; Baker, 1979: 170*]. Yet Corbridge and I completely agree; as his own citation [*1982: 100*] shows, I use 'class' only to define a group with '*lasting* common interest, actual or potential *awareness* of it, and actual or potential *capacity for action* to further it', such that the group's 'members benefit from moving, in the same direction, *the one or two key, disputed variables and the associated decisions most affecting economic structure and income distribution* over that period' [*Lipton, 1977: 109*; italics current]. This defines 'class' much more narrowly than 'as an interest group', yet does not exclude intra-class conflicts about matters other than 'the one or two key, disputed variables'. These variables are identified as rural-urban allocations of resources in public control and pricing decisions affecting corresponding privately-controlled allocations: in summary, urbanising the rural surplus.

This identification of key variables (together with the above definition of 'class') implies what I ought to have made explicit: that a class normally seeks to control or capture the state machine so as to appropriate the surplus — unless the cost to it in terms of its objectives (improved values of the key variables) exceeds the benefit to it. This is the essential difference between UB and the important Smithian parallels discussed by Moore in the introductory paper to this volume. In Smith's day it was indeed the relative success of 'merchants and manufacturers [in entering] into combinations' that enabled them by artificial 'enhancement of price' to gain at the expense of 'landlords, farmers and labourers'. Relative urban power is even stronger today — which is why, contrary to Rimmer [*1977*], UB will not be ended, or necessarily even diminished, if state intervention decreases. However, such state intervention is now a much more decisive determinant than in Smith's times of the rural-urban balance. Not only is the state now far bigger (and at least as urban); the state operates not merely by altering price-relativities (which may not affect prices actually paid, and even if it does may be cheaply avoidable via sub-stitution), but mainly by allocating physical inputs and outputs — and per-sonnel — backed in the last resort with force. These physical allocations directly affect what urban and rural people *can* do, not just what it *pays* them to do.

Classes in today's LDCs seek, therefore, to influence or control the state. And they seek, by these and other means, to appropriate surpluses: first by shifting resources, only second by shifting prices. The urban class is much better placed, not only to combine Smith-wise, but, nowadays more important-ly, to manipulate or control — directly or via a partly-autonomous[35] bureauc-racy — state power. Such better placing, unfortunately, is not related either to greater efficiency or to greater need. But the direct role of the UB bargain — including the leaders of formally-employed labour — is hardly in doubt [on food pricing, see *Hertford, 1978: 121-39; Bates, 1981*], and surely validates the underlying class alliances posited. Committed urbanites, whether capitalists or proletarians, agree on what they want the state to do about the key invest-ment allocations and relative prices.

State technology is the final, centralising cement in the strength of this urban class. Armies, police, intelligence services, media – all offer manipulative or repressive *techniques* to states, hardly dreamt of when Smith wrote. That has to be *one* reason why UB in NDCs was so much less than it is in LDCs today – though neither states nor technologies are inherently malign (consider medicine), or likely to go away at the wave of a Chicago wand. But it is centralised urban power over the rural, not 'capital' (or labour, or capitalism or socialism), that the economies of scale and agglomeration, associated with new state technology, naturally serve. That, perhaps, partly explains the sectoralisation of classes in today's LDCs.

Yet such a state, while centralised and strong, is usually neither monolithic nor all-powerful. Institutions are created within it either to compromise with the rural masses or to advance them at least to the extent that their backwardness prevents adequate rural surplus generation. Such institutions within the state are ambiguously poised between urban and rural classes. Sensible proposals to remedy UB will not, of course, assume states 'capable of Olympian detachment, of acting neutrally for the greater good of all society' [*Byres, 1979; 236*, reporting my alleged views]. However, UB is at best Pareto sub-optimal, or a bad strategy in a non-zero-sum game; at worst, self-contradictory (e.g. because one cannot milk a heifer). On these realities, and on the concessions that the urban class must make to them, it is not hopeless to build.

NOTES

1. No such succinct statement, alas, appears in Lipton [*1977a*]. In view of the occasional misrepresentation of the hypotheses there, I hope that all interested in urban bias will glance at these four pages, reproduced in J. Harriss (ed.) [*1981: 66-9*].
2. Recent pressures to curtail this costly but largely successful scheme, even in the context of patterns of public-sector activity *as a whole* favouring Bombay (and its new city) at the cost of the hinterland, are nevertheless significant.
3. To respond fully to this critique requires a dynamics of *class* in relation to *surplus*, the *state* and *technology* for rural *vis-à-vis* urban advance. This was not adequately provided – to say the least – in Lipton [*1977a*]; it can only be hinted at in the text below.
4. The analysis leading to this conclusion [*Lipton, 1977a: 154-6*] should be set against accusations that the book is 'polemical', 'forensic', etc.
5. Of course all data have their limitations. I do not believe that the problems of rural income measurement are as intractable as does Seers [*1977: 3-5*]; attempts to resolve them would probably strengthen the UB arguments anyway [*Lipton, 1977b: 24-6*].
6. On the other hand, it is sometimes overlooked; thus H. Rao, [*1978: 1702*] claims that 'intuition rather than ... any concrete exercise' underpins advice that LDCs with 70 per cent of workers and 20 per cent of investment in A should, over 5-10 years, seek to raise the latter share to 35-45 per cent.
7. This 'textbook for undergraduates', in 'introducing students to the ideas ... of Michael Lipton on urban bias', bases its approach on one detailed and hostile review of those ideas [*Byres, 1979*] – a review which 'led to [Kitching's] book being structured' as it was. Hence, without consulting me, Kitching instructs undergraduates to beware the 'sincerity of Lipton's protestations in favour of ... industrialisation' and my 'almost complete ignorance of the neo-populist tradition ... through Chayanov', whose work I have reviewed in detail [*Lipton, 1968*].
8. I am mystified by Byres's attack on my 'assertion that they [Dobbian industrialisation strategies] are "Stalinist"'. I make no such assertion. Since Khrushchev's 1956 *exposé*, Stalinism means a particular form of political criminality, not a disputable economic doctrine. In pointing out that 'Stalin's methods could not have been avoided, given Preobrazhensky's

(and Stalin's) priorities' — 'utter nonsense' for Byres [*1979: 223*] — I mean, as my previous sentence states [*Lipton, 1977a: 129*], that 'responses of peasants to price disincentives compel any government, determined to apply them *and* to extract food, to use force'. The statements are not about investment allocations at all. Byres, in claiming that I deal with Dobb's argument by a 'cheap gibe', simply fails to read the text.

9. I thus reject Friedman's 'methodology of positive economics' that, provided a theory predicts adequately, we need not worry about its assumptions.

10. Byres [*1979: 230*] referring to Mitra [*1977: 108, 122*], states, 'None of this fits the UB hypothesis, and Lipton most surely be familiar with it (Mitra's book appeared in the same year as Lipton's, but Mitra was a Visiting Fellow at IDS in 1975—6, and his manuscript was circulating throughout that period. I myself read it at that time.)'. I did not see it before publication and thus, happily, left the needed decisive rebuttal to more capable hands [*Tyagi, 1979* and *Kahlon and Tyagi, 1980*]. Byres's other implicit charges of *suppressio veri* are also incorrect. He is on safer ground in assuming ignorance.

11. If I sometimes do 'not use Indian case material when it doesn't support my argument', or use 'argument with selective evidence' [*B. Harriss, 1980: 15*] it is, once again, due to ignorance and not dishonesty.

12. However, Barker [*1983*] correctly criticises Bates for appearing at times to imply that UB processes operate only through state 'intervention' in otherwise unbiased market processes.

13. 'Participation' too often over-represents the articulate or well-off.

14. Certainly, such countries — where rural populations are typically only 30-40 per cent of totals — face acute problems of effective aggregate demand, if they seek to base rural expansion on extra output of *cheap foods* (or export crops) [*Currie, 1979: 92*]. However, the generally greater poverty and labour under-utilisation, and hence the lower k's, associated with rural and farm activity are as grave in Latin America as in Asia; and intra-rural inequality (and hence the concentration of land upon farmers who supply urban, or exportable, surplus) is much graver. Urbanisation has indeed been faster in middle-income LDCs [*Currie, 1979: 95*], as stated in Lipton [*1977a: 224*]; but much of it, there too, rests on boundary illusions and redefinitions, and has side-effects unhelpful to rural efficiency and poverty-reduction [*Lipton, 1977a: 225-6, 230-7*].

15. I doubt whether the NDCs' general avoidance of UB can be attributed mainly, not to the 'capital-cheapness' (relative to agriculture) of early industrialisation, but to its financing out of imperialism [*Esho, 1980: 3*] or out of surpluses from new lands, e.g. in North America [*Seers, 1977: 20*]. Did the post-Plassey extractions go into British industry, or into new colonial investments (plantations in the West Indies) and into land purchases and 'improvement' in England?

16. Ideally one would of course prefer 'rural-urban'; see, however, Lipton [*1977a: 296-7*].

17. Including cartel activity, etc., as well as overt state action.

18. Nor, of course, does a longer series reduce the risk of an atypical initial or terminal year — and even linear regression lines (because they minimise the sum of *squared* deviations and therefore 'seek' to approach extreme values, even if end-values) do not greatly help here. Commonsense might, of course — but it, too, cannot pare away (a) and (b), leaving the pure (c) of changes in urban (or rural) bias.

19. Both employment and wage effects depend on *why* relative farm prices rise: if due to extra non-farm demand or to reduced UB, favourable effects would be expected; if to reduced farm supply (e.g. bad years), normally not.

20. This evidence is based on correcting four major, and I think indisputable, errors in the pioneering work of Gandhi [*1966*], all tending to overstate relative *rural* capacity [*Lipton, 1978: 201, 203, and 220 (fn. 23)*]. Without discussing these corrections, Byres asserts 'that Gandhi's book was and is a thoroughly reliable piece of work' [*Byres, 1979: 225*].

21. As stated by Currie [*1979: 88*], I ascribed the source of one piece of evidence wrongly for this: the statement that $100 of Latin American fixed investment is normally associated with $40-50 extra yearly GNP, 'but only $10-12 if put into residential building' [*Lipton, 1977a: 203*]. The correct source is Breese (ed.) [*1969: 501*], not '1966' as I stated. But there is nothing 'preposterous' (as Currie alleges) about Morse's citation from Hauser in that source.

22. This is additional to a similar effect due to the generally greater labour-intensity with which marginal rural (as against urban) income is generated.

23. In two LDCs, the top quintile in urban areas has the same proportion of sectoral income as in rural areas; in two more, the proportions differ by 0.7-0.8 per cent of sectoral income, less than the range of statistical error; as Byres states, I was wrong to count one of these, and doubly wrong to misread and count the other 'in favour'. In the other six, the top quintile gets at least 1.9 per cent more of sectoral income in the 'more unequal' sector than in the 'less unequal'.

24. For lack of space a refutation of Byres's [*1979: 256*] claim that Japan's growth was based on UB has been omitted.

25. Urban corruption exists too, of course, but only rural corruption seems likely to transfer much income between rural and urban sectors.

26. This is not to deny the existence of complementarity among investments, personnel, etc. – nor of political compromises.

27. In his introductory paper to this volume, Moore rightly criticises me (and others) for political economy without politics: for a shortage of examples of '*how* the class alliances which he posits have actually operated politically', and hence for appearing to assume that 'in order to demonstrate that a class is pursuing its interest it is adequate to demonstrate that it benefits from policy'. While standard empiricist method, this badly needs supplementation with case-studies of political action on, for example, budgetary allocations or price policies.

28. The extreme UB in investment and social and public services in much of Africa, however, renders the townward drift of artisans a very serious problem there. The Kautskyan shift of income from rural to urban *circuits* [*Lipton, 1977a: 68, 117-19*] means that rural artisans, too, lose, but urban artisans gain, from UB.

29. Or, more accurately, 'agriculture-dependent': some 25 per cent of time and 33 per cent of income, in the rural micro-studies of Chuta and Liedholm [*1979*], is non-agricultural, though much of it depends on agricultural supply (processing) or demand (input production or maintenance).

30. Even land distribution in rural areas – the justified target of land reformers – is surely much less unequal than in cities?

31. And also on social welfare provision: UNICEF (Colombo) data reveal that health and educational indicators in Nuwara Eliya, the tea district with the highest concentration of Indian Tamil workers, are 30-40 per cent worse than all-island averages.

32. The dots indicate 'classes or class'; this issue is discussed below.

33. Or with the extent of socialism; I am as aware as Byres that this depends on the class nature of the state (not *just* its size), but if the apparent relative size of the state is uncorrelated with poverty or growth or urban-rural distribution, then attributing these to centralised decision-making, including state socialisms (or to decentralised decision-making, perhaps including 'Yugoslav-type' socialisms) is refuted out of hand. Byres too often accuses me of being ignorant of – or ignoring – detailed historical sequences that I do not cite simply because they are irrelevant to the argument.

34. Admittedly, the choice is skewed by discounts, bribes and advertisements; on the other hand, North-east and North-west each offer a choice of restaurants!

35. Ellis, in this volume, characterises the Tanzanian (class?) conflict as 'bureaucrats versus peasants'. Daedalus or not, I dare not enter the labyrinths of argument about the relative autonomy of a Weberian or Poulantzian bureaucratic class. But bureaucrats – class, autonomous, hegemonic or not (perm any n from three) – are certainly urban in promotion structure, authority structure and life-style, and usually in desired residence, asset-holding and allegiance.

REFERENCES

(Note that all references without a title are to reviews of Lipton [*1977a*].)

Abdullah, M.S.H., 1979, *Peasant Poverty, Agriculture and Government Policy: Peninsular Malaysia since 1957*, M. Phil., University of Sussex.

Alberts, T., 1981, *Agrarian Reform and Rural Poverty: A Case Study of Peru*, Lund: Economic Studies No. 12.

Almy, S.W., 1978, *American Anthropologist*, Vol. 80, No. 3.

van Arkadie, B., 1977, 'Town versus Country?', *Development and Change*, Vol. 8, No. 3.

Asian Development Bank, 1977, *Rural Asia: Challenge and Opportunity*, Singapore: Federal Publications.

Baker, R., 1979, *Modern Asian Studies*, Vol. 13, No. 1.

Bale, M. D. and Lutz, E., 1979, *Price Distortions in Agriculture and Their Effects: an International Comparison*, Washington D.C.: World Bank Staff Working Paper (hereafter WBSWP) No. 359.

Barker, J., 1983, 'The Fractured Debate on Agricultural Policy in Senegal and Mozambique', mimeo, Institute of Development Studies (hereafter IDS).

Bates, R., 1981, *Markets and States in Tropical Africa*, Berkeley and Los Angeles: University of California Press.

Beeson, I., 1979, 'Egyptians Go Hungry While Fields are Claimed for Urban Growth', *The Guardian*, 10 July.

Berger, S. and Piore, M. J., 1980, *Dualism and Discontinuity in Industrial Societies*, Cambridge: Cambridge University Press.

Bergsman, J., 1979, *Growth and Equity in Semi-industrial Countries*, Washington, D.C.: WBSWP No. 351.

Breese, G. (ed.), 1966, *The City in Newly Developing Countries*, Englewood Cliffs: Prentice Hall.

Breese, G., 1978, *American Journal of Sociology*, Vol. 84, No. 3.

Brown, L. R., 1978, *The Worldwide Loss of Cropland*, New York: Worldwatch Institute Paper No. 24.

Burch, D., 1979, *Overseas Aid and the Transfer of Technology: A Case Study of Agricultural Mechanisation in Sri Lanka*, D.Phil., University of Sussex.

Byres, T., 1979, 'Of Neo-populist Pipedreams: Daedalus in the Third World and the Myth of Urban Bias', *Journal of Peasant Studies*, Vol. 6, No. 2.

Cameron, J. and Ndhlovu, T. P., 1983, *Some Major Limitations of Regionalism as a Radical Development Strategy*, Occasional Paper No. 20, School of Development Studies, University of East Anglia.

Chase-Dunn, C., 1978, 'Who Gets What and Why', *Working Papers*, March-April. (No more precise reference available.)

Chuta, E. and Liedholm, C., 1979, *Rural Non-farm Employment: a Review of the State of the Art*, Rural Development Papers No. 4, Michigan State University.

Coleman, A., 1976, 'Is Planning Really Necessary?', *Geographical Journal*, Vol. 142, No. 3.

Connell, J. et al., 1976, *Migration from Rural Areas: the Evidence from Village Studies*, Delhi: Oxford University Press.

Corbridge, S., 1982, 'Urban Bias, Rural Bias and Industrialization', in J. Harriss (ed.) [*1982*].

Currie, L., 1979, 'Is There an Urban Bias?', *Journal of Economic Studies*, Vol. 6, No. 1.

Dallalfar, A., 1978, *Communications and Development*, Vol. 2, No. 2.

Dick, H., 1981, 'Urban Bias: A Good Idea But ... The Indonesian Case', *Asian Studies Association of Australia Review* (hereafter *ASAAR*), Vol. 5, No. 2.

Dizard, J., 1977, *Annals of the American Academy for Political and Sociological Science*, Vol. 433, September.

Eckholm, E. P., 1976, *Losing Ground: Environmental Stress and World Food Prospects*, New York: Norton.

Esho, H., 1980, 'Economic Consequences of Heavy-industry Policy in India – a Brief Note', mimeo, IDS.

FAO, 1984, *Agricultural Price Policies*, Rome.

Flora, J. L., 1977, *Rural America*, August.

Friedman, J., 1978, *AIP Journal*, January.

Galbraith, J. K., 1979, *The Nature of Mass Poverty*, Harvard: Harvard University Press.

di Giorgi, U., 1979, 'The Rural-Urban Dichotomy', *Ceres*, No. 68, March-April.

Grawe, R., 1980, 'Human Development in South Asia', *Poverty and the Development of Human Resources*, Washington, D.C.: WBSWP No. 406.

Griffin, K., 1977, *Journal of Development Studies*, Vol. 14, No. 1, October.

Gugler, J., 1982, 'Overurbanization Reconsidered', *Economic Development and Cultural Change*, Vol. 31, No. 1.

Habitat Asia, 1979, *Report of the International Conference of Habitat*, New Delhi.

Hanson, A. H., 1966, *The Process of Planning*, Oxford: Oxford University Press.

Harriss, B., 1981, *Transitional Trade and Rural Development*, New Delhi: Vikas.

Harriss, B., 1980, 'Criticism of Key Elements in Lipton's Explanation of the Mechanism of Urban Bias' in Baker, R. and Harriss, B., *Urban Bias in Developing Countries: Two Views*, Discussion Paper No. 67, School of Development Studies, University of East Anglia.

Harriss, J. (ed.), 1982, *Rural Development: Theories of Peasant Economy and Agrarian Change*, London: Hutchinson.

Hart, J., 1979, 'The Industrial Imperative', *New Statesman*, 21 September.

Hayami, Y. and Ruttan, V. W., 1971, *Agricultural Development: an International Perspective*, Baltimore: Johns Hopkins University Press.

Heisey, P., 1978, *African Economic History*, 5, Spring.

Herring, R. J. and Edwards, R. M., 1983, 'Guaranteeing Employment to the Rural Poor: Social Functions and Class Interests in the Employment Guarantee Scheme in Western India', *World Development*, Vol. 11, No. 7.

Hertford, R., 1978, 'Government Prices for Wheat, Rice and Tractors', in Schultz, T. W. (ed.), *Distortions of Agricultural Incentives*, Bloomington: Indiana University Press.

Hewlett, S. A., 1977, *Political Science Quarterly*, Vol. 92, No. 3.

Howes, M., 1981, 'The Creation and Appropriation of Surplus Value in Irrigated Agriculture: A Comparison of the Deep Tubewell and Handpump in Rural Bangladesh', in Greeley, M. and Howes, M. (eds), *Rural Technology, Rural Institutions and the Rural Poor*, CIRDAP: Comilla.

IDS, 1977, *Urban Bias: Seers versus Lipton*, Discussion Paper No. 116, August.

Isbister, J., 1978, *African Economic History*, 5, Spring.

Ishikawa, H., 1967, *Agricultural Development in Asian Perspective*, Hitotsubashi University: Institute of Economic Research.

Kahlon, A. and Tyagi, D., 1980, 'Intersectoral Terms of Trade', *Economic and Political Weekly*, Vol. 15, No. 52, December 27.

Karp, M., 1978, *African Economic History*, 5, Spring.

Keyfitz, N., 1982, 'Development and the Elimination of Poverty', *Economic Development and Cultural Change*, Vol. 30, No. 3.

Khan, A. R., 1978, 'Taxation, Procurement and Collective Priorities in Chinese Agriculture', *World Development*, Vol. 6, No. 6.

Kitching, G., 1982, *Development and Underdevelopment in Historical Perspective*, London: Methuen.

Klatt, W., 1977, *International Affairs*, Vol. 53, No. 4.

Lambert, T. A., 1979, 'Development and Deception', *Cornell Journal of Social Relations*, Summer.

Lean, L. L., 1978, *Income Distribution, Employment and Poverty in West Malaysia since 1957*, Ph.D., University of Malaya.

Leeson, P. F., 1977, *Manchester School*, Vol. 45, No. 2.

Lehmann, D., 1977, 'Neo-classical Populism', *Journal of Peasant Studies*, Vol. 4, No. 4.

Lipton, M., 1968, 'Back to Grass Roots', *The Times Literary Supplement*, December 19.

Lipton, M., 1974, 'Towards a Theory of Land Reform', in Lehmann, D. (ed.), *Agrarian Reform and Agrarian Reformism*, London: Faber and Faber.

Lipton, M., 1977a, *Why Poor People Stay Poor: Urban Bias in World Development*, London: Temple Smith.

Lipton, M., 1977b, 'Urban Bias: Generalisation versus Particularity', in *IDS* [*1977*].

Lipton, M., 1978, 'Inter-farm, Inter-regional and Farm-nonfarm Income Distribution: The Impact of the New Cereal Varieties', *World Development*, Vol. 6, No. 3.

Lipton, M., 1981 (reprinted in Harriss, J. (ed.) [*1982*]), 'Why Poor People Stay Poor', Sixth Vikram Sarabhai Memorial Lecture, Indian Institute of Management, Ahmedabad.

Lipton, M., 1982, 'Rural Development and the Retention of the Rural Population in the Countryside of Developing Countries', *Canadian Journal of Development Studies*, Vol. 3, No. 1.

Lipton, M., 1983a, *Poverty, Undernutrition and Hunger*, Washington D.C.: WBSWP No. 597.

Lipton, M., 1983b, *Labor and Poverty*, Washington D.C.: WBSWP No. 616.

MacRae, N., 1977, 'Asia Survey', *The Economist*, 7 May.

Mamalakis, M. J., 1970, *The Theory of Sectoral Clashes*, Economic Growth Centre, Yale University, Paper No. 152.

Mazrui, A., 1978, *Journal of Politics*, Vol. 40, No. 2.

Meesook, A., 1979, *Income, Consumption and Poverty in Thailand, 1962–3 to 1975–6*, Washington D.C.: WBSWP No. 364.

Mitra, A., 1977, *Terms of Trade and Class Relations*, London: Frank Cass.

Mitra, A., 1978, *India's Population: Aspects of Quality and Control*, ICSSR/Family Planning Foundation, Vol. 1.

Moore, M. P. *et al.*, 1983, 'Space and the Generation of Socio-economic Inequality on Sri Lanka's Irrigation Schemes', *Marga*, Vol. 7, No. 1.

Naughton, J., 1978, 'City Against Country', *The Listener*, 20 January.

Nyerere, J. K., 1979, *On Rural Development* (address to WCCARD), W/G 8723 (WCCARD/LIM/5), FAO, 14 July.

Peterson, W., 1979, 'International Farm Prices and the Social Cost of Cheap Food Policies', *American Journal of Agricultural Economics*, Vol. 61, No. 1.

Rao, H., 1978, 'Urban vs. Rural or Rich vs. Poor?', *Economic and Political Weekly*, Vol. 12, No. 40.

Rao, V., 1980, 'Urban Bias and Rural Development', *Indian Economic Review*, Vol. 15, No. 1.

Rimmer, D., 1977, 'Development's New Orthodoxy', *The Times Higher Education Supplement*, 6 May.

Rix, A., 1981, 'Lipton and Japan', *ASAAR*, Vol. 5, No. 2.

Rosen, G., 1978, *Journal of Economic Literature*, 16.

Rothermund, D., 1980, 'Epilogue', *Urban Growth and Rural Stagnation: Studies in the Economy of an Indian Coalfield and its Rural Hinterland*, New Delhi: Manohar.

Ruzicka, L., 1982, 'Mortality in India', mimeo, British Society for Population Studies, Oxford Conference, December.

Sah, R. K. and Stiglitz, J. E., 1983, *The Economics of Price Scissors*, Cambridge, Massachusetts: National Bureau of Economic Research Working Paper No. 1156.

Schickele, R., 1968, *Agrarian Revolution and Economic Progress, A Primer for Development*, New York: Praeger.

Seers, D., 1977, 'Indian Bias?: A Review Article of *Why Poor People Stay Poor'*, *Social and Economic Studies*, Vol. 26, No. 3, University of the West Indies, Jamaica, reprinted in IDS [*1977*].

Sen, A. K., 1968, *Choice of Techniques*, 3rd edn., Oxford: Oxford University Press.

Sen, A. K., 1983, 'Development: Which Way Now?', *Economic Journal*, Vol. 93, No. 4.

Sender, J., 1983, 'Analysing Agricultural Differentiation and Poverty in Guyana', mimeo, Society for Latin American Studies Conference, Cambridge, April.

Singh, I. J., 1977, 'Why Poor People Remain Poor', *Finance and Development*, December.

Southall, A., 1978, *African Economic History*, Vol. 5, Spring.

Strachan, H. W., 1978, *Business History Review*, Vol. 52, No. 1.

Streeten, P., 1977, 'Poverty and Urban Bias', *The Round Table*, 267, July.

Thamajarakshi, R., 1969, 'Intersectoral Terms of Trade and Marketed Surplus of Agricultural Produce, 1951–2 to 1965–6', *Economic and Political Weekly*, Vol. 4, No. 26, June 28.

Thomas, V., 1982, *Differences in Income, Nutrition and Poverty within Brazil*, WBSWP No. 505, Washington D.C.

Todaro, M. and Stilkind, J., 1981, *City Bias and Rural Neglect*, Washington: Overseas Development Council.

Toye, J., 1978, *Journal of Commonwealth and Comparative Politics*, Vol. 16, No. 4.

Toye, J. (ed.), 1978, *Taxation and Economic Development: Twelve Critical Studies*, London: Frank Cass.

Tyagi, D. S., 1979, 'Farm Prices and Class Bias in India', *Economic and Political Weekly*, Vol. XIV, No. 39.

United Nations, 1980, *Demographic Yearbook*, New York.

Urwick, J., 1983, *Urban Bias in an African Educational System: the Case of Secondary Education in Sokoto State, Nigeria*, D.Phil., University of Wisconsin.

Vogeler, I., 1978, *Professional Geographer*, Vol. 30, No. 3.

Vyas, V. S., 1979, 'Presidential Address: Some Aspects of Structural Change in Indian Agriculture', *Indian Journal of Agricultural Economics*, Vol. 34, No. 1.

Wade, R., 1982, 'The System of Administrative and Political Corruption: Canal Irrigation in South India', *Journal of Development Studies*, Vol. 18, No. 3.

Weiskoff, R., 1976, 'Income Distribution and Income Growth in Puerto Rico, Argentina and Mexico', in Foxley, A. (ed.), *Income Distribution in Latin America*, Cambridge: Cambridge University Press.

White, J. W., 1979, *American Political Science Review*, Vol. 73, No. 2.

Wilson, R., 1977, *Economic Journal*, Vol. 87, No. 347.

World Bank, 1981, *Accelerated Development in Sub-Saharan Africa: An Agenda for Action*, Washington, D.C.

World Bank, 1983, *Focus on Poverty*, Washington, D.C., February.

Zarenda, H., 1978, *South African Journal of Economics*, Vol. 46, No. 1.